AIRBORNE ASSAULT . . .

In Captain Siegel's aircraft, the red light near the yawning door flashed on explosively. Its haunting glare sent chills racing up the spines of the paratroopers. Four minutes to go until bailout. Siegel called out in a loud voice: "Stand up and hook up!" He took a quick peek at his luminous watch—4:18 A.M. His flight was right on schedule, always a good omen.

It took an effort by the paratroopers to stand. They felt huge and bloated with their burdensome combat gear as they staggered into position, one behind the other, and snapped static lines onto the anchor cable that ran the length of the dimly lit cabin. With the ominous red light scowling at them, the waiting stress was harder, more nerve-racking than ever. Hearts beat faster—and skipped beats. Sweat dotted foreheads. Mouths filled with cotton. It would be only seconds.

Suddenly the green light flashed on—Go!

Jove Books by William B. Breuer

DROP ZONE SICILY
DEVIL BOATS: THE PT WAR AGAINST JAPAN
OPERATION DRAGOON

OPERATION DRAGOON

THE ALLIED INVASION
OF THE
SOUTH OF FRANCE

WILLIAM B. BREUER

JOVE BOOKS, NEW YORK

OPERATION DRAGOON

A Jove Book / published by arrangement with
Presidio Press

PRINTING HISTORY
Presidio Press edition published 1987
Jove edition / November 1988

ISBN: 0-515-09805-1

Jove Books are published by the The Berkley Publishing Group,
200 Madison Avenue, New York, New York 10016.
The name "JOVE" and the "J" logo
are trademarks belonging to Jove Publications, Inc.

*Dedicated to the memory of
General Melvin Zais,
a young paratroop battalion
leader in Operation Dragoon who
rose to the top of his profession
yet never lost his touch with
or love for the fighting men
who served under him*

There was no development of that period which added more decisively to our advantages or aided us more in accomplishing the final and complete defeat of German forces than did this attack coming up the Rhône Valley [from the Riviera].

—General of the Army Dwight D. Eisenhower

Stalin . . . was one of the strongest boosters of the invasion of southern France. He knew exactly what he wanted in a political as well as a military way; and the thing he wanted most was to keep us out of the Balkans, which Stalin had staked out for the Red Army. . . . Dragoon was a major blunder.

—General Mark W. Clark

Contents

Maps

List of Illustrations

Introduction

By late July 1944, Operation Dragoon, a proposed massive Allied invasion of southern France, had been embroiled in heated controversy for months. Originally scheduled to coincide with Operation Overlord, the Normandy landings that took place on June 6, Dragoon was the invasion that almost wasn't. It had been on again, off again repeatedly, and it came within a hairsbreadth of being canceled at the final moment due to a bitter and prolonged dispute between the Americans and British at the highest levels.

Second in scope only to Overlord, Operation Dragoon would involve a force of three hundred thousand men, a thousand ships, and several thousand warplanes. A ten-thousand-man airborne contingent would spearhead the assault in the predawn darkness. The invasion was designed to seize the vitally needed major ports of Marseilles (which gave its name to the French national anthem) and Toulon, to liberate the southern two thirds of France, and to form the lower pincer to link up with Overlord armies in the North.

A shortage of LSTs (landing ship, tank) was a factor that contributed to the repeated postponements and near cancellation of Dragoon; the Allies hadn't enough of those assault craft to launch Overlord and Dragoon simultaneously.

Winston Churchill, the peppery, seventy-year-old prime minister of Great Britain, said with a growl: "The destinies of two great empires seem to be tied up in some goddamned things called LSTs!"

Churchill, the shrewd statesman, set out to scuttle Dragoon. He had more than military considerations in mind, having grown to fear the prospect of postwar Communist domination of central and eastern Europe should the surging Soviet army overrun all of that vast territory. In mid-1944, with strong Allied forces in Italy pursuing the Germans northward after seizing Rome, Churchill saw a golden opportunity to thrust northeast from there into the Balkans, then on to Vienna and Budapest and into southern Germany. The prime minister planned to beat the Soviets to the prize.

Franklin D. Roosevelt, the consummate politician, was staunchly opposed to the "Balkan adventure." Up for reelection in November as president of the United States, Roosevelt candidly confided to intimates: "I can't afford to have American armies run the risk of bogging down in the Balkans in what the American public would consider support of British postwar interests."

Josef Stalin, the cunning Soviet dictator, had strongly advocated that the Western Allies invade southern France rather than the Balkans and eastern Europe. He had already staked out that region for himself. Privately, British and a few American generals labeled Dragoon "the Stalin Plan."

Churchill, the most dogged of men in pursuit of a goal, applied all of his ample guile in trying to pursuade Roosevelt to abandon Dragoon in favor of the Balkans strategy. The president remained adamant, confiding to his son Elliott:

"Our chiefs of staff are convinced of one thing. The way to kill the most Germans, with the least loss of American soldiers, is to mount one great big offensive [in France] and then slam 'em with everything we've got. It makes sense to me."

It made no sense to Winston Churchill. He intensified his campaign to scrap Dragoon in favor of his Balkans strategy.

On June 11 (five days after the Normandy invasion) the British chiefs of staff, at the behest of the prime minister, demanded a sweeping review of the entire Allied strategy in the Mediterranean.

On June 17 ponderous British Gen. Henry Maitland "Jumbo" Wilson, Allied commander in the Mediterranean, proposed harnessing all resources for continuation of the Allied offensive in Italy on into the plains of Hungary. Snorted seventy-seven-year-old Henry L. Stimson, Roosevelt's secretary of war: "[General] Wilson is never far from a bottle."

On July 24 Churchill pleaded directly to Roosevelt: "We cannot wreck one campaign [Italy] for the sake of another [France]. Both can be won."

On August 6 the prime minister reopened arguments with Supreme Commander Dwight D. Eisenhower, an American. The British leader was rebuffed after one of the most intense personal debates of the war between the two leaders. That night, Eisenhower's naval aide, Comdr. Harry C. Butcher, penned in his diary. "The boss told The Prime 'no' in every form in the English language."

Finally, after numerous postponements over a period of three months, a new D-Day was set for Dragoon: August 15. Presumably that settled the matter. But only one week before the Riviera would be assaulted, Churchill tried again. He proposed that Dragoon forces be shifted to ports in Brittany, some of which were still in German hands, although that French peninsula was in the process of being cleared by American troops who had broken out of a Normandy stalemate on July 25.

"Impossible at this late date!" thundered an exasperated Eisenhower. Thousands of orders for Dragoon convoys and troop movements had already gone out.

Finally, the British Bulldog threw in the towel. Unbowed, he signaled Roosevelt: "I pray God you are right."

Lamented the prime minister to aides: "Southern France may well prove to be another bloody Anzio."

SPIES, DECEPTIONS, AND INTRIGUE

Instead of Operation Dragoon, the British wanted to use troops in Italy to leap the Adriatic, drive northward to Vienna and then on into southern Germany.

"There Will Be No Withdrawal"

The ancient, tranquil city of Avignon stirred uneasily in the hot sunlight of August 12, 1944. Glistening in the early-morning haze were the massive gray fourteenth-century ramparts that ringed the noble community, and within these confines was the huge, fortresslike bulk of the Palace of Popes, known as Europe's most impressive medieval building. Finding decadent Rome too boisterous, the Papacy moved to Avignon in 1307 and began building the palace. The popes ruled from this edifice until 1377, when the Papacy moved back to Rome.

Close by the ornate palace stood the twelfth-century Gothic cathedral containing the tomb of Pope John XXII. From there it was but a short distance to the hilltop gardens of the Rocher des Doms, with a spectacular view of the broad expanse of the Rhône River down below. The river rises from a glacier in Switzerland, then enters France and flows southward until it empties into the Mediterranean Sea near Marseilles, some fifty miles south of Avignon and five hundred miles from its source.

Now the flocks of visitors who had descended upon Avignon from all over the world to view the historic sights had long since disappeared in this, the fifth year of World War II. In their places were other visitors—unwelcome ones, the helmeted, jackbooted soldiers of Germany. Sentries were everywhere; for quiet, unpretentious Avignon was headquarters of the German Nineteenth Army, which was responsible for repulsing any Allied invasion along the three-hundred-mile Mediterranean coast between Spain and Italy.

This year there were no wealthy Parisians lolling on the white beaches of the breathtaking Riviera, ninety miles southeast of Avignon, which in peacetime had been a favorite playground for American millionaires, Russian grand dukes, and English lords and their ladies. There along the Côte d'Azur the idle rich had basked in the warm sunshine every day of the year, or swum in the Mediterranean, a body of water so placid and clear that one could see his shadow moving over the firm, smooth sand bottom twenty feet below. This was one of the most famous stretches of beach in the world.

At the western boundary of the Riviera stood the ancient, bawdy port of Marseilles, the third largest city in France with nearly one million residents. It had been a dominant port of the Mediterranean for almost twenty-six hundred years, since the arrival of the first Greek settlers in the superb natural harbor known as the Old Port. Now German sentries were everywhere along those historic docks.

The town of Saint-Tropez, with tall pink houses overlooking the protected bay where in prewar days the British Mediterranean fleet used to anchor, was strewn with barbed-wire barricades, and thick concrete pillboxes dotted the town and its beaches. Hyères, where the statuesque girls were dark and Saracen and the streets were lined with palm trees, resembled an armed camp, which it was. The town of Fréjus, where Julius Caesar stored supplies for his campaigns in Gaul centuries before, and Saint-Raphael, a modest fishing village gone garish with the trappings of a modern coast resort, were thick with swarms of *Feldgrau* (the German soldier was nicknamed after the color of his uniform—field gray) constantly conducting anti-invasion exercises. Cannes, its luxury hotels, meager beach, and dreams of sport fishing, yachts, and flowers, now was in the iron grip of the Wehrmacht.

In these early days of August, there was a thick pall of apprehension hovering over the entire Riviera, land of pink oleander, grassy seaside terraces, garden walls, pastel villas, lush shrubbery, ornate estates, hyacinths, and white beaches. German soldiers and French civilians alike were haunted by the specter of an enormous man-made hurricane about to strike them.

Except for the suffocating aura of droves of enemy soldiers in their midst, life had not been too harsh for the citizens of Avignon during the twenty months the Nazi swastika had flown over public buildings and the stately Dominion Hotel, living quarters of General of Infantry Friedrich Wiese, commander of the Nineteenth Army, and his staff. Unlike teeming Paris, the French capital far to the north, where the population was on a starvation ration, there was adequate food in this agricultural region of southern France. Traditional *pommes frites* (fried potatoes) could be bought at most restaurants. There were rutabaga (a turnip variety often used as cattle food) in abundance, and each family managed to scrounge a few eggs and a pound or two of meat each month. Usually the latter purchases were made from *BOFS (buerre, oeufs, fromage,* butter, eggs, cheese)—black marketeers.

Most importantly, ancient Avignon and its residents had been far removed from the massive bombings and the armed violence raging elsewhere in Europe and the Mediterranean region. That peaceful state of affairs had been suddenly shattered on July 17, when a flight of American heavy bombers plastered the Dominion Hotel, leaving it in flaming ruin and forcing General Wiese and his staff officers to flee for their lives. At the insistence of aides, Wiese moved to a château on the outskirts of Avignon, a structure considered less conspicuous from the air.

Since that first bombing nearly a month previously, air-raid sirens in Avignon and all along the Riviera wailed daily as American heavies and fighter-bombers pounded German installations, bridges, radar stations, gun batteries, troop barracks, and headquarters. Steadily the powerful Allied air force stepped up its bombardment. Nice, Cannes, Saint-Tropez, and the fortress port of Toulon all were deluged with explosives. The entire Côte d'Azur, stretching for a hundred miles along the Mediterranean, was under almost continual air attack, with Allied flights arriving so frequently that authorities ceased sounding the sirens.

American Thunderbolts, Mustangs, and twin-boomed Lightnings had been diving and swooping at will upon German coastal batteries, antiaircraft-gun positions, blockhouses, and barbed-wire minefields for nearly four weeks. On August 12, as the southern France bombing campaign reached its zenith, heavy bombers from the British Royal Air Force, and fighter planes flown by French pilots joined in the aerial pyrotechnics, pounding German airfields and supply dumps far inland from the blue coast. Few Luftwaffe fighter planes were able to rise to contest this awesome onslaught from the sky.

Now, on the twelfth day of August, a perspiring General Wiese and his able chief of staff, Lt. Gen. Walther Botsch, were poring over a huge wall map of southern France. The heat in the airless operations room was suffocating and seemed to add to the gloomy atmosphere. Wiese, regarded by his peers as a capable tactician, never for a moment believed that his 250,000-man force could repulse a full-scale Allied invasion. The Nineteenth Army had been weakened two months previously when the Allies struck in Normandy and Field Marshal Gerd von Rundstedt, *Oberbefehlshaber West* (commander-in-chief west), had pirated three of Wiese's eleven divisions in an effort to hold back the Overlord avalanche.

In General Wiese's command were three corps headquarters, which controlled the nearly seven divisions strung out along the Mediterranean coastline. West of the Rhône River were the 189th, 198th, and 716th Infantry divisions. Around the mouth of the Rhône, in the center, was three fourths of the 338th Infantry Division, the remainder of the formation having been sent to the north a few weeks previously.

Perhaps through strategic intuition, Wiese had positioned his best troops east of the Rhône, along the Côte d'Azur, where, unknown to him at the time, the powerful Allied juggernaut would strike. Under Maj. Gen. Hans Schaefer, the 244th Infantry Division defended the Marseilles sector. Schaefer, who had gained an outstanding reputation as a battle leader in Russia, where he had been wounded, was beset with one major problem: The 244th was a *bodenstandig* (static) division; it would be unable to maneuver. However, along with several field artillery batteries, the energetic Schaefer was in charge of 88 coastal guns.

Major General Johannes Baessler's 242nd Infantry Division, defending the coastline from Toulon eastward to Agay, was also a bodenstandig formation, but Baessler had at his disposal 106 coastal guns ranging in size up to .340 caliber, which could fire 700-pound shells farther than 20 miles.

The Nineteenth Army's remaining coastline division was the 148th Infantry, commanded by Maj. Gen. Otto Fretter-Pico, whose sector reached from Agay to the Maritime Alps at the Italian border. Fretter-Pico's division had but two regiments (instead of the customary three).

The mission of Col. Gen. Johannes Blaskowitz, commander of Army Group G, was to defend the two thirds of France south of the east-to-west-flowing Loire River. When the Allies struck in southern France, he would count heavily on his one armored division, the 11th Panzer, which was in reserve in the Bordeaux area, along the Atlantic Seaboard. It had seen heavy duty on the Russian Front, and its twenty-six Mark IV tanks and forty-nine Mark V's were only one half its regular strength, yet enough to create a considerable impact against Allied forces should the invaders cross the beaches.

Blaskowitz's other reserve division, the 157th, was far north of the Côte d'Azur and could be expected to be of little value once the invasion began. The 157th Division for weeks had been battling large bands of French Resistance fighters in the mountains.

Generals Wiese and Botsch had worries other than the fact that their Nineteenth Army divisions were stretched thinly for three hundred miles along the coast. They were deeply concerned about the fighting capacity of their troops. Many were war-weary men from the Russian Front who had been wounded there, then sent to garrison duty along the Riviera. In recent months there had been a heavy influx of non-German soldiers, mainly former prisoners of war from the Eastern Front whose morale was very low and whose loyalty to the Third Reich was doubtful. Led by German officers and noncoms, this Wehrmacht mixture included Poles, Armenians, Ukrainians, Georgians, Azerbaijanians, and others. Wiese winced each time he read field reports telling of the impossibility of assigning these non-Germans even to routine guard duty because few spoke German and fewer still could pronounce the passwords.

General Wiese had still more concerns in addition to the hodgepodge force at his disposal. According to a stream of reports from Admiral Wilhelm Canaris, the cagy master spy who ran the Abwehr, Germany's intelligence service, the Allies were training large numbers of assault troops in Italy and elsewhere in the Mediterranean to launch a massive invasion in the region. Canaris's left-behind spies reported that the Allies would muster some 300,000 troops, 2,000 warplanes, and hundreds of ships for the onslaught.

If the man-made tidal wave of explosives and steel struck Wiese's Nineteenth Army, he would be supported only by 186 airplanes of the Luftwaffe, and the Kriegsmarine (Navy) would be able to respond with only 28 torpedo boats, 9 submarines, 5 destroyers, and 15 patrol craft. Most of these vessels were based in and around Marseilles and Toulon, and they were grandly designated the Sixth and Seventh fleets.

In the stifling operations room at Nineteenth Army headquarters on this twelfth day of August, Generals Wiese and Botsch were solemnly evaluating their strategic situation and reached a starkly dismal conclusion: The Nineteenth Army's destiny was to stand fast and fight against overwhelming odds in a hopeless cause and be wiped out in the process.

Sobering reports were arriving hourly from the Normandy battleground, each signal more devastating than the previous one. The powerful Allied force that had invaded Normandy on June 6 had broken loose after having been bogged down in heavy fighting for six weeks. Now tank-tipped spearheads of the U.S. First and Third armies had mopped up most of the Brittany Peninsula and were dashing eastward across northern France toward Paris and on to the border of the Reich.

If the rampaging American spearheads in the North were not halted, or if General Wiese did not receive an order to withdraw promptly the five hundred miles up the Rhône Valley into Germany, the Nineteenth Army would be cut off from the Fatherland, unable to obtain reinforcements, ammunition, food, medicine, or supplies, and left to wither on the vine or be chopped to pieces by Allied invaders along the Riviera.

Wiese turned to Botsch and stated evenly, "There's no chance that a withdrawal order will be received." Wiese had known that all along.

When assigned to command the Nineteenth Army only three months previously, General Wiese had been ordered to report to the Führer, Adolf Hitler, who was also commander-in-chief of the armed forces. Hitler had sternly warned Wiese:

"There will be no withdrawal. If anything happens along the Riviera you will fight to the last man and the last bullet! Do you fully understand, Herr General?"

Despite his pessimistic outlook on the situation along the Côte d'Azur, Friedrich Wiese would do his duty. He was a professional soldier of the Third Reich, had taken a blood oath of everlasting loyalty to his Führer, and would fight to the death if need be. He was dedicated to making the Allies pay dearly should they strike at his sector.

THREE MONTHS PREVIOUSLY, in mid-May, Field Marshal Erwin Rommel—the famed Desert Fox—had sped by car to the Riviera from his headquarters at La Roche Guyon, north of Paris, to inspect defenses. The indefatigable Rommel, Germany's youngest field marshal, had been rushed to France from Italy several weeks before with a ringing order from Adolf Hitler: "Smash any Allied invasion effort!"

Roaring along the Côte d'Azur in his mud-splattered Horch, Rommel had grown increasingly furious. Defenses were minimal, and there appeared to be no plan to fortify the coastline. Rommel's anger was not directed at Friedrich Wiese, who had just arrived, but at Wiese's predecessor, General of Infantry Georg von Sodenstern, and at General Blaskowitz, commander of Army Group G.

Field Marshal Rommel loudly read the riot act to a red-faced General Blaskowitz, then raced off in a huff. Blaskowitz promptly summoned Wiese, along with engineer officers and officials of the Todt Organization, the paramilitary civilian agency charged with Wehrmacht construction projects. Blaskowitz, still smarting under Rommel's barbs, in turn laid down the law to his subordinates: "Go all-out to strengthen the *Südwall* (South Wall)—beginning immediately!"

Since that day, construction activity had been furious along the Côte d'Azur. Luxury hotels, ornate villas, and stylish restaurants that once had catered to the wealthy and the famous, had windows covered with concrete and were turned into formidable blockhouses. Mines—thousands of them—were sewn along the beaches. Any stretch of shoreline that the Allies could conceivably use to land in assault craft was saturated with sturdy iron posts just under the water surface, posts that would rip open the bellies of the tiny craft. To each of these underwater obstacles was wired an artillery shell that would explode on contact, blowing to pieces a boat and its passengers.

Along desolate sectors of the blue coast, where rocky features would preclude the landing of large numbers of assault craft, were planted tens of thousands of antipersonnel mines, designed to kill an invading soldier outright or to blow off his legs. Hundreds of miles of barbed-wire strands were strung along the beaches and covered by dug-in machine-gun positions. Up and down the Riviera deep trench networks were dug, and overlooking the beaches holes were carved out of rock to shelter flame-thrower crews.

Working feverishly around the clock in the 100-mile sector between Nice and Marseilles, some 14,000 Todt workers, many conscripted from the French population, constructed 578 casemated positions, each holding a field gun or a coastal gun.

German engineers and the Todt Organization were ingenious in their work. Aerial photos taken almost daily by Allied reconnaissance planes revealed that the French civilians had built a large, magnificent Tudor pavilion on a cliff overlooking a wide expanse of sandy, golden beach, as well as large numbers of bathing huts and beachside cafes. Actually, all of these were blockhouses or bunkers, thick-walled and made to look like harmless facilities for the war-weary natives.

General Wiese was convinced that Allied paratroopers and glidermen would strike first, so inland he installed thousands of sharp stakes, invisible in aerial photos but capable of impaling a landing paratrooper. Long, sturdy poles were placed in the ground in open fields and in vineyards to wreck gliders, and strong, thick wires were stretched taut between trees for the same purpose.

At the same time that Generals Wiese and Botsch were conferring at Avignon on August 12, a beautiful young French woman was suffering the torments of the damned. She was Helene Vagliano, a resident of the Riviera. For weeks she had been the subject of covert surveillance as she pedaled her bicycle up and down the Côte d'Azur, her long black hair and billowing skirt flowing in the breeze. Now she was in the Gestapo's torture chambers in Nice.

Helene Vagliano was suspected of spying for the French Underground—and indeed she had been. For months she had been cycling up and down the Riviera as a message courier among various cells of the Armée Secrete (Secret Army). On July 29, a long, black Citroën roared up beside her as she rode along, and three Gestapo men leaped out. They roughly jerked her off the bicycle, threw her into the back seat of the car, and took her to a prison in Nice. Fortunately, she had just delivered a message to an Underground leader and had no incriminating material in her possession.

Her protestations of innocence were to no avail. Her Gestapo interrogators repeatedly shouted at her: "Confess! Confess, you French whore! You're a goddamned spy!"

Daily for two weeks Helene had been subjected to the most atrocious treatment. Always the "interrogation" was the same. In front of several male Gestapo agents, she was stripped naked, strung up to a rafter, and beaten with a whip. Nearly every lash was accompanied with strident shouts, "Confess! Confess!"

Helene refused to confess. "Who are your accomplices?" they yelled into her ear.

The Nazi torturers persisted. The young woman screamed in agony as they burned her bare breasts with lighted cigarettes. She was cut down, and while semiconscious her hands were plunged into boiling water and held there for several minutes. When her hands were finally removed, strips of red, tortured flesh hung from them. Still she refused to admit that she was a spy or to name accomplices. She betrayed no one.

Bleeding and scalded, Helene Vagliano was thrown back into her cell, where she collapsed like a rag doll on the concrete floor. The next day the Gestapo would repeat the procedure.

A FEW DAYS after the young French woman was seized by the Gestapo, a flight of American heavies flew over a newly installed German gun battery overlooking the beaches near Cannes, where American assault troops would soon storm ashore. Bombs cascaded downward, and battery and crew were utterly destroyed. The bombing mission would save many American lives. But neither U.S. Army Air Force crews nor the German soldiers down below were aware of the source of the intelligence that had guided this mission. Details of the new German battery had been radioed by the French Underground to Allied headquarters in Naples. This was the information in the message Helene Vagliano had delivered to an accomplice just before she was captured by the Gestapo on July 29.

On the same Saturday morning of August 12, American Intelligence officers at an old Italian Army barracks in Naples were sifting through a large stack of documents. Known as the Blockhouse, the old barracks was located near the waterfront in downtown Naples. It was a large quadrangle with an interior courtyard surrounded by high walls. The building was Army, Navy, and Army Air Force planning headquarters for Operation Dragoon and was closely guarded by sharp-eyed sentries who had instructions to "shoot anyone who does not halt on your order."

The Intelligence documents contained complete information concerning German strength and dispositions along the Côte d'Azur. Not even Overlord, the Normandy invasion, could equal Dragoon's Intelligence file. So sensitive and crucial was this information that when it was necessary for those not in high command or in Allied G-2 (Intelligence) to study the documents, they first were handed a neatly typed message that said: "If you knowingly or otherwise reveal any of the top-secret information in this file you will be severely punished."

In the file was a mile-by-mile, sometimes yard-by-yard, detailed description of the Côte d'Azur, all the way from Cannes west to Toulon, together with the precise position of German gun batteries, machine-gun posts, minefields, bunkers, trench networks, barbed-wire entanglements, and headquarters. Also recorded were the caliber of guns in the concrete casements, their range and fields of fire, and the number of Germans to service the weapons at each position. In many instances there was listed the names of German officers, down through captains and lieutenants, in charge of regiments, battalions, companies, and even strongpoints along the coast.

All of this mountainous pile of information had been numbered, classified, and indexed, then filled in on a huge map of southern France that covered one entire wall of the Intelligence room. When Dragoon struck on August 15, Allied commanders would have available to them more information on German defenses and troop dispositions than would General Friedrich Wiese, commander of the Nineteenth Army.

This awesome collection of information from a hostile region was obtained from a variety of sources—the French Underground, which for years had been sending information to the Allies by radio and courier; an ingenious British machine code-named Ultra, which years before had cracked the "unbreakable" German code and constantly intercepted top-secret enemy wireless messages, deciphered them, and passed the contents on to top-level commanders and Intelligence officers; and aerial reconnaissance, which was continuous.

THAT AFTERNOON of August 12, a battered old car with large Red Cross symbols painted on all sides and on its roof chugged up to a German checkpoint on the outskirts of Digne, a bustling town inland from the Riviera. The occupants of the vehicle were four French civilians on a business trip: Armand de Pont-Leve, manager of the Compagnie de l'Electricité in Nimes; Monsieur Chambrun, an official of the French Highways and Bridges Department; Monsieur Chasuble, a civilian businessman; and the driver, Claude Renoir. Allied warplanes were pounding Digne, and men wearing the gray-green uniforms of the Wehrmacht were dashing about, shouting and waving their arms.

"Mongols!" the tall, handsome, dark-haired Chambrun called out. These soldiers were members of the Wehrmacht's Oriental Legion Against Communism, and the French civilians in the car knew it was wise to avoid them if at all possible; for even though the four civilians' papers were in order, the "Mongols" had a reputation for making indiscriminate arrests and for rough treatment.

The Mongol-manned roadblock presented a serious problem, for these travelers were in reality leaders of the French Underground in southern France who were returning to their base at Seyne-les-Alpes after meeting with two leaders of the Armée Secrete in preparation for the landings along the Côte d'Azur.

Chambrun was a British Army officer named Francis Cammaerts (code name Roger), who had been parachuted into France in March 1943, one of the 480 secret agents sent to that German-occupied country by the Special Operations Executive (SOE), the British cloak-and-dagger organization. Now a lieutenant colonel, Cammaerts was in charge of SOE operations along the Mediterranean coast of southern France.

Monsieur Pont-Leve was also a British officer, whose real name was Xan Fielding (code name Cathedrale), and although his French civilian papers identified him as manager of the electric company at Nimes, by his own admission he "barely had the knowledge to flip on a light switch." Monsieur Chasuble was a French Army officer working covertly for the American supersecret Office of Strategic Services (OSS). His true identity was Major André Sorensen.

The SOE had been the brainchild of Prime Minister Winston Churchill in 1940 when Great Britain stood alone and at bay against the mighty legions of the Third Reich. "Set Europe ablaze!" Churchill had directed the fledgling organization. "Carry the fight for freedom by sabotage and subversion behind enemy lines!'' Now, four years later, SOE had become the best-organized and most effective spy operation behind German lines.

As the Red Cross car's occupants waved their documents before the Mongols at the Digne roadblock, with the impatient air of tardy businessmen late for an important appointment, Claude, the driver, embellished the scenario by periodically revving the engine. Despite the tenseness of the situation, the four spies could barely suppress smiles when one of the Mongols closely scrutinized their identity papers—holding the documents upside down.

With imperious waves of their arms, the Wehrmacht Orientals allowed the Red Cross car to proceed.

Renoir prepared to drive off when a German car quickly pulled up behind. The Allied spies felt their heartbeats quicken. Renoir in a flash debated whether to bolt away or brazen out the latest confrontation.

''Hold it!'' Roger whispered. ''Gestapo!''

Four Gestapo men, each armed with a Schmeisser machine pistol, and a youthful German civilian leaped from their vehicle. The civilian began hurling questions at the Allied spies and examining their papers. The Gestapo agent's suspicions were aroused. One set of papers was out of date. One had no official stamp. Two of the French ''businessmen'' spoke with accents.

Roger, Cathedrale, and Major Sorensen were ordered out of the Red Cross car, hustled into the agents' vehicle at gunpoint, and hustled off to Gestapo headquarters. Claude Renoir, who actually was a Red Cross official with authentic identity papers, was allowed to continue his journey.

The three Allied spies, all assuming calm, innocent demeanors, were placed in separate cells. On the virtual eve of the invasion of southern France, when Roger's services were most crucially needed, the leader of the Allied spy network along the Riviera was in the clutches of the dreaded Gestapo. Roger's luck had run out. As he calmly awaited the atrocious fate he knew was coming, he could detect the muffled thumps of Allied bombs far off in the distance along the Côte d'Azur. The sound steeled his will. It meant that the Allies were coming—and soon.

MEN ENGAGED IN the dangerous game of parachuting as spies into German-held southern France did not have a monopoly on courage. Unlike the legendary Mata Hari of World War I, Allied female spies seldom coaxed military secrets from high-ranking German officers in the intimacy of a boudoir. Rather, women spies parachuting (or landing by boat in some instances) into southern France had to depend, not on glamor or seductiveness, but, as with their male counterparts, on their courage, steel nerves, and resourcefulness.

In carrying out their espionage function, female agents held one subtle advantage over their male counterparts: Because they were women, they could generally move more freely about the countryside without attracting as much suspicion as would males.

Several female agents were dropped by the OSS, a spy and sabotage agency headed by World War I's famed hero, Maj. Gen. William J. "Wild Bill" Donovan, a prominent New York lawyer. One of these was Virginia Hall.

Virginia Hall had previously lost a leg in an automobile accident, but she badgered the OSS to send her into Nazi-occupied France. Adding to her danger, she was well known to the Gestapo from a previous sabotage mission. Hall had parachuted into southern France in March 1944. Her artificial leg had been tucked under one arm to prevent its damage on crashing to earth.

Despite her physical handicap, Miss Hall was a human dynamo. She helped organize and train the French Underground and on occasion joined with her fighting men on sabotage and ambush missions. She joined in derailing German troop trains, blowing up bridges, and raiding Wehrmacht facilities, and she provided continual radio contact with OSS headquarters in London. The communications function was particularly hazardous due to the constant enemy DF-ing (electronic direction-finding equipment).

Miss Hall for months had been forced to keep on the go in southern France; the Gestapo was constantly on her trail . . .*

DURING THE LATE months of 1943 and early 1944, Allied agents who'd infiltrated southern France had been able to carry out their espionage activities with a minimum of German

---

*General Donovan personally requested President Roosevelt to award Virginia Hall the Distinguished Service Cross. She became the first civilian woman in World War II to receive that high military commendation.

interference. Nor had French agents of the Nazis who'd infiltrated the Underground caused much of a problem. The eyes of Adolf Hitler, the Wehrmacht, and the Gestapo had been concentrated along the Atlantic Wall in northern France, where powerful Allied forces assembling in England were expected to strike. But in March 1944, the Germans had started giving much greater attention to the French Mediterranean coast. Actions against French "terrorists" and Allied spies were greatly intensified as squads of Gestapo and Sicherheitsdienst (SD), the SS counterintelligence corps, descended upon the Côte d'Azur.

In May the Gestapo and the SD struck—suddenly, massively, and with Teutonic thoroughness. Scores of key Allied agents along the Riviera, including the leader of the SOE's Cannes *réseau* (unit), were trapped and arrested, all within a week's time. Up and down the Riviera, men and women of the Underground were caught. So precise and methodical had been the wave of arrests that SOE and OSS leaders were convinced that treachery was involved. The situation had become so perilous that leaders in some threatened reseaux were ordered to flee to the hills together with their men.

Despite the countless arrests and bestial treatment inflicted on those caught by the Gestapo and the SD, the Allied spy networks and the Underground in southern France continued to function with only minor disruptions. With Allied landings in southern France expected to occur soon, Roger, Cathedrale, Virginia Hall, and countless other such leaders refused to abandon their posts and flee to the mountains as their associates had begged them to do.

The War's Worst-Kept Secret

At his headquarters in the towering mountains of northern Italy, Field Marshal Albert Kesselring had been puzzled for several weeks. The astute *Oberbefehlshaber Süd* (commander-in-chief south) and his Intelligence officers had been pondering the significance of the disappearance of many elite paratrooper and commando-type units and three first-rate infantry divisions from Lt. Gen. Mark W. Clark's Fifth Army. Clark's force had driven the Germans out of Rome on June 4 and since that time had been locked in heavy combat north of the Italian capital with Col. Gen. Heinrich von Vietinghoff's veteran Tenth Army.

Kesselring, known to the Allied high command as Smiling Al because of his toothy grin when his picture appeared in Third Reich newspapers, had learned to fly at age forty-nine after thirty years as an artilleryman. He commanded air fleets in the Polish and Russian campaigns but later returned to ground-force command. Good-humored, invariably polite, and imperturbable, the field marshal was an expert bridge player and often entertained at dinner parties with his sleight-of-hand tricks of magic.

Experienced and shrewd, Kesselring soon had at least a partial answer to the riddle of the vanishing American units: The

Allied high command had secretly pulled these units from the front lines to launch an invasion elsewhere in the Mediterranean. By deduction, Kesselring concluded that the massive blow would strike behind German lines in Italy at Genoa or against southern France.

Mainly through left-behind spies, the "missing" American units were soon located by German Intelligence: The 3rd Infantry Division was undergoing intense amphibious training at Pozzuoli, near Naples, and the 36th Infantry Division was doing likewise on the beaches north of Naples. In the Salerno area, down the coast from Naples, the 45th Infantry Division was practicing assault landings against the precise beaches where the Allies had first forced a landing on Hitler's Fortress Europe in September 1943.

The Wehrmacht also learned that several American and British parachute and glider units were going through intense combat training at airfields scattered around Rome. As July turned into the dog days of August, high-flying Luftwaffe reconnaissance planes reported a massive collection of shipping, including scores of warships, at harbors in Italy, Corsica, Sardinia, Malta, and as far away as North Africa.

Operation Dragoon was the worst-kept military secret of the war. Maybe of any war. It was the subject of widespread gossip on the streets and in the sleazy waterfront bars of Naples, Rome, Salerno, and towns in Sardinia and Corsica. An Italian priest at Sunday mass urged his parishioners to pray for the American boys "who will soon be going into southern France." A store in Pozzuoli broke out with a new show-window display—a large stack of maps of the French Riviera. A young woman in a Naples brothel bid farewell to her longtime regular client, a member of the 45th Infantry Division: "I guess you won't be visiting again if you're going into southern France." The startled GI paid up and left.

Private Truesdell "Pat" Moser, an eighteen-year-old replacement with the veteran 509th Parachute Infantry Battalion, was listening to a popular American love song, "I'll Be Seeing You," over Radio Berlin. For days Moser had been regaled by veterans of his elite unit with "horror stories" of bloody encounters in Algeria, Tunisia, Salerno, Anzio, and elsewhere. Now he was in for another shock.

Suddenly the record finished playing and a sultry, sexy voice cooed: "Hello, all you American paratroopers at those airfields around Rome . . ."

Moser broke out of his reverie. He was stupefied. This was the Axis Sally (also known as the Berlin Bitch) whom the youth had been hearing so much about. How in the hell did she know where he and his paratrooper comrades were? Moser wondered.

"You parachute boys won't have to worry about bailing out over southern France," Axis Sally declared. "We'll have a reception committee waiting for you, and the flak will be so thick you can simply walk down on it."

By now several other GIs had gathered around the radio set. They always liked to hear what the Berlin Bitch had to say. "You fellows in Italy should be home taking care of your wives and girlfriends instead of letting the 4-Fs do it for you. Why get killed on the beaches of southern France when you could simply give up and go home after the war?" Axis Sally inquired in a solicitous tone. She then gave the name of Brig. Gen. Robert T. Frederick, leader of the 1st Airborne Task Force, a newly formed amalgamation of several independent parachute and glider regiments and battalions. Frederick's airborne men would spearhead the Dragoon assault, and its existence had been classified as top secret.

Axis Sally's revelations so bothered the thirty-seven-year-old Frederick that he drove north of Rome to interrogate personally German prisoners who had revealed to their captors that they knew the precise date and locale where the airborne force would be landing behind the Riviera beaches. With Frederick was his bodyguard, twenty-year-old Cpl. Duffield W. "Duff" Matson, Jr., a barrel-chested paratrooper who, by his own admission, was "one mean son-of-a-bitch," a vivid description not challenged by comrades.

Riding back to his headquarters outside Rome, Frederick was asked by Matson, "General, did you find out how those Kraut POWs knew when and where we're coming?"

The deceptively frail, soft-spoken Frederick, who had become a legend on the bloody Anzio beachhead for his battlefield heroism as leader of the commando-type 1st Special Service Force, replied, "They said it was a matter of common knowledge in their outfit."

Corporal Matson swallowed hard and made no comment.

Matson had been one of Bob Frederick's human reclamation

projects. The young general was not overly concerned with a man's past, only demanding that he be a fierce fighter and loyal to his comrades and his unit. A few weeks previously, Matson had been in an American military prison outside Rome, starting to serve his sentence for committing mayhem on a military police lieutenant and for assorted other acts of violence. Most of those with him were hard-timers. Some were up for murder, a few sentenced to be hanged. Matson had been court-martialed three times for attempted murder and was regarded as extremely dangerous and incorrigible. He was ready to kill on a moment's notice anyone who stood in his way—and the potential victim did not have to be wearing a German uniform.

One morning, after serving forty-five days, Matson was escorted from the prison by two of Frederick's paratroopers, Captain Pysienski and Leonard "Wahoo" Cheek, who had been an outstanding athlete at a Columbus, Georgia, high school. Matson was aware that both troopers had Tommy guns leveled at him. Forewarned of his charge's violent background, Captain Pysienski told Matson firmly, "The general wants to see you. He thinks you'll make a good fighting man. Don't try to escape or I'll blow your goddamned head off!"

Reaching the 1st Airborne Task Force headquarters, the young trooper was briefly interviewed by General Frederick. "I need a bodyguard. I think you'll do if you want to join us," he stated.

Stunned by the sudden dramatic turn of events in his life, Matson eagerly accepted. Only then were the two Tommy guns aimed at him lowered.

"This is Matson," Captain Pysienski called out to others in the office. "He's got a lot of talent we can use. He's one of us now."*

SOME ALLIED GENERALS called Bob Frederick a "crazy bastard." His men in the American-Canadian 1st Special Service Force, who idolized him, didn't mind. Left-handed praise, his hard-bitten fighters assured each other. Or jealousy. Generals weren't supposed to be up front, where the heavy shooting was

---

*After the war, Duffield W. Matson, Jr., graduated from the University of Miami, and his real-estate holdings and diversified business interests made him a millionaire. He told the author in 1985 that his association with General Frederick turned his own life around. Today (1985) Matson is a respected civic leader in Miami, Florida.

going on, and Bob Frederick had already been wounded several times in bitter fighting in Tunisia and in Italy.

Frederick's 1st Special Service Force had been known as the Black Devils of Anzio, a sobriquet pinned on them by the Germans, who grew to fear their nighttime raids when Frederick's men painted their faces black. His men paid him their highest accolade: They called Frederick the Head Devil.

Tales of Robert Tryon Frederick's courage under fire and his informal relationship with his men were legion. On Anzio one pitch-black night, the young general went with a raiding party that was setting out to raise hell behind German lines. The raiders stumbled into an enemy minefield, and several Black Devils had legs blown off and were screaming for help. Then German machine guns opened fire on the helpless Forcemen trapped in the minefield.

Two litter-bearers were lugging a legless man through the minefield when one medic was killed. Spotting a dark figure nearby, the surviving medic shouted, "Don't just stand there, you stupid bastard! Give me a hand!" The figure grabbed the other end of the litter and helped carry the legless man to safety as bullets zipped past every step of the way. Only then did the medic recognize his partner: General Bob Frederick.*

A lesser man than Bob Frederick would have been shaken by the monumental mission handed him in mid-July. Turning over command of his beloved 1st Special Service Force to his executive officer, Col. Edwin A. Walker, Frederick received a secret order to report at once to Lt. Gen. Jacob L. Devers, deputy supreme Allied commander in the Mediterranean Theater of Operations, in Algiers, North Africa. Known to his peers as Jakie, General Devers immediately got to the point with Frederick: "Bob, you're going to command our airborne troops in an invasion of southern France."

Frederick never changed expression, but his mind was in a whirl. Although a qualified paratrooper, he had no experience in planning airborne operations nor in commanding a strictly parachute and glider force.

"How long will we have to get ready for the mission?" Frederick finally asked.

"Five weeks—D-Day is August 15."

---

*By war's end, General Frederick had been wounded nine times.

Bob Frederick didn't reveal his shock. Only thirty-five days to plan, organize, and carry out a massive airborne attack, destined to be one of the largest of the war!

A few minutes later the young general asked Devers, "Well, where are my airborne troops?"

Devers looked Frederick directly in the eye and replied in measured tones, "So far *you* are the only one we have."

TYPICALLY, GENERAL FREDERICK wasted no time in hand-wringing or soul-searching over the enormity of the task suddenly thrust upon his narrow but sturdy shoulders. He established headquarters for the 1st Airborne Task Force (FABTF) at Lido di Roma Airfield outside the Italian capital, and by July 17 he had assembled all of his units at scattered airfields in the vicinity of Rome.

Its components scraped up hurriedly from throughout the Mediterranean, the FABTF would be of division size (9,732 officers and men), but there would be one notable difference in Frederick's force: Unlike other American and British airborne divisions that had trained and later fought as cohesive units, the FABTF was a collection of independent paratrooper and glider regiments, battalions, companies, and even platoons, which would have to be welded together with unprecedented swiftness. General Frederick knew few of the various units' officers, and few of them knew him.

The stakes were enormous; if Frederick's airborne force were to fail in its mission to spearhead the Dragoon assault and block off German attempts to rush reinforcements to the amphibious landing beaches, then the entire massive operation might well sputter or meet with disaster.

Code-named Rugby Force, General Frederick's command included:

The 517th Parachute Infantry Regiment (Col. Rupert D. Graves) and its attached 460th Parachute Field Artillery Battalion (Lt. Col. Raymond Cato), the 596th Parachute Engineer Company, the antitank platoon of the 442nd Infantry Regiment, and Company D of the 83rd Chemical Mortar Battalion.

The 509th Parachute Infantry Battalion (Lt. Col. William P. Yarborough) and attached 463rd Parachute Field Artillery Battalion.

The 550th Glider Infantry Battalion (Lt. Col. Edward

Sachs) and an attached platoon of the 887th Engineer Company.

The 551st Parachute Infantry Battalion (Lt. Col. Wood G. Joerg) and an attached platoon of the 887th Engineer Company.

The British 2nd Independent Parachute Brigade (Brig. C. H. V. Pritchard) and attached 2nd Chemical Mortar Battalion.

Several units slated to make the assault by glider, including the chemical mortar outfits and the antitank platoon, had not even seen a glider before, much less landed in one.

Some of Frederick's units, while keenly trained, tough, and spirited, had never heard a shot fired in anger. Although blooded in skirmishing in Italy only a few weeks before, Graves' 517th Parachute Infantry Regiment, the largest component in the FABTF, would be making its first combat jump.

ON JULY 19, General Frederick rushed Lieutenant Colonel Yarborough, commander of the veteran 509th Parachute Infantry Battalion, to the headquarters of Maj. Gen. Alexander M. Patch's U.S. Seventh Army in Naples. Yarborough was to work with Seventh Army planners in drastically revising the airborne plan that had been received by Frederick two days previously. Drawn up at the Seventh Army, the original plan was totally rejected by General Frederick, his staff, and subordinate commanders. A cardinal principle in airborne doctrine—landing troops in a concentrated mass—had been ignored.

"For chrissake," one of Frederick's officers had exploded after viewing the original plan, "they've got us landing in tiny groups all over southern France!"

Frederick had selected Colonel Yarborough for the crucial plan revision project because Yarborough was considered the most experienced and knowledgeable airborne officer in the Mediterranean. He had already planned two major parachute operations and had jumped with his troops in two of them. And because Frederick had great confidence in the thirty-two-year-old son of a regular army colonel.

Finishing his task at Naples, Yarborough hurried back to headquarters and showed the new plan to General Frederick.

"Now, that's more like it!" Frederick said, beaming.

The following day, the task force commander called his

battle leaders together to brief them on the forthcoming operation. Pointing at a large wall map of the Riviera region, Frederick said, ''See that town of Le Muy, about fifteen miles inland from the coastal town of Fréjus? All roads leading from the west, north, and east go through Le Muy. If we seize that town the Krauts will not be able to rush reinforcements to the coast and attack our seaborne forces while they are coming ashore and vulnerable. We will drop on and capture Le Muy.''

Frederick's Intelligence officer took the floor. From information gained from the French Underground and other sources, he pointed out, it appeared that some three thousand German troops would be encountered in the immediate Le Muy area.

''We'll run into a mixed bag around Le Muy,'' the G-2 stated. ''There'll be first-rate troops, including a thousand Wehrmacht officer candidates who can be expected to resist fiercely, and ragtag units of Orientals, Poles, and Russians who were dragooned into the Wehrmacht and will probably be looking for a chance to surrender.''

However, the G-2 warned, one factor would keep these non-Germans fighting: Determined, even fanatical junior officers and noncoms would have pistols in the backs of the ''volunteers.''

Lieutenant Colonel Yarborough, who had drawn up the airborne operational plan and whose 509th Parachute Infantry Battalion would spearhead the Dragoon assault, briefed the gathering on details. ''The airborne task force will strike just before dawn, ahead of the amphibious landings,'' he pointed out. ''Instead of being sprinkled around southern France in small packets, we're going to land in one big glob, around Le Muy. Our job is to block German reserves from rushing to the beaches, and to raise as much merry hell behind enemy lines as the law allows.''

Yarborough said that ''our 509th will jump at 4:15 A.M. on D-Day, land to the south and southeast of Le Muy, and capture the high ground overlooking the town. Colonel Graves's 517th Parachute Regimental Combat Team will jump fifteen minutes later and seize the high ground west and north of Le Muy and cover the main roads leading west to Toulon and to Draguignan, where a German corps headquarters is located.''

Yarborough added drily: ''Maybe with a little luck we will be able to personally invite a Kraut general at Draguignan to be a guest of the United States government.'' His words would prove to be prophetic.

At 6:00 A.M. the British 2nd Independent Parachute Brigade —the Red Devils—under Brigadier Pritchard, would jump and capture the town of Le Muy. A glider force would bring in artillery and mortars at 9:00 A.M., and at around 6:00 P.M. Joerg's 551st Parachute Infantry Battalion would jump, followed minutes later by Sachs's 550th Glider Infantry Battalion.

"Hopefully," Colonel Yarborough stated, "and I repeat the word 'hopefully,' the seaborne forces will link up with us no later than D-Day plus four."*

TRAINING WAS INTENSE for members of the airborne task force in the last part of July and early days of August. Speed marches with full combat gear, night and day. And more speed marches. Strenuous physical exercises that made tough men even tougher. Bodies became bronzed from the torrid rays of the Italian sun. Yet there was time for USO shows, with their inevitable bare-legged female dancers; goodies from the post exchange, which included Coca-Cola and cold beer; heatedly contested baseball, boxing, and soccer competition between rival outfits; and always a steady stream of paratroopers and glider fighters into eternal Rome.

Devout American airborne men had audiences with Pope Pius XII in the Vatican; others engaged in more worldly pursuits, including encounters with *vino* and with Roman ladies of the evening, who seemed to be on every corner of the fabled old city. GIs trod the cobblestones of the ancient Appian Way, viewed the crumbling Colosseum and the ancient Roman Forum, and strolled under the historic Arch of Constantine.

Then there were always the fights. Customarily the fisticuffs, often with bottles and saloon furniture in supporting roles, were between airborne men and straight-legs, as nonairborne soldiers were called. Inevitably the military police were drawn into the action.

Lieutenant Colonel Richard J. Seitz, a battalion commander in the 517th Parachute Infantry, formed up his men and cautioned them about getting into fights while on pass in Rome.

"If you get into trouble in town and less than three or four MPs are needed to take you to the stockade, I'll ship your ass out on the next train back to the straight-legs!" the twenty-five-

---

*After the war William Yarborough became commander of the Special Forces Center at Fort Bragg and later rose to three-star rank.

year-old Seitz roared.

To the paratroopers, this would be an ignominious fate, indeed. "Just to be on the safe side," a sergeant remarked to a comrade, "I'm going to make sure at least *five* MPs are needed to haul me in."*

AMERICAN PARATROOPERS WERE drawn from a wide spectrum of society. Each was a volunteer for hazardous duty. In the 1st Airborne Task Force there were dead-end kids from the slums of New York City's Lower East Side and scions of wealthy families, cowboys from Wyoming and rodeo riders from Montana, state troopers and large-city detectives, All-American football players and professional wrestlers, Golden Gloves boxing champions, lawyers, bellhops, motorcycle daredevils and circus tightwire walkers, teachers and drugstore clerks, ex-convicts and judges. They had one common denominator: Each was a fighter.

Paratroopers, a cocky and tough breed of warriors, were proud members of the world's most exclusive fraternity. Membership could not be bought or bestowed due to wealth, social standing, or political connections. Rather, entry through the hallowed portals of the paratrooper fraternity had to be earned by measuring up through the most grueling training program the human mind could create. Then one had to perform on the field of battle.

Due to the nature of the parachute business, there was a unique and close-knit relationship between officers and men, one of mutual respect and confidence in each other. Cooks, surgeons, generals, chaplains, clerks, riflemen, and medics faced identical dangers when jumping into combat. Bodies hurtling from airplanes and floating down under billowing white parachutes all looked alike to hostile gunners on the ground. A general or a colonel or a chaplain was just as likely to plunge to his death with a "streamer" (a chute that failed to open) as was the most humble private.

AT HIS HEADQUARTERS at Ciampino Airfield about six miles south of metropolitan Rome, Col. Rupert Graves, leader of the 517th Parachute Regimental Combat Team, was engaged in a

---

*Richard Seitz, from Kansas City, eventually rose to three-star rank and command of the XVIII Airborne Corps.

constant whirlwind of activities as he prepared his men for the ordeal they would soon face behind the white, sandy beaches of the Riviera. Graves, who graduated from West Point in 1924, was nearly forty-five years of age—"old" for a paratrooper. On occasion he reflected, "Good, God, I'm two decades older then my battalion commanders!" He had graying hair and a moustache that, to his teenage troopers, made him look "goddamned ancient."

Most of the time Colonel Graves was known to his officers and men as the Gray Eagle. But when they were angry at him over some real or imagined grievance, the Gray Eagle became Old Hose Nose.

Graves was not the rip-roaring, cursing, shouting type of battle leader found in some combat outfits. He was a courtly gentleman who had the rare ability to inspire his men to do their best for him. Most accorded him their highest accolade: Colonel Graves is a good man.

On the shaded slopes outside Frascati, Graves's men had pitched pup tents, and early in August they came down to the 517th Regiment's headquarters, where they were initiated into their roles in Operation Dragoon.

In closely guarded war rooms, the wide-eyed paratroopers studied large maps labeled "Top Secret" and memorized terrain features in the Riviera region, especially those on and around their DZs (drop zones). The eager parachutists peered intently at the irregular topography of painstakingly created sand-table reproductions of landing areas, etching indelibly in their minds each road, trail, ravine, creek, town, woods, lake, hill, and valley. This knowledge might be crucial when they were behind German lines.

Towns in southern France were given code names on the sand tables to keep objectives and the locale of the invasion safe from unauthorized prying eyes. The code names were Texas cities such as Houston, Galveston, and Fort Worth. A platoon sergeant in the 517th was given his troops' objective: They were to capture a town code-named "Dallas." As this particular group was leaving the briefing tent, the sergeant turned to a comrade and asked, "Say, I wonder what the population of Dallas is."

"Oh, I'd guess about a half million," the other replied, referring to the real Dallas, Texas. "Why do you ask?"

The sergeant was silent for several seconds, then declared

solemnly, "That's going to be a goddamned big job for only my one platoon."

A TEENAGER FROM Texas, Cpl. Charles E. Pugh of the 596th Parachute Engineer Company, was tuned in to Radio Berlin on a hot and humid afternoon. His tent was sweltering. Axis Sally was playing a record of "Sentimental Journey," a popular American ballad of the time. *Is she trying to tell us something?* Pugh thought. *Sentimental journey? To southern France, perhaps?*

The previous morning a battalion of the 517th Parachute Regiment, of which Pugh's combat engineer company was a component, had staggered through the outskirts of Rome after an all-night speed march and tactical exercise on the way back to their bivouac area near Frascati. Burdened by heavy combat gear and weapons, the troopers' faces were streaked with a mixture of black camouflage grease and perspiration. Thousands of Romans stared curiously at the passing American parachutists.

"Sentimental Journey" concluded, and sexy-voiced Axis Sally came on the air. "Hey, all you good-looking guys in the 517th Parachute Regiment outside Rome," she cooed, "you won't have to paint your faces black like you did yesterday when you come to southern France." Sally giggled, then added, "Because we're going to light up the sky so brightly with our ack-ack guns that the black faces won't help hide you!"

Several others joined Charlie Pugh in the tent. They were startled to know that the Berlin Bitch not only had pinpointed their location but also was aware of the locale in which Graves's men would land.

Now the female propagandist turned bitter and said with a snarl, "Our boys in southern France know how to take care of you vicious gangsters from Chicago!" To the Nazis, most Americans were gangsters from Chicago.

"Hell," called out a trooper, "the Berlin Bitch has been seeing too many goddamned old Al Capone movies!"

ON THE MORNING of August 1, the final draft of the operational plan for Dragoon was circulated to Allied commanders. The massive assault was to be launched along a forty-five-mile stretch of the Côte d'Azur between Cavalaire-sur-Mer and Agay, the targeted beaches being east of the German-held fortress port of Toulon. Shortly after midnight of D-Day, two thousand American and Canadian fighting men of Colonel Ed Walker's 1st Special Service Force—the Black Devils—would strike the first blow against the Nazis' South Wall.

Using rubber boats, electric-motored surfboards, and kayaks, Walker's men would storm ashore on the Îles d'Hyères, two pine-clad little islands just off the coast at the western flank of the assault beaches. Acting on information furnished by the French Underground, Allied Intelligence had learned that the Germans had a three-gun, 164mm battery on Île du Levant, the easternmost island, which could play havoc with the amphibious landings. The Black Devils were to silence this menacing battery—and quickly, before the main fleet arrived off the Riviera.

At the same time, a contingent of French commandos was to steal ashore on the mainland just north of the Îles d'Hyères. Code-named Romeo, this force was to block the main coast road leading from Toulon to prevent German reinforcements from reaching the landing beaches. The commandos had another crucial mission: They were to scale towering Cap Negre and destroy an enemy gun battery that could pound the ships offshore as well as the coastline in both directions.

Far to the northeast of Romeo Force, a French naval demolition team was to slip onto the mainland from rubber boats a short distance west of Cannes, blow up a coastal fortification, then establish block positions to prevent German troops in Cannes from rushing to the landing beaches. A short time later and before dawn, General Bob Frederick's paratroopers would pounce on the Wehrmacht behind the shoreline.

H-Hour for the main amphibious assault would be 8:00 A.M. After a massive pounding of German positions along the Riviera by heavy bombers, fighter-bombers, and warship guns, three Allied naval attack forces would each land an American division simultaneously and abreast. The three naval groups and the beaches on which they would deposit foot soldiers and tanks were code-named Alpha, Delta, and Camel. On the left flank, Alpha Force would carry Maj. Gen. John W. "Iron Mike" O'Daniel's veteran 3rd Infantry Division and take it ashore on two beaches thirteen miles apart, at Cavalaire and at Pampelonne. In the center, Delta Force would land Maj. Gen.

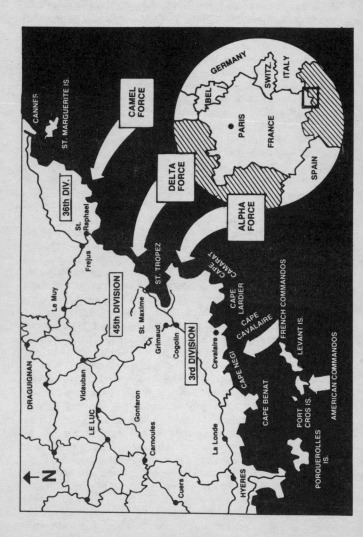

William W. Eagles's battle-tested 45th Infantry Division at Baie de Bougnon and at La Nartelle. On the right flank, Camel Force would deposit Maj. Gen. John E. Dahlquist's experienced 36th Infantry Division onto the coast at Saint-Raphael.

Once the three American assault divisions were ashore in strength, General of the Army Jean-Marie de Lattre de Tassigny's French II Corps would land and attack along the coast toward the southwest to capture the two primary objectives of Dragoon—the ports of Toulon and Marseilles.

AFTER READING HIS copy of the operation order, General de Lattre rushed to confer with Gen. Sandy Patch, commander of the Seventh Army. The French general was choked with emotion; after four years in exile, he would be returning to his homeland to help liberate it from the yoke of Nazi oppression. Yet he was angry—and deeply disappointed. His Fighting French were not to have the "honor" of joining in the initial assault against Hitler's South Wall.

The conversation was cordial yet cool. But in the end de Lattre resigned himself to a follow-up role for his corps when it was explained that there were not enough assault craft to land both the three-division American VI Corps and the French II Corps at the same time.

"Don't forget," the tall, thin Sandy Patch reminded his French subordinate, "it is you who will have the honor of seizing our two principal goals—Toulon and Marseilles!"

Patch and de Lattre shook hands and parted on friendly terms.

A Spider Web of
Espionage

Marie-Madeleine Fourcade, a petite homemaker, was peeling potatoes in the kitchen of her modest home in Aix-en-Provence on the hot afternoon of August 2 when she heard strange noises outside her door. Madame Fourcade felt her heart begin to beat faster, for along the Côte d'Azur the French civilians lived in an almost constant state of anxiety after twenty months under the heel of the hated Boche. Hardly a day went by that the natives along the wide sweep of the blue coast did not hear of savage reprisals taken against French "terrorists."

During the previous six weeks, ninety-nine hostages had been hanged at Tulle after an SS officer was shot and the "murderer" failed to come forward. In the Verdon region eleven Frenchmen, including five teenage boys, were hanged following a German troop-train derailment. Nine more boys were arrested by the Gestapo in Nice, and thirty teenagers were taken into custody in Vence. All were brutally interrogated, then shipped off to concentration camps.

Now Madame Fourcade felt a surge of terror as a heavy pounding shook her door, and moments later a squad of helmeted German soldiers and four civilians—by their felt hats obviously Gestapo—burst into her kitchen. She knew that the

German authorities had been stepping up arrests of French civilians with an Allied invasion of southern France almost certain to strike soon. But what on earth would this heavily armed contingent want with an Aix housewife in the act of preparing supper?

"Where's the man?" the Gestapo screamed at Marie-Madeleine. "Where's the man?"

The woman, white-faced with fright, dropped her peeling knife. She protested that there was no man, that she lived alone.

"You lie, bitch!" a Gestapo man screamed. "A man was seen in your courtyard."

The German stared icily at the woman. "He's tall, fair-haired, and you French terrorists call him the Grand-Duc," the Gestapo agent snapped.

"No, no, there must be some mistake," Madame Fourcade declared. "I know no one by that description, I am a woman alone, I tell you."

As casually as possible, Marie-Madeleine sauntered across the room and sat down on a sofa. One Gestapo man, who had been watching her every move, bolted across the room, kneeled down, and swept his hand under the sofa. He removed a sheaf of papers and, calling out in triumph, "Well, well, what have we here?" waved them overhead.

Madame Fourcade felt a white-hot surge of fear. These were the secret messages she had sent to London. Marie-Madeleine was a French secret agent, one of the most important, who was the founder and moving spirit behind an espionage network known as the Alliance of Animals. The Grand-Duc was one of the leaders in her spy apparatus along the Côte d'Azur. Only the previous day he had met with Madame Fourcade to discuss the distribution of six tons of ammunition, guns, grenades, explosives, radios, and other supplies that had been parachuted to a "safe" drop zone near Aix a few nights before.

Having found the incriminating evidence, the Gestapo agents slapped Marie-Madeleine repeatedly and shouted threats at her. "Confess you're a terrorist! Confess!" they yelled. "Where's the Grand-Duc? Talk, talk, if you know what's good for you!"

The Germans demanded that she give her true identity, or "We've got ways to make you talk!" Bleeding from the nose and mouth, Madame Fourcade played for time. Knowing from agents in her network that the Gestapo chief in Aix was out of town, the woman said scornfully, "I will talk only to your boss. You are too unimportant for me to talk to."

Grabbing the leader of the Alliance of Animals by the hair, the Gestapo agents, red-faced with anger, pulled her upright and hustled her outside and into a car. She was driven to Gestapo headquarters and roughly hurled into a cell, her captors still unaware that this was not just another "terrorist" but the leader of one of the biggest and most effective Allied spy networks in southern France.*

The Armée Secrète in southern France was a spider web of espionage and sabotage groups, a mysterious shadow force usually operating without uniforms or insignia. Even at the highest levels, Underground leaders chose to remain ignorant of one another's identity. What a Resistance fighter did not know could not be extracted from him or her in Gestapo torture chambers.

Each *réseau* in each cloak-and-dagger group operated independently, with a minimum of day-to-day direction from such leaders as the Grand-Duc, who was also code-named The Killer, and also known by the fictitious name Helin des Isnards. If this profusion of Underground code names was sometimes confusing to Resistance fighters, it was doubly so to the Gestapo. In the case of the Grand Duke, the Germans were not only diligently searching for him, but for The Killer and Helin des Isnards as well, all of them being the same person.

In theory, all Underground networks in southern France had been organized into one integrated organization—the État-Major des Forces Françaises de l'Intérieur (French Forces of the Interior, or FFI). This supposedly unified sabotage and Intelligence force included staff and agents of the American OSS, the British SOE, and two French spy agencies, all directed from London. In reality, there were intense rivalries and jealousies among the American, British, and French agencies, and in France, disputes among *reseaux* even within the same spy network. The internal intrigue was intense.

In June, an Allied group known as the Special Operation Center (SPOC) had been established in London. Its function was to parachute three-man teams known as Jedbourgs into

---

*That night Madame Fourcade made a daring escape from jail. She stripped naked, squeezed between two bars, dropped to the ground from the second level, and slipped off into the night to the home of a network comrade.

France to coordinate Underground actions and to help arm Resistance fighters. These Jeds (as they were called) consisted of an American OSS or British SOE officer, each fluent in the French language; a French officer; and a radio operator. In July, seven Jeds were dropped along the Côte d'Azur where Dragoon would soon strike. The Jeds would quickly learn that the true Underground situation in southern France was drastically different from that presented by SPOC briefing officers in London. The Jeds had been told that there was a cohesive force of twenty thousand to twenty-five thousand loyal Resistance fighters in the Côte d'Azur region, awaiting only the signal to spring from the shadows, armed to the teeth, onto the hated Boche. What the Jeds found were numbers only about half of those projected by SPOC, with only some five thousand of the Maquis (full-time Underground fighters) armed.

Besides fighting the Germans, the Underground in southern France competed with each other for power in postwar France. The Communists had formed the largest and best-organized Underground network, the Francs-tireurs et Partisans (FTP). Most of the FTP leaders were devoted to Moscow's leadership and regarded the Jed teams with suspicion.

A short time after parachuting into southern France, a Jed OSS officer radioed back to London: "There is no doubt that most Resistance activity in this region is being directed by Communists of the FTP." But the Jed teams worked with the FTP as well as they could, for disrupting the German defenses before Dragoon struck was still a common goal.

Two weeks before D-Day for Dragoon, American Capt. Geoffrey M. Jones, a twenty-five-year-old OSS officer and scion of a wealthy eastern family, parachuted into southern France and joined up with an FTP *réseau* of 150 Communists. Each morning, Jones reported to SPOC in London, the group loudly sang the "Internationale" (the Communist anthem) and *then* the "Marseillaise."

"They seem to be carried away with this Communist stuff," Captain Jones signaled. "They call each other 'comrade' and are always giving the clenched-fist salute."

In London, SPOC and other Allied authorities were deeply worried by field reports from southern France. They feared a massive rebellion by thousands of FTP advocates on the eve of Dragoon. André Dewavrin (code name, Colonel Passy), chief of General Charles de Gaulle's secret service in London, which dispatched many agents to France independently, on August 3 issued a top-secret report: "A Communist coup d'état [in southern France] to seize governmental power is to be expected."

ON AUGUST 4, U.S. Vice Adm. H. Kent Hewitt, commander of the Eighth Fleet, whose Western Task Force would participate in Dragoon, had a worried caller at his headquarters in Naples. The visitor, his face drawn and expressionless, was an old friend, U.S. Rear Adm. Don B. Moon. The soft-spoken, capable, well-liked Don Moon had arrived in Naples only a short time before and would be one of Hewitt's attack force commanders. For months Moon had planned the naval operation to land American troops on Utah Beach in Normandy on D-Day the previous June 6, then had commanded the assault force.

Even during the Normandy planning, Moon's friends had grown concerned over the endless hours he labored and his insistence on handling each minor detail instead of delegating them to his staff. On his arrival in the Mediterranean, he plunged into planning and rehearsals with his customary vigor. Now, after four sleepless nights, Admiral Moon trudged into Kent Hewitt's office. Hewitt was shocked by his demeanor; clearly Moon was near exhaustion.

Moon got right to the point. In a low voice he begged Hewitt to have the August 15 D-Day for Dragoon postponed, stressing that the Western Task Force was unprepared for the operation. Hewitt sought to reassure Moon that things were not as serious as they may have seemed. He promised to observe personally the final dress rehearsal for Dragoon and, if the rehearsal proved unsatisfactory, he would urgently request General Jumbo Wilson to postpone Dragoon.

The following morning an aide dashed into Hewitt's office. "Admiral Moon has just killed himself," the junior officer blurted out excitedly.

A victim of extreme physical and mental exhaustion, Don Pardee Moon, age forty-nine, was a battle casualty of Dragoon as surely as if he had been struck by a German shell while on the bridge of his flagship.

Shaken by the Moon suicide, Admiral Hewitt called in one of his experienced attack force commanders, Rear Adm. Frank J. Lowery, to seek his opinion of the readiness of the Western

Task Force. Now it was the bold Kent Hewitt seeking reassurance.

Lowry never hesitated. "All hands are so thoroughly indoctrinated in their tasks that they could make the landing without an operation order," he declared.

GERMAN SPIES VIEWING activities unfolding on a beach along the beautiful Gulf of Salerno on August 5 may have had a difficult time later trying to explain and interpret just what they had seen to their masters in the Abwehr in Berlin. The beach, nearly one hundred miles south of Rome, had been thickly studded with precise copies of the sturdy German obstacles that would be encountered along the Riviera landing beaches. Several top-secret, Rube Goldberg-type devices, recently developed in the United States, were being tested. The Mediterranean tide on D-Day in southern France would submerge the obstacles and make them difficult to demolish. How would the Allies clear the way for assault boats? These curious new devices and techniques might solve this crucial problem without having to rely on naval demolition teams.

As American generals and admirals looked on, bombers showered the experimental beach with small bombs rigged with special fuses to detonate a few feet above the surf, designed to cut wiring in the obstacles and explode mines. Then the Navy took over with a weird-looking array of new gadgets. There were the "apex" drone boat, a remote-controlled landing craft filled with tons of high explosives, to be detonated over German underwater obstacles; and the "Woofus," a rocket-equipped craft carrying seven-inch rockets with a range of three hundred yards, which would be fired into the maze of underwater beach obstacles. "Reddy Fox" was a long pipe filled with explosives to be towed over obstacles, sunk, and detonated.

At the conclusion of the experimental exercise, the American brass were not impressed. It had been proven that none of the Buck Rogers devices (as the GIs called them) were dependable. They would be used in the Dragoon amphibious assault, but the principal reliance would have to be placed on the "frogmen," the underwater demolition units. Each frogman team consisted of one naval officer, five sailors, and five enlisted Army engineers. They would be the first in; their expected longevity in the assault would be measured in minutes.

MEANWHILE, IN A closely guarded building in downtown Naples, American Intelligence officers had for weeks been poring over huge stacks of photos. In 1942, shortly after the outbreak of war, American Intelligence issued a plea to civilians to turn in old photos and snapshots taken in recent years in Europe and the Mediterranean region. Puzzled by the curious request, the home front responded with a deluge of hundreds of thousands of snapshots, most taken with home Kodaks during carefree vacations in peacetime.

Now American Intelligence officers, peering through magnifying glasses, were gleaning crucial information on the Riviera assault region. A shapely young woman pictured standing waist-deep in the surf at Cavalaire revealed that low-bottomed landing craft could reach onto the beach at that point. A faded snapshot of two children posing on the ramparts of an old fort at Saint-Tropez furnished clues about the size of warship guns needed to demolish the structure. The unknown man who snapped a photo of his wife with a background of the coastline west of Saint-Raphael permitted an artist to render a detailed drawing of the beach there.

IT WAS NEARING midnight on August 5 when several furtive figures moved into the deep shadows alongside a large green field a few miles east of the town of Draguignan, some sixteen miles inland from the Riviera beaches. One of those stealthily slipping beneath a spreading oak tree was Pierre Aumont, a forty-four-year-old proprietor of a Draguignan cafe, a popular spot for the German Feldgrau when they were off-duty. There the homesick young soldiers of the Third Reich would gulp copious amounts of *vin,* loudly sing the lilting German ballad "Lili Marlene," and engage in friendly conversation with the jovial proprietor, Monsieur Aumont.

"Good old Pierre," the boys in the rumpled gray-green uniforms and hobnailed boots told each other. "He's a real friendly guy."

In recent months, some natives of Draguignan had come to believe that Pierre Aumont was too friendly to the hated Boche. There had been ugly rumblings among the citizenry over his cozy relationship with the soldiers visiting his cafe, how late at night when the wine was flowing the cafe proprietor would be laughing and talking with the German boys, even provide a sympathetic ear to their complaints over a pompous new colonel or the fact that their unit had been alerted for transfer to the fighting front in Normandy.

Aumont was a shameless excuse for a Frenchman, some of his neighbors said with a snarl. They had no way of knowing that for more than a year the jovial cafe proprietor had been chief of the local *réseau* of General de Gaulle's Armée Secrete, nor that almost daily he sent terse reports to London on what he had learned talking to German soldiers whose tongues had been loosened by the wine he served them.

Now, around this dark field outside Draguignan, Aumont and his men tensely waited. Soon there was the drone of a large aircraft; then the engine noise got louder as the plane began circling the field. A series of blinking lights came from the C-47; then Pierre stepped out of the shadows and replied with the muted blue glow of his flashlight. Moments later, several large white parachutes blossomed in the sky and floated to the ground. Each had several large containers attached to it.

Aumont and his shadowy comrades felt their heartbeats quicken. If the Gestapo were secreted in the vicinity, this was the precise point in the proceedings that they would strike. The Underground men dashed from their hiding spots, grabbed up the containers, and began lugging them to two trucks parked in the underbrush along a nearby road. The parachutes were gathered in and buried. Inside the containers were grenades, explosives, Tommy guns, and vast amounts of ammunition— enough to arm Aumont's entire *réseau*. An hour later Pierre was back in his cafe, laughing and joking with late-drinking Feldgrau. Good old Pierre.

Onto designated fields up and down the Riviera region on this and succeeding nights, more than one hundred thousand containers of weapons, explosives, and ammunition were parachuted to Resistance groups, their reception and distribution guided by the Jedbourg teams of Allied secret agents. There was one restriction placed on the enormous parachute operation: Under no circumstances were the containers to fall into the hands of the Francs-tireurs et Partisans, the Communist Underground.

* * *

UP AND DOWN the Allied-occupied boot of Italy, fighting men of diverse backgrounds and cultures were preparing for the assault against the Nazis' South Wall. One of these groups, the Goumiers, were fierce Berber tribesmen, skilled in mountain fighting and feared by the Germans for their knife-wielding talents. Recruited from the Atlas Mountains of Morocco, the Berbers fought under French officers and had gained wide fame for battlefield heroism in Italy.

The red-turbaned Berbers, who would land in southern France with de Lattre's French corps, were unsmiling, kept to themselves, and seldom spoke to outsiders. The Americans noticed that the Berber tribesmen were constantly sharpening their nasty-looking knives. It was whispered that the Moroccan fighters cut off the ears of victims and were rewarded in cash by the French for each ear turned in.

GIs gave the tribesmen a wide berth. "Do they get cash for German ears or for American ears also?" an outsider asked, only partly in jest.

Fond of drinking goats' milk, the Berbers took goats into battle with them. But this extra encumbrance did not prevent the tribesmen from being terrors in combat.

"I'm glad those mean-looking bastards are on our side!" a GI said, summing up the sentiments of the Americans.

IT WAS THE lot of Iron Mike O'Daniel's 3rd (Rock of the Marne) Infantry Division to suffer the first casualties of Operation Dragoon—far from the fortified beaches of the Riviera. Already veterans of three major amphibious assaults, the 3rd Division was preparing to conduct a full-scale dress rehearsal. O'Daniel, square-jawed and tough, and his subordinate commanders considered realistic rehearsals crucial, omitting nothing but enemy troops firing live ammunition back.

The site chosen for the practice landing was north of Naples, near the mouth of the Garigliano River. All during the previous winter, this region had been part of the Germans' defensive line, and Wehrmacht engineers had planted mines so thickly that the area bristled with fiendish explosives and booby traps. As part of the realistic training for Dragoon, it fell upon the 10th Engineer Battalion to clear mines from beaches and roads leading inland to permit the 3rd Division to conduct its practice landing. It proved to be a nasty job—and a bloody one. But the 10th Engineers completed the "noncombat" mission—at a cost of eighteen men killed and forty-three wounded.

At the conclusion of the Dragoon assault rehearsal, the 3rd Division was assembled in an enormous olive grove near Naples. Major General Lucian K. Truscott, Jr., leader of the VI Corps and known to his men as the Green Hornet after a dashing comic-strip character, spoke over a loudspeaker:

"Men, I'm not asking you to hate the Germans. I'm only telling you that you've got to win this war! Win it, I tell you! Win it!"

Iron Mike O'Daniel, the firebrand, took the microphone from his boss, shook his fist violently, and roared: "You can take it from me, boys—hate the Germans! Hate the bastards! Cut your initials on their goddamned faces!"

A mighty roar from fourteen thousand throats echoed across the landscape. "Give 'em hell, Iron Mike," a soldier shouted, "give 'em hell!"

ON AUGUST 10, at his tree-shrouded old château on the outskirts of Avignon, Gen. Friedrich Wiese was handed a top-secret signal from Oberkommando der Wehrmacht in Berlin. It was the latest Intelligence analysis of the situation in the Mediterranean. Wiese's trained eye quickly caught the key sentence: "No large-scale landings are contemplated by the Allies for the time being."

The Nineteenth Army commander pitched the report onto his desk, already piled high with a deluge of previous Intelligence estimates. For three weeks he had been bombarded with predictions of impending Allied landings in the Mediterranean. Now, overnight, OKW had executed a complete flip-flop—no landings were expected for the time being.

"Botsch," the frustrated Wiese remarked resignedly to his chief of staff, "considering our limited means for reconnaissance, the only way we're going to know Allied intentions for certain is when they hit the beaches."*

AT THE SAME time General Wiese was reading the OKW signal at Avignon, hundreds of miles to the south a small convoy of

---

*General Walther Botsch narrowly escaped an Adolf Hitler-ordered firing squad seven months later. It would be the capable Botsch's misfortune to be in command of the Rhine River sector where the Americans seized the Remagen bridge and poured across the water barrier.

Allied vessels was steaming out of the ports of Taranto and Brindisi, deep in the heel of the Italian boot. One of the transports, the *Princess Beatrix,* a Royal Navy vessel skippered by Capt. J. D. King was carrying a seven-hundred-man force of French commandos. They would strike in the darkness shortly after midnight of D-Day, at Cap Negre.

Commanded by Lt. Col. Georges-Regis Bouvet, a tough, demanding battle leader, the commandos were a select group, chosen after the most intense screening, then hardened by an arduous training program. Day after day Colonel Bouvet had driven his men to the limit of their endurance. At night they climbed the steepest cliffs, snaked their way through minefields in pitch blackness, assaulted thick-walled bunkers and blew them up with dynamite charges. There were arduous forty-mile speed marches under a torrid Mediterranean sun while burdened with full battle gear. Colonel Bouvet knew German tanks would be encountered. So he had his men scoop out shallow slit trenches, lie down in them, and have light tanks roll over them. Later medium tanks and then heavies would follow suit.

There were casualties on occasion in this grueling training in preparation for the commandos' return to their native land. But those who endured emerged as tough, hardened, steel-willed, and resourceful fighting men, ready for any ordeal they would face on the shores of southern France.

For the preceding month, Colonel Bouvet had been the only one in his force who was permitted to know the exact target of his French commandos. Only within the preceding 24 hours had his men been let in on the secret: They would scale the precipitous, 350-foot-high face of Cap Negre, destroy German positions there, then establish positions blocking the coast highway at Cavalaire against German reinforcements heading for the landing beaches from Toulon.

As the convoy that included the *Princess Beatrix* set a course for the Riviera beaches on August 10, one of those lining the railings of the transport was M. Sgt. Noel Texier. As fighting men go, Texier was "old"—tough, durable, resourceful, yet getting along in years. Hand-to-hand combat and scaling sheer cliffs as high as a forty-story building were endeavors for the young.

Sergeant Texier had been seriously wounded in North Africa the previous year and had already reached retirement age for his rank. There were only three weeks remaining in his active duty, and he would finish out the war in some cushy rear-area assignment. But Texier had begged Colonel Bouvet to permit him to take part in the midnight assault against his homeland. Bouvet finally gave in.

The aging sergeant was filled with deep emotion. He peered out across the endless expanse of blue sea toward his beloved France. After four years, he would be returning, along with his seven hundred fellow commandos, to help free his country.

There against the railing of the *Princess Beatrix*, Texier in his mind's eye could already see the shores of his native land, even though it was still hundreds of miles over the distant horizon. Even now tears welled up in his eyes. Neither Noel Texier nor his comrades had any way of knowing that in less than five days he would be dead—possibly the first Allied soldier to be killed in the liberation of southern France.

Hitler Makes a Fateful Decision

At his headquarters at Rouffiac, near Toulouse, on the evening of August 10, Col. Gen. Johannes Blaskowitz had grown increasingly frustrated and irritable. Messages had been pouring into the communications center of his Army Group G headquarters all day. But not the one he had been urgently anticipating for nearly a week.

Convinced by early August that the Allies would not strike in the Bay of Biscay area of southwestern France, Blaskowitz had sought approval from Oberkommando der Wehrmacht to rush his first-rate 11th Panzer Division from the Bordeaux region, along the Atlantic Seaboard, to the Marseilles-Toulon area near the Riviera. There the 11th Panzer would be in position to launch an immediate counterattack against the Allies on the landing beaches.

Blaskowitz had already alerted the commander of the 11th Panzer Division, Maj. Gen. Wend von Wietersheim, to roll on two hours' notice. But for seven days and nights now, von Wietersheim had been cooling his heels at his CP in the village of Languedoc, vainly waiting for the order to take to the roads for the Riviera. The 11th Panzer was the only armored reserve in southern France and like all Wehrmacht tank formations could not be committed nor moved without the specific approval of the Führer himself.

Blaskowitz on this hot, sultry tenth day of August railed to his staff over the stupidity of the Wehrmacht command structure. The system often left battle commanders powerless to react until Adolf Hitler reached a decision at Wolfsschanze (Wolf's Lair), his headquarters outside Rastenberg in East Prussia. Blaskowitz was unaware that the Führer's indecision was the result of Hitler's having been taken in completely by a British deception, a ploy code-named Operation Ironside.

The Ironside stratagem was the brainchild of the XX Committee,* a shadowy organization based in Great Britain and whose function was to confound and confuse Hitler and the Wehrmacht about Allied intentions. A creature of MI-6, the British secret service agency, the XX Committee consisted of the finest—and most devious—intellects that could be congregated from throughout the empire. One of the XX Committee's crowning glories was Operation Fortitude, an incredibly complex and sophisticated ploy intended to deceive the Wehrmacht about the time and locale of Overlord, the massive cross-channel invasion of Normandy.

So successful had been the Overlord deception plan in bamboozling Hitler that the Führer ordered his strong Fifteenth Army to remain idle for seven weeks along the Pas de Calais while his Seventh Army was cut to pieces by the invaders only a day's road march to the west. Hitler had been convinced through the XX Committee's stratagem that the Pas de Calais, only twenty miles from England, would be struck a second and more powerful blow by an army group led by Lt. Gen. George S. Patton, Jr. Listed on battle maps at OKW as a one-million-man unit assembled in southeastern England, Army Group Patton was a phantom force created solely through the nimble minds on the XX Committee.

As part of the ingenious Normandy deception ploy, Operation Ironside was given birth. Ironside was designed to convey to the German high command that the Bordeaux region would be invaded after Normandy, with the hope of pinning down General von Wietersheim's 11th Panzer Division as long as possible. It was believed that the Ironside stratagem would keep the 11th Panzer near Bordeaux and away from the Normandy

*Unofficially better known as the Double-cross Committee.

landing beaches for a few days or a week at most, until the invading Allies were firmly established ashore. But so completely had Hitler and his military advisers been hoodwinked by Ironside that two months later the 11th Panzer was still sitting idle at Bordeaux.

The principal actress on the Ironside stage was a beautiful young Latin American. Her father had been assigned to the Argentine embassy in Nazi-controlled Vichy, France, in 1942 when his eye-catching daughter visited him there. At a cocktail party, an Abwehr official suggested that she slip into England as a German spy. The young woman, apparently flattered at the offer, smiled broadly and accepted the proposition.

Two days later she departed for England by way of neutral Spain. When she reached Madrid she made a side trip to the British embassy. There she told her story, and MI-6 arranged for her entry into England. But first it would be necessary for British security authorities in London to detain her for a few weeks to allay German suspicions.

In due time, the lady, now code-named Bronx, began corresponding with the Abwehr through letters written in invisible ink and mailed at a Lisbon bank where she had an account. The ''neutral'' Spaniards would see that the letters reached their destination—they were more friendly toward the Reich than they were toward the Allies. MI-6 supplied her with a steady flow of harmless information which, to the Germans, appeared authentic and valuable. Her Abwehr controllers were so impressed with her spy work that they put her on a comfortable salary and sweetened it with regular bonuses.

For nearly a year, Bronx had been reinforcing Abwehr confidence in her thorough regular reports furnished by MI-6. Finally, in mid-May 1944, Bronx sent an urgent commercial telegram (through the regular Lisbon service) to the Abwehr, using a secret code given her by the Germans. Innocuous to the unknowing eye, the message was deciphered by the Abwehr: ''I have definite information that the Allies will invade the Bay of Biscay [Bordeaux] on or about June 15, 1944.''

IN BERLIN ON the afternoon of August 11, Admiral Wilhelm Canaris, who had gained a towering reputation in the First World War as a clever and productive spy for the Kaiser, was poring over urgent signals received from his Abwehr agents at

Gibraltar and in Madrid. The coded messages stated: "Large Allied convoys have left North African ports with troops and supplies. Destination unknown." Canaris rushed this alarming information to Hitler and his advisers at Wolfsschanze.

Late that night at Avignon, General Wiese was handed an urgent message from OKW. They had turned 180 degrees from the previous day's flip-flop: "Allied convoys carrying troops have departed North Africa. Might land at Genoa [Italy, behind Kesselring's lines] or in southern France or at both locales at the same time." Wiese pitched the latest estimate of Allied intentions in the Mediterranean onto his desk.

SHORTLY BEFORE MIDNIGHT on August 11, General Blaskowitz stuck his head into the office of his chief of staff, Maj. Gen. Heinz von Gyldenfeldt, at Army Group G headquarters near Toulouse, 240 miles west of the Riviera. "Any word from Wolfsschanze on shifting the 11th Panzer?" Blaskowitz inquired. "Nein, Herr General" was the reply. The army group commander already knew that only silence had prevailed at Hitler's headquarters concerning his urgent request of a week before. So crucial was shifting the 11th Panzer to the Riviera, his chief of staff would have rushed to him with word once the Führer had reached a decision. Muttering to himself, Blaskowitz stalked out of the room and headed upstairs to steal a few hours of sleep.

Ominous rumblings in the Mediterranean were now beginning to worry Wehrmacht commanders. Shortly after daybreak on August 12, a pair of Luftwaffe reconnaissance pilots radioed back that they were flying over a large Allied convoy of some seventy-five to one hundred vessels, including a number of troop transports. The sea armada was steaming steadily along the coast of Corsica.

AT THE OFFICERS' mess at General Wiese's headquarters in Avignon at noon that day, excited diners were intently discussing the latest reports reaching the Nineteenth Army. From traitors in the French Underground, it had been learned that the Allies might strike along the southern coast of the Mediterranean on August 15. Most German officers were relieved that the suspense would soon be over. Waiting for the other shoe to drop (the first had fallen in Normandy) had been a nerve-racking ordeal, for General Wiese on down to the privates on guard at machine-gun posts along the Côte d'Azur.

OUTSIDE THE U.S. Seventh Army's headquarters in the Flambeau Building in Naples was parked a curious-looking truck of British manufacture. A twenty-six-foot antenna reached for the sky in the center of its roof. Uniformed personnel, most wearing the blue of Britain's Royal Air Force or the brown of the Royal Corps of Signals, rushed busily from the truck into the headquarters and back out again.

The camouflaged British truck and the activities of the pleasant but tight-lipped English servicemen involved with it were so thickly shrouded in secrecy that its presence at an American Army headquarters was a source of ceaseless speculation. Only General Patch, the Seventh Army commander, his chief Intelligence officer, and two other top staff officers were aware of the communications truck's function. Vehicle and crew were known as an SLU (special liaison unit), and it furnished General Patch with a continual flow of deciphered top-secret German wireless signals. Often Patch would be reading the Wehrmacht messages at the same time their intended German recipients were poring over them in Avignon and Rouffiac, in Berlin and at Wolfsschanze.

On a regular basis, an RAF officer would hand General Patch a pirated German signal the SLU had received from its base in a large stone Victorian mansion just outside the quiet little town of Bletchley Park, forty miles north of London. At this top-secret center—referred to in hushed tones as Station X—coded messages flowing among Hitler, his generals, and assorted Wehrmacht headquarters were intercepted, deciphered, and sometimes evaluated.

Central to the Bletchley Park operation was one of the most closely guarded secrets of the war—the Ultra decoding machine. Just before the outbreak of hostilities in Europe, British spies, with the aid of Polish Intelligence, had stolen a precise copy of a highly secret and complex German encoding machine code named Enigma. So ingenious and sophisticated was Enigma that Hitler and the Wehrmacht considered its code unbreakable.

A team of Great Britain's foremost mathematicians and cryptanalysts, working for months in intense secrecy, had solved the "unbreakable" Enigma code with the aid of their own highly sophisticated machine, Ultra. From that point, German secret signals were intercepted by the British, decoded, and distributed to key commanders and governmental officials.*

Now, at the SLU truck at the Seventh Army's closely guarded headquarters building early on the morning of August 12, a Royal Air Force officer slipped out of the truck, clasping a secret German message in one hand. He glanced at the sole of first one boot, then the other. He could not risk the off chance that bits and pieces of ultrasecret material in the wireless truck had stuck to the bottom of his boots. These scraps might shake loose and be found by unauthorized persons.**

Reaching General Patch's office, the RAF officer marched past three sharp-eyed military policemen and handed the decoded German signal to the Seventh Army commander. Patch studied the intercepted message closely as the British officer stood by silently. Without a word, the general gave the message back to the officer, who took it to the SLU truck and immediately burned it.

Patch called in his chief of staff and G-2. "Just read a couple of Wehrmacht Intelligence signals," the low-key commander told his staff officers. "The Germans can't decide if we're going to hit Genoa, the Riviera, or both places at the same time."

Sandy Patch was not the bombastic, two-fisted, hell-for-leather-type combat leader. Yet, in his soft-spoken manner, he brought out the best in those serving under him. Patch mixed easily with his fighting men, often chatted with them while rolling a cigarette from a sack of Bull Durham. In World War I he saw action on the Aisne and the Marne, at bloody Saint-Mihiel and in the Meuse-Argonne. Shortly after Pearl Harbor, Sandy Patch was rushed to the Pacific, where he whipped a hodgepodge collection into shape as the Americal (America-Caledonia) Division, then led it to Guadalcanal, where it relieved elements of the Marines and helped drive the Japanese from the island.

---

*Not until thirty years after the end of World War II was the secret of Ultra's existence disclosed by the British government. The Western Allies thought Ultra might be needed if war were to break out with the Soviet Union.

**In recent weeks the British had reluctantly agreed to the integration of American officers into the SLUs. But the Ultra operation was still primarily British.

Now in Naples, in the Flambeau Building surrounded by a high wall and security guards, Sandy Patch was facing the greatest challenge of his life—commanding an entire field army in the crucial invasion of southern France. Only a few close friends knew that he was harboring a gut-wrenching personal worry: His only son, Capt. Alexander M. Patch, Jr., like his father a West Pointer, was in the thick of the heavy fighting with his infantry outfit in Normandy.*

LATE ON THE evening of August 12, large numbers of bulky LSTs carrying men of Iron Mike O'Daniel's 3rd Infantry Division began slipping out of crowded Naples Harbor. Starting to darken, the sky was cloudless. A soldier named Patelli called out to comrades on a crowded deck: "Take it from me, the first wave is the best to be in. If you don't like the machine guns shooting at you from a pillbox on the right, you have your choice of attacking the pillbox shooting at you on the left. But the second wave has no choice. They have to attack whatever pillboxes were bypassed!"

It was grim dogface humor. The soldiers around Patelli, many of them battle-hardened veterans of three previous amphibious assaults, continued to play poker on the deck. Somehow, humor had gone out of their lives.

Soon another voice was raised: "Okay, fellows, take your last look at beautiful, sunny Italy!" No one budged. "Deal the cards!" a soldier grumbled without looking up.

Inwardly, the men were tense. Stomachs were queasy. Many felt a thinly veiled sense of doom. These were what the Army called assault troops. They would be the first to hit the beach, and there would be nothing between them and spitting German machine guns but the buttons on their shirts. This could be a rough one. And every man on board knew it.

Inside a wardroom on a troop transport carrying elements of the 3rd Division's 7th Regiment, Capt. Ralph M. Flynn and Lt. Glenn E. Rathbun were teamed up in a hot and heavy card game against Captain Sladick, a battalion surgeon, and the ship's Navy doctor. Stakes were two cents a point, and in short order Flynn and Rathbun had cleaned up on the two medical officers.

Suddenly the card players heard rousing cheers from soldiers

---

*Later Capt. Alexander M. Patch, Jr., would be killed in action.

jammed onto the decks. "What in hell's that?" one officer asked.

"Hitler's probably learned the 3rd Division's coming and has killed himself," another replied drily.

Rathbun and the other three rushed out on deck and tried to edge through the excited olive-drab throngs as the cheering continued to echo across the placid seascape. "It's Winnie!" the men shouted. "It's Winnie!" Standing on his toes behind a group of GIs pushing against the railing, Rathbun could see the British destroyer *Kimberley* sailing along parallel to the transport only some fifty yards away. Bare-headed, beaming, and with the ever-present oversized cigar stuck in his mouth, Winston Churchill stood on the *Kimberley's* bridge and repeatedly flashed the V for Victory sign to the cheering multitude of American soldiers sailing to battle.

The British Bulldog had fought against Dragoon for months, right up to one week before D Day, and had pleaded his case before the highest American tribunals, Eisenhower and Roosevelt. Now, outwardly at least, the prime minister had scuttled his own personal hostility toward the southern France invasion and was on hand to wish the Allied fighting men well.

As Churchill assumed his customary role in the spotlight, another man standing next to him on the *Kimberley's* bridge remained unnoticed by the GIs in the convoy. Dressed casually, in Navy work clothes, was one of the United States' highest-level military authorities, Undersecretary of War Robert P. Patterson. Had anyone been mildly curious as to the identity of Patterson, he probably would have passed him off as an elderly deckhand seeking to edge into Churchill's limelight.

THAT SAME DAY in Berlin, a junior officer of the Kriegsmarine staff penned in the organization's war diary: "A large-scale Allied landing, either near Genoa or in southern France, is imminent." One of the Abwehr's "most dependable" left-behind spies in Naples signaled that the American cruiser *Augusta,* a headquarters ship bristling with antennae, had just weighed anchor. The *Augusta* had been floating headquarters for the invasion of Normandy, so the Abwehr's Canaris reasoned that so sophisticated a ship would not be employed merely to help bombard the Italian coast.

The final entry in the war diary of Rear Adm. Heinrich Ruhfus, naval commander at Toulon, on August 12, stressed that the whole Mediterranean coast was "in great danger . . . It can hardly be hoped that an invasion can be beaten off by our forces." In Paris that day, Adm. Theodor Krancke, commander of Kriegsmarine West, predicted that an invasion of southern France would begin on August 15 and added, "It will probably hit in great strength on the Rhône delta," an accurate estimate that events would prove.

BY THE EVENING of August 12, Gen. Lucian Truscott's entire assault corps was afloat—the 3rd, 36th, and 45th Infantry divisions and attached units. At 9:00 P.M. Truscott was piped aboard the command ship for the amphibious assault, the *Catoctin,* which was bristling with radar and radio antennae.

For the first time ever (including the enormous Normandy invasion), a command ship for an invasion carried top Army, Navy and Air Corps leaders and their staffs, those responsible for the operation. On board the *Catoctin* were Gen. Sandy Patch; Adm. Kent Hewitt; Brig. Gen. Gordon P. Saville, leader of the U.S. Twelfth Air Force, whose warplanes would lend massive support to the invaders; and General Truscott. When Truscott hopped off the gangplank and onto the deck, he was greeted by his boss, General Patch. Knowing that no battle leader wants a superior officer looking over his shoulder, Patch said, "Truscott, I have to come along on the *Catoctin,* but I want you to know I do not want to embarrass you in any way. I am not going to interfere with the way you fight your battle. I want you to know it."

Truscott was moved by Patch's typically considerate gesture. "Well, thank you, General," Truscott replied. "I have no desire but to work in the closest possible cooperation with you, and I'll always be glad to have your advice."

The *Catoctin* was the ultimate in sophisticated command ships, equipped in and sent directly from the United States for the southern France invasion. The ship's maze of communications equipment was the kind that leaders of previous Allied invasions had only dreamed about. The *Catoctin's* radar equipment was the most accurate that scientists and engineers could create. Her radio communications room held nearly fifty sending sets, and newfangled luminous screens for announcements were incorporated into banks of teleprinters. Her switchboard would allow battle commanders to follow every minute detail of the unfolding operation, both on the landing beaches and on the water. An enormous luminous dial would furnish a minute-by-minute accounting of all floating vessels, including the tiny assault craft. Never before in warfare would invasion commanders have such a wealth of ongoing information at their fingertips and before their eyes.

Nearly a thousand soldiers, sailors, and airmen, most dressed in work fatigues, were jammed onto the decks along with the immaculately clad generals and admirals, their neatly pressed uniforms, gold braid, and silver stars gleaming in the fast-fading rays of the Mediterranean sun. Unnoticed in the human crush aboard the *Catoctin* was a slight, gray-haired man in khaki trousers and shirt open at the neck. His nose, flattened by a blow years before, gave him the appearance of a retired welterweight boxer. He did nothing to attract attention to himself, but here was the man largely responsible for the creation of this enormous American fleet. Secretary of the Navy Jim Forrestal was going along on the amphibious assault.

Unassuming James Vincent Forrestal—World War I aviator; president of the New York investment firm of Dillon, Read & Company; and one of the chief administrative architects of the mightiest fleet mankind had ever known—did not even complain when he was assigned modest-sized sleeping quarters on the *Catoctin*, jammed in with three others.

As a bright sun peeked over Naples Harbor the next morning, General Lucian Truscott was already up and out on deck. Like nearly all on the *Catoctin*, the VI Corps commander had spent a sleepless night in his hot, airless stateroom. And like any battle leader soon going into a desperate struggle with a determined enemy, Truscott's mind had been awhirl as he tossed and turned through the night.

At 11:00 A.M. the *Catoctin* hoisted anchor and began to edge out of Naples Harbor. The bay for days had been filled with ships and smaller craft of every description; now it was virtually deserted. The slower-moving LSTs, LCIs, and LCTs, with their warship escorts, had departed the previous evening. The headquarters ship would be part of a speedier convoy. As hundreds of Americans lined the decks, a high-powered speedboat was seen knifing through the waters of the Bay of Naples, heading for the *Catoctin*. Its sleek bow, rising out of the water, was gushing spray to each side. Nearing the command ship, the speedboat halted and suddenly a huge chorus of cheers erupted from the decks of the *Catoctin,* as if on cue, for none could mistake the roly-poly figure standing up in the approaching craft, with his Frank Buck sun helmet; rumpled, ill-fitting seersucker suit; and cigar tightly clenched between the teeth. The omnipresent, indefatigable British Bulldog, Winston Churchill, had dashed by to flash his famous V for Victory sign and, over a loudspeaker, wish the command group good luck.

AT PICTURESQUE AVIGNON, headquarters of the German Nineteenth Army, on the afternoon of August 13, General Wiese was growing increasingly edgy. Along with the oppressive heat, there seemed to be some sort of indefinable aura of doom hovering over the Riviera region, perhaps the calm before the storm. Reports continued to flow into his communications center from high-flying Focke-Wulf pilots who'd sighted numerous Allied convoys off Corsica, Sardinia, and the boot of Italy. And the French civilians seemed to be restless, flitting about on unknown missions. Allied bombers had stepped up their attacks, pounding German gun batteries and rail and road centers as far east as Genoa in Italy.

At 4:00 P.M. Wiese called in his chief of staff, Walther Botsch, and instructed him to check with his division commanders along the Côte d'Azur. Wiese put in a call to Maj. Gen. Johannes Baessler, commander of the 242nd Division at Brignoles.

"Except for the regular bombing raids, all is quiet here," Baessler reported. "In fact, it's so damned hot that many of my men are swimming in the Mediterranean."

Along the shore at Cavalaire, German soldiers, most stripped to the waist, were idly lounging on the white sand dunes and gazing out over the glistening blue sea. Here and there little knots of bronzed Feldgrau—totally naked—splashed about joyfully in the gentle swells of the surf. Nearby, French girls and young women were also frolicking through the water, oblivious to the naked German soldiers cavorting about.

The carefree bathers on this warm afternoon of August 13 were careful not to wander into the minefields all along the shore. Here and there was the ominous sign *"Achtung, Minen!"* (Attention, Mines!). About fifty yards inland two machine guns, each weapon's field of fire interlocking with the other's, were positioned to rake the beach. Behind those positions the knowing observer could vaguely detect the menacing snout of an 88mm gun barely poking out the window of a "bathhouse," actually a concrete bunker camouflaged to look like an enclosure for changing clothes.

Unknown to General Baessler, many of these sun-browned, laughing young soldiers of the 242nd Division would be dead or mangled in thirty-six hours; for the 242nd would absorb the brunt of all the bombs, shells, and bullets the Western Allies could hurl at them.

Had these young German fighting men of the 242nd Division been able to see two hundred miles beyond the horizon, they would have been stupefied by the view, for out there in the Mediterranean, bearing down on them, were a thousand Allied vessels of every description—the mightiest fleet ever assembled in this part of the world.

During the preceding three days, ten large convoys had poured out of harbors all over the Mediterranean—from Malta, Oran, Bizerte, and Algiers, from Palermo, Naples, Salerno, and Pozzuoli, from Taranto, Brindisi, Nissida and Baia, Propriano and La Maddalena. There were five battleships: the aging *Nevada, Texas,* and *Arkansas;* the British *Ramillies,* and the French *Lorraine;* the heavy cruisers *Augusta, Quincy,* and *Tuscaloosa;* a force of aircraft carriers (seven British, four American); warships from a French Navy proud once again, the *Fantasque, Montcalm, Terrible,* and *Mailin,* among others; several destroyers manned by Greek and Polish sailors and flying the flags of those countries; and scores of other cruisers, corvettes, destroyers, and antiaircraft ships. There were a hundred transports, each jammed with American and French soldiers; Norwegian, Greek, and Polish cargo vessels; trawlers, minesweepers, hospital ships, headquarters ships, tugboats, and hundreds of landing craft.

High overhead, tiny specks in the cloudless blue sky, Luftwaffe reconnaissance planes snooped on the ten convoys bound for a rendezvous south of the Côte d'Azur. The appearance of the Focke-Wulfs always set off an ear-piercing drumfire of antiaircraft guns from scores of ships before the enemy snoopers fled for home. Dragoon commanders on the *Catoctin* were unworried by the Luftwaffe spying; they knew it would have been impossible to conceal such a massive armada.

* * *

THIRTEEN HUNDRED MILES from the Riviera that night, Adolf Hitler was conducting his regular strategy conference at Wolfsschanze, a camouflaged, closely guarded headquarters complex tucked away in an East Prussian pine forest. The Führer's meetings were almost invariably in the hours of darkness, for he was essentially a night person. He would harangue his generals until nearly dawn, then sleep for a few hours. A hot bath; and injections by his personal physician, Dr. Theodor Morell (who was considered a quack by his colleagues), and Hitler was ready to hold forth again. He had enormous stamina.

Unknown to Hitler, for several weeks Allied authorities in England had been debating whether to try to kill the Führer. Through Ultra, the Allies knew his every move. A concentrated air attack almost certainly could have done the job. But after exhaustive discussion, the decision went against the proposal, mainly because of the strong protests of Winston Churchill.

"We would make him a martyr in the eyes of the Wehrmacht and the German people," the prime minister concluded. "And it would stiffen their will to resist. Besides, with Hitler dead the conduct of the war might return to the hands of his professional generals."

Now, on this night of August 13, the rapidly deteriorating German situation in France was under intense discussion. Two entire Wehrmacht field armies, the Seventh and Fifth Panzer, were in the process of being surrounded by the Americans and British in Normandy, raising the haunting specter of another Stalingrad. At the same time, General George Patton's tank-tipped spearheads were racing eastward in pursuit of retreating German units and would soon be reaching Paris.

Far to the south, evidence had been overwhelming for several days that the Allies were about to launch a powerful invasion of the Riviera, which could result in General Blaskowitz's entire Army Group G being cut off from the Fatherland and systematically destroyed.

Five days previously, a set of contingency orders had been drawn up by General of Artillery Walther Warlimont of the OKW operations staff, authorizing total withdrawal of the Wehrmacht from France. He had rushed these plans to Gen. Alfred Jodl, the OKW chief of operations, whose primary job in the Nazi scheme of things was to translate Hitler's strategic desires into field orders. Jodl, whom many Wehrmacht generals

considered a toadie for the Führer, was a powerful man in the
Third Reich. He decided which military matters would be
brought before Hitler and which would not be.

For five days General Jodl could not bring himself to present
the draft withdrawal orders for the Führer's signature. Like all
German generals, Jodl knew that Hitler had a standing edict in
the West: Don't give up one foot of ground. Now even Jodl
realized total disaster in France was facing the Wehrmacht. On
this night he presented Warlimont's withdrawal plan to the
Führer.

As Jodl and other generals present had anticipated, Hitler
glanced through the document and without a word tossed it
aside. Then he began perusing other contingency orders. One
provided for "resistance by all available means" along the
shores of southern France.

"This is the one I will sign," Hitler said evenly.

The momentous decision, one fraught with peril, had been
made. The German armed forces would fight it out along the
Côte d'Azur.

"Nancy Has a Stiff Neck"

At Ombrone Airfield outside Rome late in the afternoon of D-Day minus one, Maj. Thomas R. Cross, executive officer of the 2nd Battalion of Graves's 517th Parachute Infantry, was inspecting equipment bundles being packed on C-47s. These bundles were crucial, for they contained mortars and shells, small-arms ammunition and medical supplies. It was only ten hours before Cross's battalion would lift off for its first combat jump.

Out of the corner of his eye Cross caught sight of a figure dashing up to him. It was Capt. Robert Newberry, a company commander. Newberry clearly was agitated.

"This is a hell of a note," Newberry said, snorting. "The machine-gun ammo is badly corroded, it will take a miracle for it to fire, and the 60-millimeter mortar shells are from different lots, so the firing tables are different for each lot. We won't know which range table to use with which lot!"

The two officers roundly cursed the "idiots" who had issued defective ammunition to a paratroop unit that, behind German lines, could not be rapidly or easily resupplied—if at all.

Cross and Newberry rushed to the battalion commander, Lt. Col. Dick Seitz, who joined in turning the air blue. The thought of his seven hundred paratroopers being isolated behind German lines with faulty ammo caused him to shudder.

Seitz rapidly lined up a C-47. Together with two men he had quickly collared—Lieutenant Miley and Corporal Higginbotham—Cross leaped aboard, and the aircraft flew to an ammunition dump at Civitavecchia. With time running out before the lift-off for the Riviera, the three troopers began feverishly loading scores of heavy ammo containers as the boiling sun beat down on them.

Arriving back at Ombrone Airfield, Cross and others quickly unloaded the ammo. It had been a frantic race with the clock. Some of the ammo bundles were being fitted to the para racks under the C-47s even as C-47s loaded with parachutists were taxiing out to lift off for southern France.

AT OMBRONE AND Orbetello airfields that afternoon, the antitank company of the Japanese American 442nd Infantry Regiment was making final preparations for the glider assault on the morrow. The Nisei, as they were called, had volunteered to fight for their country even though back in the States some of their families, relatives, and loved ones were penned up in detention camps.

After Pearl Harbor, President Roosevelt signed an executive order requiring that Americans of Japanese descent on the West Coast be rounded up and herded into barbed-wire enclosures, there to sit out the war in flimsy shacks. If they were bitter about the treatment given their families, the Nisei fighting men took it out on the Germans. Inspired by the 442nd Regiment's motto, "Go for Broke!," the Japanese Americans were determined to make the ultimate demonstration of their loyalty to their country. In so doing, the towering mountains of Italy had been saturated with their blood, and the Germans had learned to fear the indefatigable Nisei warriors.*

Nothing fazed the Japanese Americans, not even when, a few weeks before, members of the antitank company were told that they would become instant glidermen and take part on Dragoon—and none of them had even seen a glider before. They were given two glider rides, awarded glider wings, and told, "Okay, you're ready to go!"

Now, on D-Day minus one, the Nisei were loading six-

*At war's end, the 442nd Infantry Regiment was said to be the most decorated unit of its size in the U.S. Army.

pounders into Waco gliders. These British antitank guns had been hurriedly substituted a few weeks before when it was discovered that the regulation 57mm guns would not fit into Wacos. Even this alarming development was taken in stride by the Nisei.

GATHERED IN THE shade of a building at Montalto Airfield, C-47 pilots of the 437th Troop Carrier Group, veterans of D-Day in Normandy, were listening intently to a final briefing on the next day's mission. There was hardly a breath of air, and the men were clad in shorts and T-shirts. After the group operations officer detailed the flight plan, the weather officer took over.

"It appears that the weather will be good for the run to the drop zones," the meteorologist declared. "But"—there was always a "but" in weather predictions—"there is a good chance that the DZs might be obscured by cloud cover."

The young fliers winced. It was difficult enough trying to locate a drop zone without it being "obscured."

A G-2 took over and pointed out that "all German flak guns along the coast have been spotted, and our fighter-bombers and warships will try to knock them out before our paratrooper flight arrives over the Riviera."

Leaning over to a comrade, a pilot whispered, "The key word is *try!*"

The G-2 concluded on a sour note: "One thing is certain— the Krauts will be expecting you. They'll probably even know what the 437th Troop Carrier Group is going to eat for supper tonight!"

AT GROSSETO AIRFIELD near the Tyrrhenian Sea northwest of Rome, a free-spirited glider pilot (GP), Flight Officer Jack "Deacon" Merrick, and his fellow fliers were intently poring over aerial photographs of their landing zones (LZs). Merrick was encouraged; the LZs appeared to be devoid of man-made obstacles. Yet Merrick felt uneasy. Before Normandy, he and other GPs had been told that their landing zones there were surrounded by three- to four-foot hedgerows—which turned out to be forty-foot trees.

Merrick's skepticism, the healthy doubt of a man who had already been through the mill, would prove to be well founded. Unknown to the Dragoon GPs, the photos had been taken

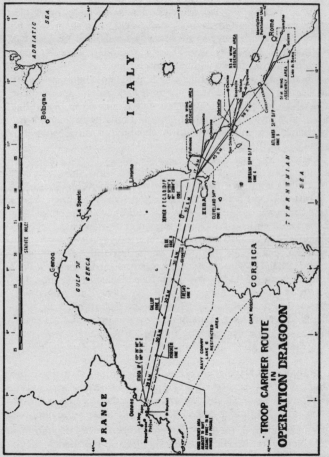

Map 13

eighteen days previously. In the meantime, the Germans had been hard at work. Using conscripted labor, they had pock-marked Riviera LZs with antiglider obstacles.

Other factors worried Merrick. He and his fellow glider pilots had been at Grosseto for two weeks, and there were no restrictions or secrecy, as there had been before Overlord in Normandy. The GPs were free to wander wherever they wanted, mixing freely with Italian civilians.

Then there were the gliders he and his comrades would fly the next day. They had been assembled in Rome—by whom he had never learned—and were ferried to Grosseto. They had never been test-flown, so the GPs could only hope that steering mechanisms would function properly and that wings would not break off in flight.

Deacon Merrick would not sleep soundly that night.

American glider pilots were a breed unto themselves, a mixed bag of backgrounds and reasons for flying motorless aircraft into and behind enemy lines to crash landings. There were those who could not make it as cadets at flight school, and those bored with desk jobs in some other branch of the service. Many volunteered to be GPs because they wanted to fly and fight (once a glider pilot was on the ground he became an infantryman). These men, high-spirited, irreverent, with a unique esprit all their own, often had been barroom brawlers who held an intense dislike for military discipline. Many were attracted to the smell of adventure much as a moth is attracted to a flame. Now their moment of truth was at hand once again. There were few occupations in war more fraught with peril than that of a glider pilot in combat.

AT 4:00 P.M. at Naples, a weather forecaster was shown into the office of Lt. Gen. Ira C. Eaker, an American commanding Mediterranean air forces. This would be the decisive forecast. There was still time to cancel the airborne assault if conditions were unsuitable. "A high-pressure area might be over the objective [the Riviera] in the morning, producing a heavy ground fog," the meteorologist explained.

Eaker frowned. This was a gloomy report for an impending airborne attack. The general briefly discussed the report with his staff, then declared: "We'll go as planned." Fog or no fog, the die had been cast.

*   *   *

THAT AFTERNOON A ghastly apparition was half-dragged, half-carried into the office of the chief of the Gestapo in Nice. Even her best friends would have had a difficult time recognizing once vivacious and beautiful Helene Vagliano. This would be the sixteenth consecutive day that she was "interrogated" since her arrest by the Gestapo. Now her ashen face was puffed, her eyes blackened, and her hair was matted with dried blood. Her body was covered with welts and bruises, and burns from lighted cigarettes. Still she refused to confess that she was a spy or to disclose her accomplices.

The daring courier for the French Underground along the Riviera now received another sickening blow. The Gestapo told her that her mother and father had been arrested as "spies." Unless Helene admitted that she herself was a spy, her parents would be shot. If she confessed, her parents would be released. With that, she broke down and signed a confession that she had indeed been a courier for a British spy network in southern France and that she had radioed information to London and to Naples. Helene knew she had signed her own death warrant.

Under a barrage of threats, she wrote down a list of names and addresses of her Underground contacts throughout France —all of them fictitious.

AT ABOUT THE time Helene Vagliano was scrawling her shaky signature on a confession, General von Gyldenfeldt burst into the office of his boss at Army Group G headquarters at Rouffiac, near Toulouse. "Herr General," he called out excitedly to Johannes Blaskowitz, "here it is. The Führer has approved shifting 11th Panzer to the Riviera."

General Blaskowitz would have heaved a sigh of relief, but he knew that the Führer's approval had come too late—eight days too late. Even under the lash of the hard-driving General Wend von Wietersheim, it was not likely that the 11th Panzer could traverse some three hundred miles in time to influence the outcome of the looming clash along the Riviera.

Von Wietersheim had his panzer division on the road as dusk began to enfold southern France. Stretched out for a hundred miles along the coast at Bordeaux, the tanks, armored cars, trucks, and other vehicles of the 11th Panzer headed for the Riviera along secondary roads. Vehicles were camouflaged with fresh foliage against the dreaded Allied Jabos (fighter-bombers) that had been marauding over southern France the preceding week.

General von Wietersheim was infuriated by the snail-like pace of his columns picking their way in the darkness over back roads in order to avoid Jabo packs after daylight. The panzer leader knew he was in a race with the Allied fleet for the Riviera beaches, and the stakes were enormous. He ordered his armored columns to get onto Route Nationale 13 and dash along it toward the Côte d'Azur.

"But Herr General," a colonel protested. "The Jabos . . ."

"To hell with the Jabos!" von Wietersheim shouted into his radio transmitter. "Get the hell moving!"

MEANWHILE, LATE THAT afternoon of August 14, Adm. Kent Hewitt's huge convoy was knifing majestically through the calm blue waters of the Mediterranean, heading in a generally northerly direction. Those on the bridges and lining the rails could see the hazy, rugged coastline of Corsica fading in the distance. Overhead scores of sausage-shaped barrage balloons, secured by sturdy steel cables, hovered six hundred feet above many of the ships to discourage low-flying Luftwaffe pilots. Between ships a constant stream of messages was being flashed by sailors furiously manipulating semaphores in Morse code.

Among the 247 warships in the Allied fleet were many battle-scarred vessels. The proud old American battleship *Nevada,* dating back to World War I, had survived the Japanese sneak attack on the Pacific fleet at Pearl Harbor on December 7, 1941, and had contributed its powerful fourteen-inch gun batteries to pounding the Normandy coast during the D-Day assault. The graybeard of the fleet was Britain's battleship *Ramillies,* which had been plowing the waters of the globe for nearly three decades. Its fifteen-inch guns would be the largest to bombard German positions along the Riviera.

THE VENERABLE BRITISH cruiser *Ajax* had joined in electrifying the free world in December 1939 when it joined in forcing the commander of the mighty German battleship *Graf Spee* to scuttle her when cornered in the neutral port of Montevideo, Uruguay. The American cruiser *Tuscaloosa* had run a gauntlet of *Stuka* dive bombers in August 1942, when it helped escort a crucial convoy of American and British weapons and supplies to Murmansk and thus helped keep a beleaguered Soviet army in the war. Later the *Tuscaloosa* added its firepower to the bombardment of the Normandy coast on D-Day for Overlord, as did the British cruiser HMS *Black Prince* and the aging battleship USS *Texas*.

Few sailors or soldiers on board the ships of the mighty armada, so immense that it covered more than fifteen thousand square miles of the Mediterranean, realized that they had been sailing along routes once used by Phoenicians, Carthaginians, and Romans who had set out to conquer ancient Gaul.

IT WAS NEARING 4:00 P.M. when the *Catoctin* began steaming past the destroyer *Kimberley,* flagship of the Mediterranean naval commander, Admiral Sir John Cunningham, which was holding north of Corsica. The *Kimberley* was preparing to dash back to Ajaccio in Corsica to pick up Winston Churchill, who had insisted on being present to observe the assault on the Riviera.

Cunningham flashed a signal to Admiral Hewitt and Generals Sandy Patch and Lucian Truscott aboard the *Catoctin* as she headed for battle: "All convoys have passed at the planned moment. An operation so well organized must succeed. Good luck. May God be with you."

AT 7:30 P.M. on the mainland, thirty-eight-year-old, red-haired André Bouchard was huddled in the musty cellar of his home in Fréjus, listening to the nightly litany of coded phrases broadcast by BBC from London to the Resistance in France. Bouchard had to be extremely cautious; anyone caught listening to the BBC would be executed if caught. The Frenchman kept his old radio hidden under a large pile of turnips in the cellar.

For the preceding eighteen months, Bouchard had been living a perilous double life. By day he eked out a living for himself; his petite blonde wife, Francine; and the couple's three children. By night he was the leader of a local *réseau* and slipped through the shadows with his fellow Resistance members to harass the Germans and obtain information for the Allies.

Like thousands of others in the Resistance there, André Bouchard had been aware for three days that a massive Allied invasion would soon strike somewhere along the Mediterranean coast. But neither Bouchard nor anyone else in the French Underground knew precisely when or where the invaders would come ashore.

It was monotonous sitting there alone in the dark cellar night after night, listening intently to a lengthy string of seemingly innocuous messages in the French language. Some of the phrases had a meaning for the Underground at some locale in France, other phrases meant nothing and were sandwiched in to confuse the Germans monitoring BBC broadcasts.*

On this night once again the BBC messages were meaningless to Bouchard: "Rain will damage the wheat crop . . . Joe's old motorcycle will not run . . . Crickets are chirping in the grass . . . Nancy has a stiff neck . . ."

André Bouchard caught his breath. "Nancy has a stiff neck!" Did his ears deceive him? There, he heard it again: "Nancy has a stiff neck."

That was the secret code phrase to alert the Underground that the Allied invasion would hit the Côte d'Azur within twenty-four hours.

Bouchard leaped to his feet, barely able to restrain an impulse to shout with joy. He quickly covered the radio in the turnip pile and rushed upstairs to tell Francine the news. Then he hauled out the pistol concealed under the floorboards of the kitchen and dashed off to alert his *réseau*.

All up and down the Riviera, the men and women of the Underground were springing into action. North of Le Muy that night a key telephone cable linking General Blaskowitz with his opposite number in the North of France, Field Marshal Guenther von Kluge, was severed. Near La Motte, shadowy figures removed long poles that had been stuck in the ground by the Germans as antiglider obstacles. A small but important bridge leading to the beaches was weakened so that the first German vehicle that moved onto it would collapse the span. Hundreds of thousands of broad-headed tacks were scattered over roads known to be used by Wehrmacht trucks and other rubber-tired vehicles. Large numbers of huge boulders mysteriously appeared in the middle of main highways leading to the coast. Telephone lines were cut. German couriers and staff cars were fired on from out of the shadows.

AT AVIGNON, NINETEENTH Army headquarters was a beehive of

---

*The Gestapo for weeks had been making strenuous efforts to identify the code phrase that would inform the Underground that the southern France invasion was imminent. Apparently the Gestapo failed.

activity. Reports on the outbreak of Underground violence were pouring into the communications center from locales throughout the Riviera, convincing General Wiese that the anticipated Allied blow was nearly ready to fall. At 9:55 P.M. he ordered the Nineteenth Army onto full alert.

MEANWHILE, ADMIRAL HEWITT'S huge blacked-out armada was steadily burrowing through the gentle swells of the Mediterranean, heading directly northward from Corsica toward Genoa, Italy. German radar stations that had survived the massive aerial bombing were carefully tracking the convoy's course and making almost minute-by-minute reports to various headquarters. Suddenly, at 10:15 P.M., the one thousand vessels sharply altered course sixty degrees and steered toward the northwest for a thirty-seven-mile strip of Riviera beaches code-named Alpha, Delta, and Camel.

The death struggle for southern France was about to erupt.

The Phantom Guns of Whale Island

Ten to twelve miles off the Côte d'Azur, the ghostly hulks of hundreds of Allied ships, their dim silhouettes outlined against the sky, were rolling gently in the calm water. Under the protective blanket of night, the vast armada had stealthily edged into position off Alpha, Delta, and Camel beaches at the little towns of Cavalaire-sur-Mer, Sainte-Maxime, and Saint-Raphael. It was 11:00 P.M.

Deep in the hot, stuffy, cramped holds of squat transports and in the long, gray LCIs, tense assault troops of O'Daniel's 3rd, Dahlquist's 36th, and Eagles's 45th Infantry divisions were dozing fitfully, conversing softly with each other, or poring over tiny pocket Bibles. The moment of truth was near at hand. Each man, in his own way, was preparing himself for the ordeal just ahead.

At the western end of the thirty-seven-mile stretch of the Riviera to be assaulted, Task Force Sitka, under the overall command of Rear Adm. Lyal A. Davidson on the *Augusta,* was standing by a few miles from the offshore islands of Île du Levant (Whale Island) and Île de Port-Cros. Several transports, including the *Prince Henry, Prince David, Prince Baudouin,* and *Princess Beatrix,* were jammed with two thousand grim-faced men of Col. Edwin A. Walker's 1st Special Service Force (the Black Devils of Anzio) and Lt. Col. Georges-Regis Bouvet's seven hundred French commandos. These two elite formations in Task Force Sitka would strike the first blows against Hitler's Riviera.

Two of the three small islands making up the Île d'Hyères lie five miles off the major port of Toulon. One of these, the Île du Levant, had been a peacetime favorite for nudists. Its rugged coastline of sheer rocky drops and the thick stands of pine trees and knee-high underbrush made it an ideal locale for those who preferred to cavort about *sans* clothing. The other island, Port-Cros, was similar in many respects to the Île du Levant.

It was the predawn mission of Ed Walker's 1st Special Service Force to assault and capture these two islands before the main landings at 8:00 A.M.* There was particular concern over the presence on Ile du Levant of a German long-barreled gun battery that could pound the landing beaches and the vulnerable troop transports offshore.

Prior to sailing for southern France, Colonel Walker had reached a crucial decision. Aerial photos had revealed the presence of numerous sandy beaches ideal for an amphibious assault, and they disclosed rugged, forbidding terrain of sheer cliffs and rocky ridges on the seaward side. Walker chose the difficult terrain on the seaward side for his troops to assault the Île du Levant.

"The Old Man's finally gone off his rocker entirely!" one of his troops had said, fuming; he expressed the sentiment of his comrades. Others called it a "suicide mission."

Walker's staff vigorously urged him to change his mind about sending his men against this seemingly insurmountable terrain. The Black Devil commander refused to budge from his decision.

"Your objections are precisely why we will assault as planned," Colonel Walker told his staff. "The Germans undoubtedly have reached the same conclusions and will not expect us to attack the seaward side. So they will have only token, if any, defenses there."

Besides, Walker had great confidence in the ability of his Black Devils to overcome these inhospitable, rocky cliffs. Hadn't they scampered up and down towering mountain peaks in Italy like bands of mountain goats, often in the teeth of heavy enemy fire?

The plan called for some thirteen hundred men of Lt. Col.

---

*The designation 1st Special Service Force had once caused a great deal of confusion for German Intelligence. The Germans could not understand why commando-type missions would be assigned to U.S. Special Services, a branch of the Army whose primary function was to entertain troops.

Robert S. Moore's 2nd Regiment and Lt. Col. R. W. Becket's 3rd Regiment to paddle ashore in rubber boats and begin scaling the rugged outcroppings on the Île du Levant. Should Colonel Walker's analysis of German defensive positions be faulty, these rocky heights could be dripping with Black Devils' blood.

At the same time Walker's troops were clawing their way up those heights, the seven hundred men of Lt. Col. J.F.R. Akehurst's 1st Regiment would be going ashore on Port-Cros, and Lieutenant Colonel Brevet's French commandos would be storming the mainland nearby, at Cap Negre.

The seizure of the Île du Levant and the destruction of the ominous 164mm (6.5-inch) German gun battery could be decisive for the main amphibious assault at the Alpha landing beaches. Yet for weeks an argument had raged at General Patch's Seventh Army headquarters over whether these three enemy guns even existed. Countless aerial photos had clearly shown the big artillery pieces, with their menacing snouts pointing out to sea. And the French Underground had reported the battery on the Île du Levant. Yet a French naval officer had for weeks been engaged in violent arguments with Patch's staff. He claimed that the gun battery at Titan lighthouse on one tip of the Île du Levant had been blown up by the French in November 1942 when Hitler had sent his legions to occupy all of France after the Allies invaded North Africa.

"Look at them!" an exasperated staff colonel at the Seventh Army had shouted at the French naval officer, waving an aerial photo of the three-gun battery in the adamant adversary's face. "Just look at those barrels! Three 6.5-inch gun barrels. Count 'em."

The French officer was unmoved. "Those three guns were destroyed in 1942," he responded. "If by some chance they are still there, they can't fire."

A typical emotional Frenchman, was the consensus among Patch's staff. The assaults on the Île du Levant and Port-Cros were to be carried out as planned to eliminate this serious threat to the landings. The plan called for the two islands to be seized no later than dawn, approximately two hours before the main landings at Alpha, Delta, and Camel.

AT 1:25 A.M., twenty-four-year-old Maj. Edward H. Thomas, commander of the 1st Battalion of Lieutenant Colonel Moore's 2nd Regiment, was standing on the deck of his transport. Thomas was peering intently in the direction of the Île du

Levant, trying vainly to part the inky blackness to view the rocky heights he and his men would soon have to scale. It would be two more hours before a pale quarter moon would shed a bit of light.

Ed Thomas was young to be a battalion commander. But he had performed with distinction in Italy, and Col. Ed Walker had great faith in his ability. Yet Thomas felt a vague uneasiness. In addition to the confusion certain to result from the darkness, there were other unknown factors, including the strength of the Germans on the Island of the Whales.

Around him on deck Major Thomas could discern the dim silhouettes of his Devils. Each had daubed his face black with burned cork, taped equipment to keep it from rattling, and wore a knit cap instead of a steel helmet. Daggers had been sharpened, as orders were to dispatch sentries silently.

Thomas glanced at the luminous face of his watch. It was 1:30 A.M. "Okay, let's go!" he called out as he threw a log over the railing and began scrambling down the rope ladder. He could hear rustling noises as his men also headed down the side of the ship for the rubber boats below. As soon as each inflatable raft was loaded with ten men, several of the craft were connected to powerboats that pulled them to within a thousand yards of the Île du Levant. There the rubber boats were cast off and the Black Devils hastily, but as silently as possible, paddled toward the shore.

Major Thomas and the others could feel heartbeats quicken as they neared the island and could detect the dim outlines of the heights along the shore. Soon the rubber boats beached—and all was silent. The only sound was the gentle lapping of the surf against the rock outcroppings. Stealthily, like swarms of locusts, the Black Devils began scrambling up the heights. Reaching the top, they deployed into skirmish lines and headed for the Titan lighthouse and its three big guns. The going was arduous and slow. Thick underbrush, which covered the island, made each step difficult. Still not a shot had been fired.

A patrol was sent out to scout the gun battery. About a hundred yards from the German position, the scouts halted and kneeled. There they were, no doubt about it: the three menacing barrels of the 164mm guns outlined against the sky and aimed at the mainland landing beaches.

"I don't like it!" one soldier whispered to another. "It's too goddamned quiet. There don't seem to be any Krauts around the guns."

An attack was rapidly organized and the troops charged the gun battery. No Germans were there. The three big guns, which had been the objects of so much concern and planning at Seventh Army headquarters in the Flambeau Building at Naples, were dummies. Ordinary drain pipes had been skillfully contrived by the Germans to resemble gun barrels when photographed from the air. Camouflage paint had added a dash of realism.

"Another goddamned dry run!" a Black Devil called out in the darkness, reflecting the sentiment of most men. Seconds later a flurry of mortar shells began exploding around the Titan lighthouse and the drain pipes, causing the Americans to drop to the ground. The Île du Levant would not be a dry run after all. Holed up in a cave at the other end of the island was a German garrison of more than two hundred armed with several machine guns and thousands of rounds of ammunition, along with eight or ten mortars and a large stockpile of shells. As the troops deployed to assault the German stronghold, guns of the British destroyer *Lookout* began pouring in salvos to blast the enemy force out of the cave.

Edging toward the cave, Lt. William S. Story and his platoon, of Maj. Stanley Waters's 2nd Battalion of the 2nd Regiment, suddenly were pounded by enemy mortars. Story leaped into a ditch, and as the explosions rocked the ground around him, he looked back to say something to a reporter for the *Maple Leaf*, the Canadian Army's equivalent of the *Stars & Stripes*.

Story had taken the Canadian reporter under his wing, and for days the correspondent had been anxiously looking forward to being able to file an eye witness account telling in graphic terms of the seizure of the Île du Levant and its big guns. He had even brought his bulky typewriter ashore in a rubber boat with Story.

Now, in the ditch with the mortar rounds exploding on all sides, Story saw that the reporter was no longer with him. The scribe had vanished. When the brief barrage ended, Story asked if anyone had seen the *Maple Leaf* reporter. "Yeah, I saw him," a Canadian called out. "He took off like a jackrabbit for the rear."

A short distance away, Maj. Ed Thomas was observing the explosions of shells from the *Lookout*. "They're no doubt scaring hell out of the Krauts in the cave," he remarked to a company commander. "But the shells aren't getting inside. We're going to have to go in the cave and root them out of there."

As the first specks of gray began to fracture the black Mediterranean sky, heralding the imminent arrival of another hot summer day, Black Devils had moved in on three sides of the German-held cave and were peppering the opening with machine-gun and rifle fire. A few bazooka men crept forward and sent rockets hissing into the mouth of the cavity. Suddenly a German waving a large white piece of cloth emerged from the smoke-filled opening and cries of "Cease firing!" rang out from the attackers' positions. The battle for Île du Levant was over.

On the nearby island of Port-Cros, Lieutenant Colonel Akehurst and his men had also stealthily slipped ashore from rubber boats and rapidly fanned out over the brush-covered island. But there were no signs of a German presence. Akehurst, of Kirkland, Ontario, ordered his men to set up positions on several dominating ridges, reported to higher headquarters that Port-Cros had been secured, and awaited orders. Many of his troops, exhausted from the night's arduous activities, promptly fell asleep.

Offshore on his command ship, Col. Ed Walker was furious that his elite group of fighting men had been utilized for "two dry runs."

"Those goddamned islands were of no consequence after all," Walker said, fuming.

Colonel Walker promptly sent a radio signal to Adm. Lyal Davidson, the Task Force Sitka commander, on the *Augusta:* "Two islands totally useless. Suggest immediate evacuation. 240 prisoners. Enemy battery dummies. Request permission immediate departure."

The terse message reflected the colonel's disgust and a vague sense of humiliation. Capturing dummy guns and confronting a relatively small German force holed up in a cave was not his idea of the "heavy opposition" forecast for his crack 1st Special Service Force. Walker wanted his men shifted to the mainland, where they could come to grips with the enemy.

Only General Patch could issue such an order. The Seventh Army commander signaled the frustrated Walker: "Stay put for the time being."

A short time later, two of Colonel Akehurst's troops on Port-Cros were idly meandering along a path through a wooded area on their way to the beach. The vegetation was so thick that it reminded them of pictures they had seen of the Guadalcanal jungles where American Marines had fought earlier in the war. As no Germans had been discovered on Port-Cros, the two soldiers had left their rifles behind.

Rounding a sharp bend in the path, the two men froze. Standing in the middle of the path, only some twenty-five feet away and looking directly toward them, was a helmeted German sentry, a Schmeisser machine pistol hanging by its strap over a shoulder. The Feldgrau's jaw dropped. He was as startled to find himself suddenly confronted by two enemy troops as they were to see him.

For several seconds the adversaries stood motionless, staring at each other. Then, as if on cue, the German and the commandos spun about and fled in opposite directions. Within minutes Colonel Akehurst would learn that there were enemy troops on Île de Port-Cros after all. And the German commander on the island would discover that black-faced Allied troops had slipped ashore during the night.

Within a half hour, General Patch on the *Catoctin* was handed another signal from Colonel Ed Walker, this one couched in tones of mild concern:

"Urgent. Request heavy bombardment on citadel [on Port-Cros]. [We are] under heavy attack, having difficulties."

Indeed, Lieutenant Colonel Akehurst and his troops were having difficulties. Numbering but fifty-eight men, the German force on Port-Cros was entrenched inside three very formidable old stone forts built in the Napoleonic era. The walls were twelve feet thick, and twenty feet of hard-packed earth topped the ceilings. Over the decades, tangles of wild greenery had covered the forts so that they were nearly invisible to the casual observer.

Behind these thick-walled enclosures, German machine gunners and riflemen poured withering bursts of fire against Akehurst's men trying to storm the ancient citadel. Although far outnumbering the Germans, the commandos were out in the open and had armament no heavier than bazookas.

Navy fire-control parties on Port-Cros hurriedly called for gunfire from the *Augusta,* and minutes later the cruiser's eight-inch shells were rustling through the air in the direction of the holed-up German force. There were enormous explosions, but Akehurst's men watched in dismay as the shells bounced harmlessly off the thick walls of the old fortress.

The struggle for the tiny, rugged island of Port-Cros, which Colonel Walker had thought ended by default, continued to rage.

French Commandos Scale Cap Negre

At the same time that the American-Canadian 1st Special Service Force had shoved off from bulky transports to assault the Île du Levant and the Île de Port-Cros, Lt. Col. Georges-Regis Bouvet was impatiently standing on the dark deck of the *Prince David*, only a few miles from the offshore islands. Bouvet was gripped with emotion, as were the black-faced French commandos barely discernible around him. After four long years in exile, Bouvet and his fighting men would soon be stepping onto their native soil.

These men, bound on a mission of great peril for which they had trained arduously for many months, would rely on surprise and stealth. Where possible, the enemy would be dispatched by knife and bayonet.

Waiting for the signal to depart, Colonel Bouvet once again went over the attack plan in his mind. He and his commandos were to land on a stretch of beach between Rayol and Cavalaire, then scale nearby Cap Negre, towering 350 feet into the black sky, and knock out a German gun battery covering that sector of the Côte d'Azur. Those missions accomplished, the Frenchmen were to block the coast highway to keep German reinforcements from rushing to the landing beaches from Toulon and Marseilles. At the same time he was to send a detachment to seize a key height one mile inland.

A short distance away from Bouvet, two old friends, Sgt. Georges du Bellocq and M. Sgt. Noel Texier, were solemnly shaking hands and wishing each other *bonne chance*. Theirs would be the most perilous task of all. Each was to lead a nine-man patrol onto the beach at Rayol to seize a large blockhouse there one hour before Colonel Bouvet and his main body of commandos were to come ashore.

Both men knew it would be Texier's final combat mission. He had reached the retirement age for his rank but had begged to go along on this historic invasion of his homeland.

Soon a British voice boomed over the loudspeaker: "French commandos, board your landing craft."

Silently Sergeants Texier and du Bellocq and their eighteen men slipped over the railings and slithered down the rope ladders and into their rubber boats. Each dinghy was fastened to a PT boat which, operating at low speed, set a course for the mainland, six miles off in the hazy distance.

PERHAPS A MILE ahead of the two spearhead patrols, U.S. Ens. Ralph Johnson and Maj. Marcel Rigaud of the French commandos were feverishly paddling their rubber boat toward the little bay at Rayol. Between them they carried only a .45 Colt and a Thompson submachine gun. Their crucial role was not to fight, but to flash green lights seaward to guide in Texier's and du Bellocq's patrols, then repeat the process one hour later for the main body of French commandos. Rigaud, who at forty-six was nearly twice the age of his American counterpart, and Johnson would be the first Allied soldiers to set foot on Hitler's Riviera.

The two men in the rubber dinghy now were close enough to glimpse the shoreline and the dim configurations of the terrain behind it. A deep surge of near-panic swept through Rigaud. In peacetime he had been to the bay at Rayol many times and knew the coastline intimately. He did not know where he and Johnson were touching shore, but this was *not* the bay at Rayol.

Time was crucial. The clock was ticking. After a half hour of feverish effort to orient himself, Rigaud whispered to Johnson, "We're one mile west of our target." Leaping into their dinghy, the two men frantically paddled along the shoreline. Reaching their destination, Rigaud again whispered, "This is it. No doubt about it."

The desperate pair began to blink the green glow of their flashlights out to sea. As the minutes raced by, Marcel Rigaud was flooded with waves of anxiety. There was only darkness. Now the flashlight batteries gave out. Tears of grief, rage, and frustration rolled down the French officer's ruddy cheeks.

NEARING SHORE, SERGEANT du Bellocq and his nine men had been peering intently through the blackness in search of the flashing green lights. Seeing none, they paddled ashore and despite his many hours of intense study of a sand-table model of the targeted coastline, du Bellocq did not recognize the place. On the beach, the only sound was the gentle lapping of the waves. "I don't know where in the hell we are, but we can't stay here," the sergeant whispered to his men.

Moving out in single file, the black-clad commando patrol began clawing up the sheer face of a rocky hill that hovered ominously over the shore. Soon the physically tough men were huffing and perspiring profusely from the exertion. As they neared the top, a powerful flashlight beam suddenly exploded just above the Frenchmen's heads. The invaders froze. Heartbeats quickened. Breathing grew heavier. Had they been detected?

As the commandos pressed against the steep, rock-filled incline, the bright beam began playing to and fro over their heads and to each side of them. Du Bellocq sneaked a peak upward and discerned the dark outline of a coal-bucket-shaped helmet. The German holding the flashlight was no more than fifteen feet from him. Each commando deftly removed his dagger and prepared to spring. Moments later the German turned off his flashlight and melted into the darkness.

Onward the Frenchmen stole through the night, more cautious than ever. They stumbled onto barbed-wire entanglements, cut their way through the barrier, and reached a line of trenches. Preparing to cross the excavation, du Bellocq and his men were startled by a nervous voice piercing the blackness: "Ludwig! Ludwig!"

Instantly crouching, the ten commandos whipped out daggers. Mouths went dry. Stomachs churned. Still seeking Ludwig, the frantic German voice drew nearer, and now du

Bellocq could see the enemy's shadowy figure. Suddenly, like a large cat, the sergeant leaped onto his prey. Three quick thrusts of the dagger, accompanied by grunts, then a gurgling noise and the German fell to the ground, dead. He may have been the first Wehrmacht soldier killed on the mainland in Dragoon.

In the meantime, Sgt. Noel Texier's rubber dinghy had gone ashore, nearly a mile to the west of du Bellocq's landing. Texier's boat had also been victimized by navigational errors of the Navy. Texier strained his eyes to try to orient the little group. He recognized no landmark; this was not the intended beach.

Looming up directly in front of him was a dark, ominous mass, the sight of which sent a chill through him: This was the towering bulk of Cap Negre, the objective of the seven-hundred-man commando force and far from the blockhouse his squad was to knock out. Texier was in a quandary. How could he and nine men scale the almost perpendicular face of Cap Negre, wipe out the machine-gun nests that studded the elevation, then assault and capture the three-gun battery on top? The commando squad had only light weapons and daggers.

The graying Sergeant Texier paused only briefly. He and his men began the arduous task of scaling the sheer face of 350-foot-high Cap Negre. Clawing and pulling their way upward, Texier and his men reached a protruding rock formation that encircled the elevation, some 180 feet above the beach. The rocky overhang had been filed and sharpened by the Germans to prevent Cap Negre from being scaled on its seaward side. Texier began pulling himself up over this razor-sharp surface, the rock slashing deep gashes into his arms and hands.

Suddenly the tranquillity was shattered. Grenades began exploding around the sergeant and his men clinging desperately to the forbidding side of the cliff. White-hot steel fragments ripped into Texier, causing him to lose his tenuous grip and fall. He bounced from rock to rock like a rag doll before coming to rest on a narrow ledge. Texier remained motionless, bleeding profusely from ugly wounds of the head and body, semiconscious. Trapped, the other nine members of the patrol clung desperately to the cliff as the Germans in the blackness above continued to shower them with grenades. Between explosions, Texier's men could hear him moaning softly. Their hearts were pierced with anguish, for they could not risk the patrol's being wiped out by going to the aid of a wounded comrade. Sergeant Texier himself had issued these strict orders, not once but many times.

Noel Texier, the overage sergeant who would have been forced to retire at the conclusion of this mission, lay there alone and in agony as his life ebbed away, with the explosions of German grenades ringing in his ears. Killed while trying to take an objective assigned to seven hundred commandos, the aging sergeant's last conscious thoughts may have been that he was dying on the soil of his beloved France.

Noel Texier may have been the first Allied soldier to make the supreme sacrifice in the invasion of southern France.

AT 1:00 A.M. at about the same time Sergeant Texier was dying on a ledge high up Cap Negre, Rear Adm. Heinrich Ruhfus, Kriegsmarine commander for the southern coast of France, was awakened at his headquarters at Baudouin, near Toulon. An urgent signal from an outpost near Rayol was handed to him, its terse message indicated that fighting had broken out on Cap Negre and that the long-anticipated Allied invasion may have begun. As with other German leaders in southern France, Ruhfus felt a curious form of relief after so many months of anxious waiting. The other shoe had finally dropped.

Meanwhile, Capt. Paul Ducournau and a sixty-man force of French commandos were heading for shore in two landing craft. These were the men assigned to knock out the German guns atop Cap Negre before Colonel Brevet and his main body of commandos arrived at the shoreline one hour later. Ducournau would have to work fast.

On nearing the shore, Captain Ducournau felt a pang of anxiety—peering through the darkness, he could not discern the looming mass of formidable Cap Negre. Nor could he spot the blinking green guidelights.

"Turn around and head back in the direction from which we just came," the captain called out to the Canadian officer steering the landing craft. "This isn't the right beach!"

Seeing the dim outline of Ducournau's craft reversing course, the skipper of the second boat thought the first vessel had put its thirty men ashore and was returning to the open sea. The young Canadian officer in charge of the second boat ordered his craft to land. Splashing ashore, the Frenchmen were suddenly raked by machine-gun fire and pounded by mortars and grenades. In the darkness, the commandos had stumbled onto another gun battery, one protected by barbed-wire entanglements and covered by a force of Germans.

Taking whatever cover they could find, the Frenchmen fired back, and for the next three hours a furious fight raged. Trapped and isolated, the thirty-man commando force suffered heavily. Cries pierced the night air as German bullets and grenade fragments ripped into fragile flesh and bone.

In the meantime, Captain Ducournau had located the ominous bulk of Cap Negre and had landed at its base with his thirty men. The captain believed that his second landing vessel with half of his force had been following him, but when it failed to appear, apparently swallowed up by the night, Ducournau ordered his thirty men to start clawing up Cap Negre. Burdened with heavy combat gear and weapons, the commandos arduously pulled themselves up the vertical cliff, expecting a shower of hand grenades to descend upon them at any moment. Hands, faces, arms, and legs were slashed by the sharp rocks that studded the promontory. But each Frenchman moved onward, compelled by a single thought: "Get those German guns!"

After prodigious effort, their clothing saturated with blood, Captain Ducournau's commandos reached the top and, one by one, began stealthily edging over the lip of the cliff. The night was silent now and seemed haunted. The German defenders had apparently concluded that Sergeant Texier's patrol was but a random raid to keep the Wehrmacht on edge and had relaxed their vigilance.

Ducournau waved his men forward. Groping through the dark, the Frenchmen cut barbed wire, picked their way around huge bomb craters that saturated the landscape, and skirted what appeared to be minefields. Not a shot had been fired. Nor a sentry spotted. Suddenly, Ducournau felt a surge of exultation. Just ahead he could vaguely detect the shadowy outline of two menacing gun barrels. But where was the third gun he had been told was on Cap Negre?

The tranquillity was shattered. Out of the inky blackness, German machine guns sent withering streams of tracers toward the commandos. White, yellow, and orange flares brilliantly illuminated the lunar landscape and starkly silhouetted the intruders. The harsh sounds of exploding grenades echoed across the clifftop.

As if on cue, Captain Ducournau and his men charged the enemy positions, shooting and pitching grenades as they ran. Whipping out trench knives, the Frenchmen pounced on the Feldgrau and for long minutes a savage, wild, face-to-face brawl raged. Grunts were heard as daggers found their marks.

Several commandos reached the first gun and destroyed it by dropping thermal grenades down the barrel. Pushing onward, six Frenchmen reached the second gun and dropped bangalore torpedoes into its mouth. The subsequent blast knocked all six men to the ground, but they scrambled to their feet, stunned but grinning broadly. The long, menacing barrel was in shreds, resembling, they thought, the appearance of a trick cigar that had exploded in the mouth of some unwary victim of a prankster.*

Soon the bitter struggle for the guns of Cap Negre was over. An intensive search for the third gun was futile. Captain Ducournau concluded that the Germans had recently moved it. Twenty-two Germans defending the battery had been killed or wounded, and the remainder taken prisoner. Despite the rigors of scaling the cliff with its razorlike outcroppings, and their savage fight with the enemy troops, Ducournau and his commandos were gripped by a euphoric surge of achievement. When the main body of Colonel Bouvet's force would land in a few minutes and when the U.S. 3rd Infantry Division stormed ashore on Alpha Beach after dawn, German gunners atop Cap Negre would not be pouring direct fire into their exposed ranks.

It was 1:20 A.M. as the 20 landing craft carrying the 620 commandos of Lt. Col. Georges-Regis Bouvet's main force was nearing the shore. In the bow of the lead vessel, Bouvet was deeply concerned. He could not detect the flashing green lights from Major Rigaud and Ensign Johnson on the beach along the bay at Rayol. Had they been killed? Or captured?

Colonel Bouvet could recognize no coastal landmark but decided to beach his flotilla. "Okay, take them on in here," he instructed the Canadian officer in charge of the group of landing craft.

"Can't do it," was the reply. "My orders are to wait for the

---

*A bangalore torpedo was a metal tube some eight feet long and filled with explosives. Its principal use was to blow up barbed-wire barricades.

flashing green lights on shore before landing.''

Colonel Bouvet was furious. He whipped out his pistol, stuck it in the Canadian's stomach, and roared, ''Well, here's *my* orders: Now take the damned boats onto the beaches!''

The Canadian shrugged his shoulders, and minutes later the twenty landing craft were on the sandy shore. Leaping stealthily onto the beach, the 620 Frenchmen were nearly overcome with emotion on returning to their native land after years of exile. Many scooped up handfuls of wet sand and, with tears streaming down their blackened faces, pressed the soil of France to their lips.

Bouvet quickly oriented himself; he knew that he was a mile west of where he was to have gone ashore. Now the long-rehearsed plan for the main force to push rapidly inland to its objectives was useless. As silently as possible, officers formed their men into platoons and, with Colonel Bouvet in the lead, the column began stealing toward high hills lying behind the beaches.

It was quiet as a tomb at midnight. The only sound was the happy chirping of crickets. Where were the Germans? Nearing the shore, Bouvet had seen the flares and fiery grenade flashes atop Cap Negre where Captain Ducournau and his men were destroying the big guns. Surely the intense racket and the pyrotechnics on that dominating elevation would have alerted the Wehrmacht for miles up and down the coast.

One commando company, commanded by Capt. Albert Thorel, arrived at the short railroad line that ran along the Côte d'Azur between Toulon and Saint-Raphael. Thorel spotted a light flicker in the tiny train station in the village of Le Canadel, and with his men remaining in the shadows, the captain strode forward and banged on the door.

Inside, the stationmaster, Antoine Pergola, was on duty. The ominous knock in the night caused his heart to skip a beat. The Gestapo? This was the time that they customarily struck. He ambled to the locked door and called out, ''Who is it?''

''The French Army!'' Captain Thorel replied.

Pergola was in a quandary. Was this a Gestapo trick to see if he would give aide to ''terrorists''? Timidly, he opened the door.

Thorel explained his situation: His commandos had landed on the wrong beach, the fleet would soon be shelling the coastline, and he and his men needed guidance to filter their way inland through German positions.

Seeing the shadowy figures of scores of French soldiers, Pergola agreed to guide the invaders to the coastal highway. Just as Thorel's column with the stationmaster in the lead started to march, an intensive crescendo of machine-gun fire and grenade and mortar explosions erupted far to the rear. Thorel could see the flares that bathed the shoreline. A savage fight seemed to be in progress at the site where Colonel Bouvet's main force had landed a short time before.

Only hours later would a puzzled Captain Thorel learn the cause of the uproar on the beach to his rear. A patrol of the 918th Grenadiers—a unit consisting mainly of Armenian, Ukrainian, and Polish volunteers—had discovered many items of equipment discarded by Bouvet's commandos and rapidly spread the word that an Allied force had landed.

Rushing to the scene, other Wehrmacht foreign volunteers grew panicky, and in minutes pandemonium had erupted along the beach. The defenders dashed to and fro. Flares lighted the sky. Shouted orders rang out over the sand dunes. The nervous Feldgrau riddled shadows with Schmeisser machine pistols and in the mass confusion began firing at each other.

There was not a French soldier within a mile of the violent outburst; all of Colonel Bouvet's men had already slipped far inland.*

When daylight broke over the magnificent shores of the Côte d'Azur, the French commandos had achieved their crucial objectives. The big guns atop Cap Negre had been destroyed and the main force was dug in on its objective, a ridgeline over which ran the coastal highway leading from Toulon and Marseilles to the Alpha, Delta, and Camel landing beaches.

---

*Capt. Albert Thorel was killed in action the next day.

Mission: Hoodwink the Germans

At the eastern end of the three beaches where American assault divisions would storm ashore at 8:00 A.M., the Operation Rosie task force under Lt. Comdr. Douglas E. Fairbanks, Jr., had moved into position offshore, a short distance west of the popular peacetime resort of Cannes. Fairbanks's flotilla included the British gunboats *Aphis* and *Scarab,* fighter-director ships *Stuart Prince* and *Antwerp,* three seventy-foot motor launches, and four swift PT (Patrol torpedo) boats.

The handsome young Fairbanks had been one of Hollywood's most famous stars. Despite his status as a reserve officer, he had been assigned to command a crucial mission in the invasion.

In military terms, Operation Rosie was called a diversionary action, designed to attract the Wehrmacht's attention from the site of the main landings by stirring up as big a ruckus as possible. Rosie's role would be crucial to the success of the invasion.

It was 1:25 A.M. In the blackness, sixty-seven Frenchmen of the Groupe Navale d'Assaut de Corse (Navy assault commandos) under Capt. de Fregate Seriot climbed over the sides of Fairbanks's PT boats off Pointe de l'Esquillon and slipped into rubber rafts. Each man was burdened with sixty pounds of explosives, a Tommy gun, and several extra clips of ammunition. The Navy commandos would have to scale a rocky cliff, blow up key bridges along the Corniche road, and then rapidly march inland through German positions and demolish spans on Route 7. The demolitions were to prevent the Wehrmacht from rushing troops from Cannes and Nice westward to the Allied landing beaches.

Captain Seriot's mind was free of one haunting specter—that of his force stumbling into a minefield in the darkness. Less than twenty-four hours before arriving off the Riviera, Seriot had been advised that last-minute reports from the French Underground had revealed that there were no mines along the beach where the Navy assault team would slip ashore. But during the few hours following reception of the Underground signal, German engineers had descended onto the Pointe de l'Esquillon shoreline and saturated it with an assortment of fiendish mines.

At 1:40 A.M. the French Navy men reached shore and silently scrambled onto the golden sands. Not a sound could be heard other than the gentle, rhythmic lapping of the surf. Seriot and his men heaved sighs of relief. Faces blackened and wearing dark clothing, the commandos formed up quietly and began to steal inland. Suddenly, explosions pierced the night air and orange flashes leaped skyward. The Frenchmen had walked into a minefield.

Mutilated men, legs and arms blown off, intestines hanging out and draped across the wet, sandy beach, were crying out for help. Eleven in the assault team were killed, seventeen others seriously wounded.

A nearby German unit, on alert for just such a landing by Allied forces, rushed to the scene and began peppering the trapped Frenchmen in the minefield with machine-gun fire. Some of Seriot's men tried to crawl forward, and others fired back at the enemy force. Wounded and bewildered by the sudden holocaust that in moments had struck down more than 40 percent of the assault team, the sole surviving French officer surrendered most of those still alive.

Fate continued to frown on the ill-starred Navy commandos. A few men, including several who were wounded, had scrambled into the rubber boats and tried to paddle back to the offshore vessels. The sound of powerful motors echoed over the seascape as two Allied fighter planes zoomed in and strafed the dinghies, killing three occupants and collapsing the boats. Some commandos swam ashore, where they were taken prisoner.

BARELY ONE HOUR after the French disaster at Pointe de l'Esquillon, the surviving junior officer and one of his sergeants were seated under a glaring light in an austere room at a German Army command post at Grasse. The pair of Frenchmen were still weak and shaken from their ordeal on the beach. Stern-faced enemy Intelligence officers were forcefully interrogating the hapless prisoners. This could be the break the Wehrmacht had been hoping for. Surely these French commandos had to know where the main Allied landing would hit.

Both Frenchmen refused to talk. "Reveal the landing site or you'll promptly be shot," the pair were told. Finally the two Navy men broke down: The Allies would land in the vicinity of Port Vendres.

Smiles of smug satisfaction wreathed the faces of the German Intelligence officers. The prisoners were locked in a small room.

Port Vendres was near the Spanish frontier—some two hundred miles west of where Dragoon's three assault divisions would storm ashore shortly after dawn along the Côte d'Azur.

In the meantime, Fairbanks's gunboats *Aphis* and *Scarab* fired a few rounds from their four-inch guns at the coastal highway as the Operation Rosie commander and all hands tensely huddled over radio receivers for word from the French Navy commando force. As the tense minutes ticked by and ran into hours, the shipboard radios remained mute.

Just before 2:00 A.M. Lt. Comdr. John D. Bulkeley was standing on the bridge of the destroyer USS *Endicott* that was racing through the darkness toward the bay at the little port of La Ciotat, a break in the rugged coast midway between Toulon and sprawling, drab Marseilles, the sin-city of southern France, and some sixty-five miles west of the nearest Dragoon landing beach. Brash, cocky, and tough, the thirty-two-year-old Bulkeley had gained widespread fame more than two years earlier as the PT-boat skipper who had rescued General Douglas MacArthur and his staff from Corregidor as the Japanese were ringing that fortress in Manila Bay. For that "impossible" feat and other achievements in the Philippines in those black early days, John Bulkeley had received the Medal of Honor from President Roosevelt.

As the recipient of America's highest decoration for valor, Commander Bulkeley could have waited out the war in cushy jobs. But he insisted on going back into action, led PT boats again in the Pacific, commanded PT boats during the Normandy invasion, and then was given command of *Endicott* for Operation Dragoon. Now he was leading a deception mission crucial to the entire southern France invasion.

"John's always trying to figure out some new way to get himself killed," an admirer had exclaimed, reflecting the viewpoint of most.

Now, in the blackness of the Mediterranean, Commander Bulkeley peered periodically to both sides and to the stern, instinctively trying to gain a glimpse of the vessels in his tiny, high-speed flotilla— eight PT boats and seven motor launches. But he could not see even dim outlines of the other craft, for they were spread out over an area eight miles wide and twelve miles long. *Endicott* and the powerboats were simulating for German radar screens a major convoy, heading hell-bent for the Baie de la Ciotat. Bulkeley's little force was playing a major role in Operation Ferdinand, a combined sea-and-air *ruse de guerre* designed to hoodwink the Wehrmacht as to where the main Allied blow would fall.

German commanders at Marseilles had been convinced for two days that the Allies would land in force in the bay at La Ciotat, whose smooth, sandy beaches made it ideal for a massive amphibious operation. Ferdinand was to reinforce that faulty enemy impression.

Since before midnight, the hazy night air in the Baie de la Ciotat region had been filled with the sounds of Allied aircraft engines as warplanes pounded ancient Marseilles, Toulon, and German installations around La Ciotat, being careful not to destroy the German radar station on a hill at the mouth of La Ciotat Bay. Four other Wehrmacht radar stations along the Marseilles-Toulon coastline had been knocked out, but this one was permitted to survive so it could pick up Commander Bulkeley's "fleet" as well as the swarms of Allied aircraft marauding about overhead in the darkness.

At 2:15 A.M., German technicians at the radar facility on the heights at Cap Sicie passed along an alarming report: A large Allied naval force had somehow infiltrated floating minefields in the mouth of La Ciotat Bay and was now steaming inside the harbor. This "large naval force" was Bulkeley's *Endicott* and fifteen powerboats.

Aiding in the ruse that convinced the Germans that Bulkeley's force represented a formidable landing threat were three Corsica-based Wellington heavy bombers of the Royal Air Force. They had been circling over the little flotilla dropping "window," thin strips of a metallic substance that caused images to blur on enemy radar screens so that the precise number of vessels could not be counted.

Word of the looming landing was flashed to German gun batteries along the coast between Marseilles and Toulon, and soon heavy concentrations of shells were splashing into the dark, placid waters of the Baie de la Ciotat. None of the projectiles hit Bulkeley's craft. After cavorting about in the harbor for nearly an hour, the phantom fleet dashed back out to the open sea, its role in Ferdinand concluded.

At La Ciotat, a jubilant German commander promptly signaled a higher headquarters at Marseilles: "Attempted Allied landing beaten back!"

MEANWHILE, FIVE C-47 transport planes flown by British pilots took off from an airfield outside Ajaccio, Corsica, bound for the Marseilles-Toulon region. It was 1:55 A.M. The aircraft were loaded with parachutists in American garb. Flying due north toward Genoa, the C-47 flight suddenly altered its route and headed for La Ciotat, ninety miles to the west. In order to convey to German radar screens that the approaching flight was much larger, each C-47 flew at five-minute intervals, and air crews tossed out "window."

Flying at 600 feet with a speed of 110 miles per hour, the lead C-47 knifed over the coastline near the La Ciotat radar station and was fired on by a German ack-ack battery. With other C-47s following on course, the aircraft headed for the drop zone between Rougiers and Signes, about fifteen miles north of Toulon.

At 3:49 A.M. the dark skies were awash with blossoming white parachutes as the fully equipped American parachutists drifted earthward. Immediately the cries echoed through the dark, rolling countryside: *"Fallschirmjaeger!*

Fallschirmjaeger!" (Paratroopers! Paratroopers!) Periodically, for twenty minutes, the invaders from the sky spilled out behind Hitler's South Wall until three hundred had landed.

German defenses were thrown into confusion by the airborne drop. Within minutes word was flashed up through the Wehrmacht chain of command: Hundreds of Allied paratroopers had landed north of Toulon. At each echelon the numbers were inflated, and by the time the report had filtered up to Gen. Johannes Blaskowitz at Army Group G near Toulouse, *thousands* of enemy paratroopers had touched down.

At the same time the three hundred parachutists were being dropped, the destroyer *Endicott*, together with eight PT boats, a dozen air-sea rescue craft, and some British Fairmiles, were racing along the Mediterranean coastline within radar range of the Baie de la Ciotat. Under the command of Capt. Henry C. Johnson, this small, decoy naval force was streaming reflector balloons to confuse the German radar about the true size of the flotilla. Johnson's task force made as much din and commotion as possible to simulate the motions of a major landing, and it was rewarded by drawing a heavy concentration of fire from German shore batteries.

AT 3:47 A.M., Comdr. W. C. Hughes on the American destroyer *Somers* tensed as his radar picked up two unidentified ships heading toward the hundreds of Allied vessels poised quietly in the blackness off the Alpha, Delta, and Camel beaches. Patrolling south of the Île du Levant, where Col. Edwin Walker's 1st Special Service Force men were in a firefight, *Somer's* mission was to protect the sitting convoy from German warships.

Commander Hughes had been firmly cautioned by Admiral Davidson, the Task Force Sitka leader, not to "give away the show" by premature gunfire. For an hour, Hughes shadowed these two vessels and several times had signaled them by blinker light to identify themselves. There had been no response. Hughes grew increasingly concerned. If these two shadowy ships were torpedo boats, they could fire their huge projectiles in the general direction of the anchored armada and hardly miss this sprawling target.

Hughes reached a crucial decision. If he opened fire on the pair of unidentified ships—he was now convinced that they were German—he might well "give away the show." If he did not sink the two craft, their torpedoes could play havoc with the giant fleet lying silently in the blackness.

"Open fire!" he ordered the *Somers's* gunnery officer.

Hearing the order, an excited young ensign in the flagship's combat information center called out, only half in jest, "Maybe it's the *Tirpitz!*"*

The first salvo from *Somers* scored a bull's-eye on a German auxiliary ship named *Escaburt.* An enormous orange flame spiraled into the black sky, illuminating the seascape for miles in each direction. The blast blew sailors on deck far out into the calm waters of the Mediterranean. Others were killed outright. The *Escaburt* burned fiercely.

Her protector, *UJ-6081* (the former Italian corvette *Camoscio*), promptly abandoned the doomed vessel and raced off as fast as her engines would propel her. The *Somers's* guns poured salvo after salvo at the fleeing *UJ-6081.* Only after daylight would Commander Hughes learn that *UJ-6081* had taken more than forty hits, had stalled in the water, and had been abandoned by her crew.

Meanwhile, the flaming torch that was the *Escaburt* had alerted every German ashore.

AT ALL HIGH-LEVEL Wehrmacht headquarters, commanders were desperately trying to evaluate the ominous reports of heavy Allied sea, air, and ground activity along the Côte d'Azur. In Paris, Adm. Theodor Krancke's command post—Marinegruppenkommando West—nervously noted that the "thousands" of Allied paratroopers dropped north of Toulon not only threatened that key German-held port but Marseilles as well. Nearly all of the German warships on the Mediterranean coast were based at one or the other of these two ports.

At sleepy Avignon, Gen. Friedrich Wiese and his chief of staff, Walther Botsch, were staring fixedly at the giant wall map of the Côte d'Azur in the Nineteenth Army operations room. It was a puzzling situation. A rash of red spots had sprouted over the map by 4:00 A.M. An Allied force had landed at the twin islands of du Levant and Port-Cros and were fighting there. Other heavy clashes had erupted on towering Cap Negre, and a

---

*The *Tirpitz* was the German Navy's most powerful battleship. Strenuous efforts had been made by the Allies to locate and sink the warship, as its huge guns, speed, and thick hide presented a constant menace to Allied shipping.

French naval assault unit had been decimated near Cannes. A fleet had steamed into the bay at La Ciotat, then turned and headed out to sea, and large numbers of paratroopers had been dropped north of Toulon.

"What do you make of it, Herr General?" Botsch asked his boss evenly. "Where do you think the *Schwerpunkt* [main thrust] will be?"

Wiese pondered the questions momentarily, rubbing his chin thoughtfully. "I don't know, Botsch," he replied. "I simply don't know. We'll have to wait and see what develops."

Alarming reports from naval stations along a hundred miles of the Côte d'Azur continued to deluge Wiese's airless headquarters. Using sound-direction apparatus and any radar equipment that had not been knocked out, the stations were picking up large numbers of ships maneuvering twelve to twenty miles offshore. The Nineteenth Army commander could only watch and await the looming sledgehammer blow. He had done all he could to meet the threat. His fighting men along the coast had already been on *Alarmstruffe I* (full alert) for six hours.

In the meantime, a hodgepodge force of grenadiers had been rapidly thrown together in the Toulon region and dispatched inland at great speed with orders to wipe out the Allied paratrooper force that was a threat to Toulon and Marseilles. Closing in on the fields between Rougiers and Signes, where scores of collapsed white parachutes were strewn across the dark terrain, the Feldgrau opened fire and were puzzled by the failure of the enemy airborne force to shoot back. Charging the mass of white chutes, the Germans reached their quarry: three hundred lifelike rubber dummies dressed in precise replicas of helmets and other American paratrooper gear. Attached to each dummy were strings of firecrackers that had exploded on landing, conveying the impression to nervous Germans in the locale that an all-out firefight had erupted.

Curious to inspect the dummies, several German soldiers picked them up. There were sharp explosions followed by shrieks of pain from the Feldgrau whose hands had been blown off. The rubber figures had been booby-trapped.*

---

*The Germans had long been diabolical geniuses in booby-trapping everything from bedpans to baby buggies. Yet the next day Radio Berlin denounced the deception as "a dastardly deed which could only have been conceived in the sinister Anglo-Saxon mind."

THE RUBBER-DUMMY hoax was the airborne component of Operation Ferdinand. As with Bulkeley's naval force in the Baie de la Ciotat, the fake paratroopers were not expected to deceive the Wehrmacht for long, only to throw the Germans off balance. Ferdinand was like a clever boxer who would feint a left hook to draw his opponent's attention in that direction before landing a haymaker with his right fist.

The Allied haymaker was about to be launched.

"We'll Hold 'til Hell Freezes!"

Standing there in the darkness of a bivouac of his 509th Parachute Infantry Battalion at 1:00 A.M. on D-Day, Lt. Col. Bill Yarborough was outwardly buoyant and confident. But Yarborough was a truly worried man. For days he had been praying for fair weather on this crucial morning in order to have good visibility to sight the hill masses around the village of Le Muy as the C-47s approached the Côte d'Azur. Only minutes before, the thirty-three-year-old leader of the battle-hardened outfit had learned that a dense fogbank had descended over the entire target area—and was going to remain there. Now the winds were beginning to shift by some ninety degrees, and after the C-47s with their cargoes of paratroopers got in flight, the navigators would find the checkpoints difficult to see—if they could be seen at all.

Yarborough's mind flashed back to the airborne attack on German-held Sicily in July 1943 in which he participated as a battalion commander in the 82nd Airborne Division. Due to gale-force winds, the American parachutists, instead of landing in a neat pattern on a single large DZ, were scattered for sixty miles along the coastline. Was southern France to be a repeat of that episode?

The air was strange that night in the bivouac amid the olive trees. It had an unfamiliar lack of movement, utterly devoid of the customary crisp breeze that swept over the boot of Italy from the Tyrrhenian Sea. Woven into this sultry, lifeless atmosphere was the suffocating, invisible cloak of foreboding that hovered over every parachute unit ready to bail out into the black unknown behind enemy lines.

Yarborough, of Staunton, Virginia, had gathered his tough but grimfaced troopers around him. Their shadowy outlines were barely visible, as faces and hands had been stained with black and green grease.

"Troopers," the tall, blue-eyed leader began in a calm and confident voice, "you have been chosen to spearhead the invasion that may break the Krauts' back. You know now where we are going. We are going to hold there 'til hell freezes over or we are relieved, whichever comes first!"

Yarborough paused briefly, then continued: "In case anything happens, I want you to know how proud and glad I am to be with you. I'll see you in France! God bless you all!"

As the Five-O-Niners dispersed to head for their C-47s, a civilian war correspondent representing the combined American press was feeling pangs of anxiety. Robert Vermillion had never jumped out of an airplane, but in a few hours he would be bailing out behind the Riviera with men who were young, tough, and battle-tested.

How did I ever get into this? flashed through Vermillion's mind. A few days before, Capt. George McCall of Salt Lake City had led the reporter into a hangar and pointed to a canvas-covered pack. "This is what's known as a parachute," McCall stated. Then the captain took Vermillion to a C-47 and showed the reporter how to jump, adding, "If you don't do it the right way or freeze in the door, the guy behind you will kick you out."

That concluded Bob Vermillion's parachute training.

Similar scenes were being repeated at ten airfields carved out of the flatlands in the vicinity of Rome. Squat, camouflaged C-47 troop carrier planes sat on hard-surfaced and dirt runways. Solemn paratroopers slumped down on the ground beside each one. Members of Gen. Bob Frederick's 1st Airborne Task Force were quietly preparing themselves for the ordeal that lay ahead. Rifles, Tommy guns, and BARs were checked and rechecked. Then they were checked again. Each combat soldier had been told in his first day of small-arms training: Care for and protect your weapon as though your life depended on it—which it does!

General Frederick himself, who bore on his thin yet sturdy shoulders the ultimate responsibility for the airborne assault on Hitler's southern bastion, in customary fashion was coolly making his own personal preparations for the flight and jump. Frederick would share the dangers of his men in equal measure, for a parachute general could be shot in descending, break his back or crush his skull on landing—or be the mangled victim of a "streamer." Parachutes were unimpressed by rank.

Earlier that afternoon, the unflappable Bob Frederick had made a quick trip into Rome from the nearby airfield at Lido di Roma. For five weeks he had feverishly labored around the clock to plan and mount the airborne invasion, along with having to whip together several crack independent airborne regiments, battalions, and companies into a cohesive force. With the jump into southern France only hours away, General Frederick had gone into the Eternal City to get a message.

Despite Bob Frederick's almost legendary status as a front-line general who was always at the hottest spots and had already been wounded several times, the FABTF commander was no robot. During a lull on the hellhole of Anzio beachhead earlier in the year, Frederick had admitted to a reporter: "I try to get out where the going is heavy and light a cigarette so my men can see me. I have a hard time keeping my hands from trembling when I'm lighting up."

If Frederick's hands ever trembled, his Black Devils had never been aware of it.

Standing near General Frederick on a black airfield was his bodyguard, Cpl. Duff Matson, who was carrying a Sicilian dagger and four other razor-sharp knives. His pockets were full of grenades, and he would bail out carrying several blocks of TNT. Like scores of others around the Rome region airfields that night, Matson tried not to dwell upon the nasty mess that would ensue if German machine-gun bullets ripped into the explosives as he was parachuting down.

As with most major landings on hostile shores, Allied Intelligence had come up with last-minute information that Hitler might use poison gas when southern France was invaded. Strict orders had filtered down the chain of command: All troops must carry a gas mask at all times.

Alongside Matson was a friend, Walter Turner. In the

darkness, Matson could discern that Turner had pitched away his gas mask and had filled the empty canvas container with coffee and cigars.

"What're you throwing away your gas mask for?" Matson inquired idly.

"Because I'm a hell of a lot more concerned about having a hot brew and a good smoke when we land than I am of any gas Hitler may throw at us!" was the candid reply.

At the same dark airfield, Sgt. Charles B. Rawls, Jr., a member of the Intelligence section of headquarters company of the 1st Airborne Task Force, was checking his personal equipment and mulling over his encounter earlier that day with one of the most prominent officials of the Roman Catholic Church in the United States, Archbishop Francis Spellman of New York City. Early in the war, President Roosevelt had agreed to the appointment of Spellman as apostolic vicar to the United States armed forces. Now he was on hand to give his blessing and to lend encouragement to Dragoon assault troops.

Catholic paratroopers and glidermen were blessed at Lido Airfield, but members of all denominations had been invited to participate. Sergeant Rawls, a Protestant, attended the procedure, telling a comrade, "What can I lose? We need all the help we can get." Rawls was duly blessed by the archbishop.*

Elsewhere in the vicinity of Rome, Capt. Tims Quinn of Joerg's 551st Parachute Infantry Battalion was lying on the ground beside the C-47 he would soon board for the flight to southern France. The 551st would not bail out until 6:00 P.M. on D-Day, but Quinn would go in with the spearheading 509th Parachute Infantry to prepare the DZ for the arrival of Joerg's paratroopers. Quinn would alternately gaze up at the dark sky and read selections from the *Book of 101 Best Poems* to a reclining comrade, Frank Serio. The captain utilized the muted blue glow of a small flashlight to see the pages.

"Here's a poem you'll like, Frank," Captain Quinn remarked. "It's named, 'I Have a Rendezvous with Death.'"

Several moments of silence greeted Quinn's macabre observation, coming as it did only a few hours before a parachute jump into the dark and ominous unknown over hostile territory.

---

*On returning to New York after the Dragoon assault, Archbishop (later Cardinal) Spellman wrote personal letters to the parents, wives, or next of kin of the many hundreds he had blessed, including the parents of Protestant Sergeant Rawls.

Somehow things didn't seem as funny as they once were. "Let's be serious for a minute, Captain," Serio finally stated. "There's something I'd like for you to do for me."

"Sure, Frank. What is it?"

"If anything happens to me, I want you to contact my wife."

"You can count on me. But nothing's going to happen to you."

Quinn laid aside the *Book of 101 Best Poems,* reclined onto his back, and gazed skyward into black infinity. He wished he were all that certain that "nothing was going to happen" to Frank Serio—or to himself.

AS THE FIREBALL Mediterranean sun was sinking into the depths of the western horizon, British Lt. T. W. Williams and his comrades in the 1st Independent Parachute Platoon joined with their American C-47 pilots in drinking a record number of cans of fruit juice "liberated" from unit kitchens when cooks conveniently turned their backs. Williams' platoon was to serve as pathfinders for Brigadier Pritchard's 2nd Independent Parachute Brigade. A gifted musician, Williams strummed his guitar until sore fingers finally stopped him.

There was great gaiety on the surface. But a thinly veiled specter of foreboding hovered over the gathering: Before the sun came up the Red Devils would be fighting for their lives behind the Nazis' South Wall, and there was always the possibility that the C-47 pilots could go down in flames. Whatever cards Fate might choose to deal them in a few hours, for now the little group of British and Americans would drink fruit juice, sing, and make merry.

Like their American paratrooper counterparts, Lieutenant Williams and his fellow British parachutists often marched to a different drummer—not the same one heard by those soldiers known as straight-legs, who did not choose to leap from flying airplanes. Williams was a particularly good friend of Capt. Peter Baker, a huge, tough, and mean-looking trooper who somehow reminded Williams of a healthy ox, and of an amiable glider pilot named "Ape" Mockeridge, whom the lieutenant considered to be "halfway around the bend."

For months Williams and Ape had had something of a running feud while at the same time holding each other in great esteem and affection. At Comiso Airfield in Sicily, Ape pounded on Williams's bedroom door at 5:00 A.M. and shouted, "All subalterns [lieutenants] on parade!" The path-finder reached under his pillow, pulled out a revolver, and, hoping Ape was not standing on a chair, shot a hole through the top of the door.

A few days later, Ape challenged Williams—or maybe it was the other way around—to a jeep "dog fight." They both leaped into jeeps and chased each other at high speeds around the perimeter of the airfield. The duel came to a sudden end when Williams sped through the open door of a hangar with Ape right on his tail. Ape lost control and crashed into an airplane, escaping with a few cuts and a dressing down from his commander.

On one occasion the pathfinders had been relentlessly needling Mockeridge and finally locked him out of the dining room at mealtime. Ape, undaunted, poured kerosene around the door and set it on fire.

Life still got boring at hot, dusty Comiso, from where Captain Baker and his pathfinders had departed for the Rome area a few weeks before D-Day for Dragoon. A British judge who was passing through was invited to dine with Baker, Williams, and other pathfinder officers. A judge's life must be terribly unexciting, they decided, so the parachutists were determined to liven things up. Several of them went to the ammunition dump and returned before dinner with a variety of deadly explosive gadgets that would be used as table decorations in honor of the distinguished judge.

At dinner that evening, the jurist seemed to be impressed that so much effort had gone into honoring him. If the gray-haired guest was ever curious about the gadgets on all sides, he said nothing. The judge's chair legs rested on four Teller mines. In the center of the table a bowl of fruit sat gracefully on the prongs of an S mine. The dignified, friendly judge seemed to enjoy himself, although he may have wondered why his paratrooper hosts seemed to be having a difficult time restraining impulses to laugh.

Baker, Williams, and Ape were all pistol enthusiasts. They had been students at the famed "killer school" conducted by a legendary British lieutenant colonel named Grant-Taylor. The course, conducted near Comiso Airfield, was designed to demonstrate the most thorough and rapid methods for dispos-ing of enemies with firearms. Colonel Grant-Taylor was delighted when he would learn that some of his "pupils" had applied his techniques to eliminate home-grown traitors in occupied Europe.

In the evenings after dinner, Baker and Williams would sit on the veranda and fire at a large pile of .20-caliber and machine-gun ammunition stacked outside the building, in an effort to explode an occasional round. Williams was not happy with the results. One evening he told Baker, "To hell with it!" and squeezed off several rounds. The ammo pile began smoking, and the two pathfinders decided it was time to take off.

Now, at the Dragoon D-Day eve fruit-juice socializing, the chief pilot of the C-47 that would fly the British pathfinder platoon to France, U.S. Capt. Dick Jacobsen, took Lieutenant Williams to one side. "After studying aerial pics and other data," the Air Corps officer stated, "I feel confident that we will drop your platoon right on the DZ outside of Le Mitan—certainly within a mile of it and maybe even closer."

Soon—all too soon—word came that it was time to go. Williams, two officers, and their fifteen men marched the short distance to their C-47, singing. On the way the Red Devils passed the French pathfinders who were sitting on the ground, dejected because they were being left behind.

Swinging along, the British platoon broke out with the "Marseillaise," and the French paratroopers, with tears streaming down their cheeks, leaped to their feet, and their lusty cheers echoed across the dark airfield.

The platoon was met at their C-47 by Captain Jacobsen, who gathered his British comrades around him. Whatever may have been the discord and jealousies among the Allied high command, at the level of the fighting man the Americans and the British meshed in harmonious accord and even affection.

Hoping that his voice did not betray his emotion, Jacobsen declared, "You know what a kick we've got from flying you boys around [on recent practice missions], and there's one thing we want to say. When the green light goes on over the Riviera it doesn't only mean 'Go'—it means happy landings and the best of luck."

Lieutenant Williams, deeply touched by these few simple but meaningful words, made no reply. He merely took his American friend's hand and shook it warmly.

At an airfield near Grosetto, Capt. Ernest T. "Bud" Siegel, who had been a member of the New York State Police, was conversing earnestly with the three platoon leaders of his A Company of the 509th Parachute Infantry Battalion. This would be the first combat mission for Siegel since he had been promoted to captain and made a company commander, and he wanted to make certain that his unit succeeded. The A Company would lead the airborne assault, and Captain Siegel would be the first to jump.

Siegel, whose almost perpetual smile belied his tenacity on the battlefield, held great confidence in his battle-tested paratroopers (plus some new replacements), but his bold spirit had not been strengthened by an episode he had witnessed that afternoon. Siegel and his platoon leaders, Lieutenants William Pahl, Kenneth Shaker, and Hoyt Livingston, had attended a final briefing for C-47 pilots of the Troop Carrier Command, who would fly the paratroopers into battle.

Captain Siegel and his three parachute officers were surprised at the extreme youth of the pilots. "I don't think some of them have shaved yet," Siegel whispered.

When the Air Corps briefing colonel had concluded, he asked the customary, "Any further questions?" A rosy-cheeked young pilot from a Southern state drawled, "When the plane is throttled back on the left side to lessen the parachutists' opening shock, is the tail up or down?"

Siegel and his three paratroop comrades were startled. "A real prejump confidence builder!" the captain muttered. They didn't know if the young pilot was serious or was making a straight-faced joke—a tail-down position for a C-47 would result in disaster for the paratroopers as they bailed out, for each parachute could become entangled on the tail surface.

One of the Troop Carrier Command outfits that would fly General Frederick's paratroopers and glider fighters into southern France was the 50th Troop Carrier Wing. On July 16, as Dragoon was hastily being thrown together after months of bickering and indecision at the highest levels of government and command, the 50th Trooper Carrier Wing took off from England in a mass flight to Italy. The wing flew south across the Bay of Biscay into Marrakech, Morocco, then moved northeast across the Mediterranean to several bases around Rome.

Official communiqués had called the long flight "routine, with no interception by enemy aircraft." But the terse, cold words of official communiqués did not reflect the feelings or emotions of the American airmen. The statements failed to paint a vivid picture of interminable, weary hours in the air, plowing through a black void with a violent electrical storm ripping the night apart. And always there loomed the peril of interception by Focke-Wulf fighter planes. The lumbering, unarmed C-47s, whose gas tanks exploded when struck by bullets, would have been shot down in great numbers had such a Luftwaffe interception occurred.

A routine flight. That's what the official communiqués called it.

In these early hours of darkness on D-Day for Dragoon, Lt. John Goodwin of Col. Irvin Anderson's 95th Squadron was painstakingly inspecting his C-47. Goodwin would fly the No. 2 slot off Colonel Anderson's right wing. Anderson, the skipper, was a good man to follow in a combat flight, the air corps lieutenant reflected.

They called Johnny Goodwin a kid. That he was, if age were reckoned only on the basis of the twenty years he had spent on earth. But anyone peering into his blue eyes could detect a tenseness, a maturity far beyond his two decades of life, for Johnny Goodwin had been through the horrors of war. He had carried a cargo of American paratroopers into Normandy in the hours of darkness on D-Day morning, stoically maintaining his No. 2 slot as German ack-ack fire burst around him and rocked his C-47. He came over Normandy again on D-Day plus one, when a shell blew him out of the sky. Goodwin landed in the cold, turbulent English Channel but was miraculously rescued and returned to his squadron.

Now, at age twenty, the thin, sallow Johnny Goodwin held an impressive title: deputy commander of the 95th Squadron. Soon he would be going into action again. This flight gave promise of not being "routine."

AT A DARK airstrip near Marcigliana, Lt. Dan A. De Leo, who would lead a pathfinder team that would jump about one hour ahead of the main body of the 509th Parachute Infantry Battalion, glanced at his luminous watch. It was 12:55 A.M., nearly time to board his C-47. De Leo's black-faced team would be one of nine such trailblazer units for the 1st Airborne Task Force. Once they had touched down, these vanguard troops, all picked men, would have less than sixty minutes to reconnoiter the ground and plant portable beacon signals on the drop zones to guide in the original flight of 396 troop-transport planes.

Dan De Leo, in nearly two years of combat duty, had led a charmed life, even more so than had most other experienced combat paratroopers. On Christmas Eve 1942, the young native of Chicago bailed out in the darkness at the head of a twenty-nine-man raiding party ninety miles behind German lines in Tunisia. His parachute raiders had the mission of blowing up a key bridge at a hamlet named El Djem. Over this span ran the north-south railroad that supplied Field Marshal Erwin Rommel's Afrika Korps.

De Leo's comrades called it a suicide mission. "Get back the best way you can," the 509th Parachute Infantry Battalion raiders were told. After blowing up the tracks, De Leo and his men split up into pairs. Eight made it back safely, including the raiders' leader.

In September 1943, Dan De Leo, along with the rest of the battalion, had jumped some twenty-five to thirty miles behind German lines at Salerno, Italy, to relieve the pressure on Gen. Mark Clark's Fifth Army, which was on the verge of being thrown back into the sea. Most of the battalion had been scattered over four hundred square miles of rugged Italian terrain. Many avoided coming down right on the enemy, but De Leo and his stick* were dropped on top of a German position, and several of his men were killed or wounded seriously in a savage firefight.

Now the quietude of Lieutenant De Leo's airfield was shattered by shouts in the darkness: "Okay, load 'em up!" Even among the battle-scarred vets these words sent chill twinges up spines. There was something ominous in the call piercing the night air as the harsh roar of revving airplane engines rolled across the landscape.

Each burdened by seventy pounds or more of combat gear, De Leo and his pathfinder team waddled up a short ladder and through the open doorway of a C-47, its cabin bathed in the muted glow of a blue light. Wedging himself into a bucket seat, the lieutenant was careful not to glance toward one end of the cabin. He wanted to avoid "seeing" two AWOL men who were stowing away on the aircraft in order to make the jump into Southern France. Neither was authorized to go along.

---

*A stick is an arbitrary number of paratroopers, usually fifteen to eighteen men, who jump out of one airplane.

The two stowaways were Sgt. Emanuel Serano, who had made the parachute raid at the El Djem bridge in Tunisia and had been captured by the Germans, escaped, and spent fourteen months with Italian Partisan bands raiding German installations, and 1st Sgt. James Prettyman, who had no training as a paratrooper but had been assigned to the pathfinder team in an administrative capacity.

Both men had begged Lieutenant De Leo to take them with him in his C-47. He repeatedly refused their request, but they were persistent.

"Hell, I can't do that," De Leo replied. "You'd be AWOL. And if I would *see* you in the plane I'd have to have you removed."

The accent on the word *see* was not lost on Serano and Prettyman. They'd make sure that they slipped into the aircraft while De Leo "happened" to be looking in the other direction.*

There were three C-47s in the initial pathfinder flight, carrying the vanguard of the 509th and 551st Parachute Infantry battalions and the 550th Glider Infantry Battalion. Each pathfinder team had been assigned its own DZ in the same general area around the village of Le Muy. The trio of aircraft zipped down the runway and lifted off for southern France.

---

*A few hours after bailing out, stowaway Emanuel Serano would be seriously wounded, but he survived the war.

Ordeal of the Pathfinders

As the pathfinder vanguard of 396 troop transports plowed through the dark Mediterranean skies, the few thousand inhabitants of Le Muy were deep in slumber, never dreaming that their peaceful little community would soon be the focal point of a bitter struggle between the invading Allies and the German Wehrmacht. Both adversaries coveted this key locale.

Le Muy lies twelve miles from the sea and commands one of the few valleys that cut through a high ridge running along the coastline between Nice and Marseilles. Whichever side held Le Muy controlled one of the passages leading from the Mediterranean into the interior. A hard-surfaced road ran from the coastal town of Saint-Raphael northward through Le Muy and on deep into France. General Wiese at the Nineteenth Army recognized the tactical significance of this road and Le Muy and had dispatched two regiments there to defend the village. Likewise, the Allied high command had concluded that if Gen. Lucian Truscott's divisions coming in by sea were to drive northward rapidly, Le Muy had to be seized from the Germans.

As Lieutenant De Leo's pathfinder C-47 neared the French coast just before 3:00 A.M., the parachute leader stood in the open doorway, gazing toward the murky terrain outline of the Riviera. He felt a surge of alarm: The entire region was shrouded in a thick blanket of fog. Landmarks De Leo had studied on sand-table mock-ups for countless hours could not be detected.

Moments later violent explosions rocked the lumbering, low-flying C-47 as German antiaircraft gunners concealed in the fog opened fire on the intruders. There were eerie sounds in the plane, like those when a small boy tosses a handful of pebbles against a wall—shrapnel ripping through the tender hide of the C-47.

"The pilot can't make out a thing on the ground!" a nervous Air Corps crew chief hollered at De Leo above the roar of wind rushing through the open doorway. "He's going to circle out to sea and take another crack at it."

Twice more the pilot circled in an effort to locate the DZ, each time drawing a barrage of flak from German gunners. On the third try, the crew chief yelled, "He can't find the goddamned DZ! You'll have to jump now!"

De Leo shrugged his shoulders. Orders had read that each FABTF paratrooper was to jump—regardless. Turning to his pathfinders, who had been standing in the aisle with static lines hooked up, the troops under the burden of heavy combat gear for nearly thirty minutes, De Leo shouted, "Okay, let's go!" Clearing the C-47, De Leo was greeted by the vast expanse of black sky and the angry hurricane blasts tearing at his body. Moments later there was a tremendous jerk as his white parachute popped open. Suddenly De Leo felt a searing pain and lost consciousness. A chunk of shrapnel had grazed his head, ripped off his helmet, and caused blood to stream down his face.

An undetermined amount of time later, he slowly regained his senses. Although his head was spinning, with hair matted with blood and eyes refusing to focus in the darkness, De Leo became aware that his parachute had caught on a tall tree on the side of a hill and that he was dangling in his harness some twelve feet off the ground.

As he labored to shake the cobwebs from his mind, the lieutenant heard a rustling noise in the brush. It grew louder. Then he spotted the shadowy outline of a helmeted figure stalking toward him. On came the figure, closer and closer. De Leo tried to reach his pistol but could not do so. "This is the end!" the helpless trooper reflected.

Only thirty feet from the dangling pathfinder leader, the

shadowy figure halted. De Leo could discern a rifle or automatic weapon held at the ready. For moments the other man stood motionless. Then he called out in a stage whisper: "Lafayette!" De Leo heaved a sigh of relief on hearing the American password. "Democracy," he responded with the countersign.

The lieutenant also recognized the other's voice: It was that of one of his pathfinders, Charles McDonald.

The trooper quickly cut De Leo down and, seeing De Leo's hair, face, and jump suit saturated with blood, remarked in a low tone, "Damn, you're a hell-of-a-looking mess!"

"Yeah, I guess I am," the lieutenant agreed. "I was knocked out, but I think the shrapnel only grazed my head. I'm ready to go."

The question was: Go where? The first Americans to set foot behind Hitler's South Wall had bailed out "blind." Neither man knew where he was.

IN THE MEANTIME, other of General Frederick's pathfinders were having their troubles. At about the same time that Dan De Leo was dangling unconscious from a tree, nineteen-year-old Trooper Roger P. Carguerville of Lt. Col. Wood Joerg's 551st Parachute Infantry Battalion was groping around in the blackness, trying to locate the two pathfinders he had jumped with, Lt. Russell Fuller and Sgt. Hugh C. Roberts. Carguerville, of Oak Park, Illinois, had no way of knowing at the time that he had jumped eighteen miles from his drop zone.

This was the youth's first combat jump, and despite his tender years he found that he was calm and collected. As he stumbled along in the night, he periodically heard voices deep inside the thick, forbidding woods. But when he moved in the direction of the voices, they fell silent.

Through no fault of his, Roger Carguerville's mission had been a failure. He buried the heavy guide beacon he had been arduously lugging around and started trudging southward, heading for the American landing beaches along the Côte d'Azur. After covering a mile of rough going, the teenager paused to drink from his canteen. Gray was by now speckling the ink-black sky. Holding the water container to his lips, Carguerville somehow sensed peril. He whipped around to see a shadowy form lunging toward him and brandishing a long knife.

Carguerville dropped his canteen and went for the dagger in

his jump boot. Just at that moment in the gathering light, both men lowered their guard—they had at the last moment recognized each other as American paratroopers.

Carguerville was flooded with a sense of relief. Now he knew for the first time that he had not been the only American paratrooper to bail out over southern France, a prospect that had begun to worry him. The parachutists did not know each other, as they were from different outfits. As they hurriedly discussed their plight, the loud bark of a rifle split the air, and a bullet hissed past their heads. The two troopers flopped to the ground.

"The bastard's up on that hill," Carguerville stated, pointing toward a nearby elevation. "You go around one side of the hill and I'll go around the other, then we'll meet at the far end and close in on him."

Each parachutist began stalking toward his assigned side of the hill. Ten minutes later, Carguerville reached his destination and waited anxiously for his fellow trooper. The other American never arrived, and after waiting for a half hour, Carguerville resumed his trek toward the coastline.

THERE WAS GOOD reason why the youthful Carguerville could not locate his fellow pathfinder Sgt. Hugh Roberts. A communications sergeant, Roberts had landed on a rock-studded hill a considerable distance away. Just before crashing through the branches of a towering pine tree, Roberts heard the eerie wail of air-raid sirens up and down the valley. Lying there while trying to clear a head made foggy by the impact of the landing, Roberts took an azimuth reading with his compass on the moon and the stars.

"Goddamn!" he exploded, "we're way off. We aren't anywhere near where we're supposed to be!"

He quickly pondered why he had said "we"—apparently he was alone in the blackness.

Reflecting on his situation, Roberts concluded that the heavy radar equipment he was lugging to guide in the main body of his battalion would have to be destroyed. Adolf Hitler would be willing to give a large chunk of Poland or Czechoslovakia if his Intelligence experts could get their hands on this supersecret piece of sophisticated Allied technology.

The portable radar had a built-in destruct cartridge that could be detonated by pulling a pin. But around him he could hear German voices—off in the distance, to be sure, but an explosion would send them racing to the scene. So Roberts ripped out the explosive device, battered the radar with a rock, and buried it in a shallow grave covered by leaves and twigs.

Sergeant Roberts stole off in the night toward his DZ, undoubtedly many miles away, he was convinced. Minutes later he ran into a fellow pathfinder, Duke Spletzer, and then a third man, whom they did not know. The newcomer had a broken leg, so they dragged him into thick underbrush, propped him against a tree, and continued onward.

At daybreak, Roberts and Spletzer halted to rest. The going had been arduous—up one hill covered with vegetation tangles and down another equally rugged incline. Suddenly they tensed. Loud German shouts pierced the gathering light. Peeking through a thicket, the Americans spotted the source of the shouts—no more than fifty feet away Germans were establishing what appeared to be an outpost for antiaircraft guns, Roberts and Spletzer could discern the menacing gun barrels on two hills in the distance.

Four Feldgrau were setting up a machine gun close enough to the Americans that Roberts felt he could reach out and shake hands with his adversaries. Duke Spletzer grew impatient. ''Let's shoot the bastards!'' he urged in a hoarse stage whisper.

''Jesus Christ, don't shoot!'' an alarmed Roberts whispered back. ''We're in enough trouble as it is. If we shoot, we'll alert every Kraut for miles!''

The two pathfinders cautiously slipped away, and as they resumed their trek they ran into a lieutenant and three others who had jumped from their C-47. A short distance onward, an enemy machine gun suddenly opened fire on the six paratroopers. Spletzer, Roberts, and a youth from Texas dashed off in one direction; the other three scattered in other directions. The other three would never be seen again by Roberts and Spletzer.

FAR OFF IN the inky night, another pathfinder of the 551st Parachute Infantry Battalion, T. Sgt. William W. Lumsden of Hollywood Hills, California, was descending under his blossoming canopy. As the dark terrain rushed up to meet him, Lumsden could vaguely detect that he was heading directly toward high-tension wires. He slipped his chute frantically in an effort to miss the looming peril, but to no avail. Lumsden plunged right onto the potentially lethal wires.

The sergeant could feel electric shocks nipping at his body, and a second later he fell onto railroad tracks below. His binoculars had landed under him and were smashed almost flat, so great had been the impact. Lumsden was stunned by the electric shock and the force of his fall, but he was hazily aware that another American paratrooper had landed on the high-tension wires at about the same time that he had.

Lumsden and the other trooper had come down directly on a railroad yard. Seconds later, pandemonium broke out. Men were dashing about, shouting and wildly firing machine pistols. The panicky German force guarding the rail yard apparently was convinced that a major parachute assault had been launched against the facility, unaware that only two Americans had been misdropped there.

A German brandishing a Schmeisser machine pistol rushed up to where the dazed Sergeant Lumsden, still wearing his parachute harness and combat gear, was sprawled across the tracks. Firing from point-blank range, perhaps fifteen feet away, the German emptied the clip at the prone American. Lumsden felt a searing pain in his arm, as though a white-hot poker had been inserted into his elbow. A bullet had torn into his flesh and bone, and he felt warm blood flowing from the wound.

Having depleted his ammunition, the German spun around and began running. Still prone on the tracks, Lumsden pulled out his .45 Colt with his good arm and fired one round at the fleeing figure. A bullet tore through the back of his head, and the Feldgrau fell over dead.

As the wild shooting melee raged, Sergeant Lumsden struggled to his feet. His knees felt jellylike and his head was groggy. A stream of tracer bullets hissed past him as he staggered to a nearby woods, which swallowed him up. Only after dawn would he discover four bullet holes in the reserve parachute pack worn on his chest. All the holes were in front. The tightly packed chute had absorbed the Schmeisser's four slugs and prevented them from ripping into Lumsden's body.

EARLIER, CAPT. PETE Baker, Lt. T. W. Williams, and other men of the British pathfinder platoon were hooked up and standing in their C-47, waiting for the red light to turn green. Baker had a firm hold on each side of the door and behind him was Williams, then Pvt. Terry Morley. Williams glanced back over

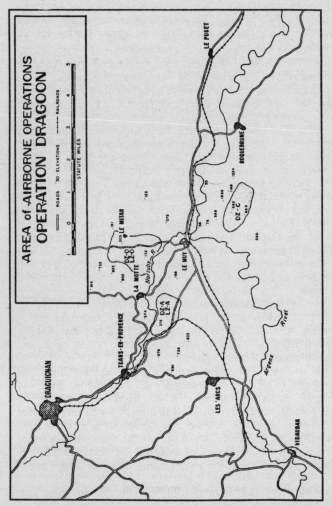

AREA of AIRBORNE OPERATIONS
OPERATION DRAGOON

ROADS   '50' ELEVATIONS   RAILROADS

STATUTE MILES

Map 14

his shoulder into Morley's grim visage, and a trace of a smile flashed across both men's faces. Good old Terry, the lieutenant reflected, he's probably the most popular man in the platoon. And despite his tender years, Williams knew, Morley was one of the best fighters.

The green light flashed on—out went Baker and Williams, with Morley right on their heels. Parachutes of the first two men opened, but the two officers were horrified to discern a dark bulk speeding past them toward the black earth. It was Terry Morley plunging to his death with a "streamer."

Lieutenant Williams landed hard on his back and through hazy eyes looked upward at the windows of a farmhouse. Shucking his parachute harness, he pulled out his pistol, cocked it, and stole out onto a road. The only sounds were far off air-raid sirens. Stalking down the road, Williams caught a glimpse of a shadowy figure coming toward him. The lieutenant did not give the password for fear of revealing his nationality. The other figure reached him, and Williams and Capt. Pete Baker found themselves staring into the muzzle of the other's pistol.

Rapidly, about fifteen of the forty-five pathfinders assembled nearby, and Baker led them to the house beside which Williams had landed. Before waking the owner to determine their precise location, the Red Devils scouted the grounds for telephone lines; they could not take a chance that the householder was a patriot. He might phone the Wehrmacht and give the alarm.

Pebbles were tossed at an upstairs window, and moments later a man dressed only in a shirt opened the door. When Captain Baker asked their location, the farmer replied in Italian. Cold chills surged through the paratroopers' veins; they thought for a fleeting moment that they had been dropped in Italy. The man actually was Italian, but then he began speaking in French.

He told the British that a German headquarters was only some two hundred yards down the road, that armored cars regularly patrolled past his house, and that Le Mitan was only a short distance away. Baker ordered the farmer to put on his trousers and shoes and guide the pathfinders into Le Mitan. A rope was placed around the man's neck to keep him from bolting away, and the Red Devils set off through the night for

Le Mitan. Along the way they frequently had to leap into ditches to avoid German patrols.

When only some four hundred yards outside Le Mitan, the beacon that would guide in the following C-47 flights carrying Brigadier Pritchard's main force was sited and turned on. That accomplished, the pathfinders set up the landing lights on the drop zone. Their work done for the moment, the parachutists rested in tall grass and waited for the first wave of their comrades. Hearing the sky armada approaching, the pathfinders flipped on the DZ lights, which glowed brightly through the darkness and predawn mist.

Minutes later, the black sky was filled with billowing white parachutes, and Captain Baker and his men peered skyward with deep satisfaction. Pritchard's parachutists were dropping right on the button.

A short distance away the sounds of a sharp firefight erupted but soon evaporated, and the drop zone was quiet. Lieutenant Williams caught the shadowy silhouette of a figure standing nearby. He pulled out his pistol and cocked it. Not wishing to call out the password and give away his nationality, the pathfinder officer stood motionless.

A voice from the silhouetted figure said, "Who are you?" Apparently he did not wish to give away his nationality, either. Or was it a German? Many of the enemy spoke flawless English.

Williams called back: "Who are you?"

"I'm Brigadier Pritchard," came the reply. "Who are you?"

Lieutenant Williams heaved a sigh of relief. He had come close to plugging the thirty-seven-year-old leader of the 2nd Independent Parachute Brigade.

DESPITE THEIR EARLY euphoria, the British pathfinders would learn that their brigade's drop had not been totally successful —through no fault of theirs. With the arrival of the sun and subsequent partial clearing of the fog, it was discovered that the landing outside Le Muy had been made virtually on top of a local German headquarters; one sergeant had actually landed on the roof. But due to a faulty electronic mechanism in the lead plane, which prevented it from picking up the beacon on the DZ, one entire flight carrying most of the 5th Parachute

Battalion was scattered over a wide area some twenty miles inland of where it should have been.

MEANWHILE, PATHFINDERS FROM all the 1st Airborne Task Force units were wandering around through the black night and the murky forests and over the rugged hills, desperately seeking their drop zones. Bedeviled by the darkness and the thick fogbank, pilots of the Troop Carrier Command had dropped their trailblazers, in most instances, far from their targeted areas. None of the American pathfinders was able to reach the Le Muy region in time to set up beacons to guide in the approaching C-47 flights loaded with paratroopers.*

---

*Later the Mediterranean Allied Force headquarters and the Provisional Troop Carrier Air Division pronounced the pathfinder operation a success.

A
JUGGERNAUT
UNLEASHED

Blind Leap Into a Fogbank

Complete blackout was in effect as the gigantic sky train carrying the initial elements of Gen. Bob Frederick's 1st Airborne Task Force burrowed through the calm Mediterranean night. Operation Albatross, the massive parachute assault against Hitler's Riviera, was under way. Visibility was good. Hanging in majestic aloofness in the black heavens was a sliver of a crescent moon.

The C-47 armada, stretching out for more than 100 miles, had aboard 5,607 infantry and artillery paratroopers and more than 150 pieces of artillery. The balance of Frederick's airborne force, 3,400 men, would come down behind the Côte d'Azur later in the day. These warriors from the sky would bail out at altitudes ranging from 1,500 to 1,800 feet, twice as high as the customary 600 to 750 feet for combat jumps.

In the leading aircraft of the lengthy formation, Captain Bud Siegel of the 509th Parachute Infantry Battalion, a veteran of many scraps with the Wehrmacht, was on his first operation as a company commander. Siegel was dozing—or pretending to doze. Only Siegel knew for sure.

So far all had gone well. There had been no sign of the Luftwaffe, nor had the sky train been fired on by Allied vessels over which the aircraft had passed. Lurking in the back of each paratrooper's mind was the Sicily disaster in which twenty-three

121

troop transports loaded with men of the 82nd Airborne Division were shot down by "friendly fire" when mistaken in the darkness for German bombers.

Here and there in Siegel's C-47 the grim face of a paratrooper cast an eerie glow, lighted by the fire on a cigarette, before slipping back into the darkness moments later. A sergeant was nervously fiddling with his harness strap and gear. Some lips were moving almost imperceptibly in prayer, invoking the protection of the Great Jumpmaster in the Sky. On occasion subdued, mirthless laughter, shaky and contrived, would break out among a knot of troopers. Moments later that, too, was gone. Mostly there was only the monotonous throbbing of the powerful engines and the frantic rush of Mediterranean air through the open doorway.

Through the small windows the Five-O-Niners would periodically twist their necks to gain a glimpse of the vague outlines of other C-47s. But the efforts were useless. It was dark, and difficult to glimpse other aircraft. Yet the solemn-faced men knew they were out there; and it was reassuring to know that comrades were whisking through the night with them on the way to battle.

Each trooper, in his own way, was steeling himself for the ordeal just ahead. What would Fate deal him? A streamer? A broken back or neck? A head split open on a stone wall? A burst of Schmeisser fire in the gut as he hung helplessly from a parachute caught in a tree? The clock ticked on. . . .

A short distance from the French coast, the crew chief shook Captain Siegel awake. "Guess our good luck couldn't last forever!" he shouted above the roar of the engines and the wind. "The entire coast and far inland are blanketed with thick fog!"

Siegel waddled to the open doorway and looked out. Indeed, there was a heavy fog. It looked to him like the pallor of death, totally obliterating landmarks Siegel and other parachute officers hoped to locate.

Pilots of the 442nd Troop Carrier Group were facing a dilemma. They had on board the entire 509th Parachute Infantry Battalion that would spearhead the invasion. Yet the DZ was invisible. No beacon signal was received from pathfinders, who had been scattered far off target and were wandering through the black woods. But off in the hazy distance, projecting above the blanket of fog, the pilots spotted the dim outlines of jagged hills surrounding the DZ. These peaks resembled those on the sand-table mock-ups of the region that they had studied diligently for countless hours.

An instant crucial decision was reached: The C-47 pilots would drop their paratroopers based on estimates of their flight position as suggested by the hilltops.

In Captain Siegel's aircraft, the red light near the yawning door flashed on explosively. Its haunting glare sent chills racing up the spines of the paratroopers. Four minutes to go until bailout. Siegel called out in a loud voice: "Stand up and hook up!" He took a quick peek at his luminous watch—4.18 A.M. His flight was right on schedule, always a good omen.

It took an effort by the paratroopers to stand. They felt huge and bloated with their burdensome combat gear as they staggered into position, one behind the other, and snapped static lines onto the anchor cable that ran the length of the dimly lit cabin. With the ominous red light scowling at them, the waiting stress was harder, more nerve-racking than ever. Hearts beat faster—and skipped beats. Sweat dotted foreheads. Mouths filled with cotton. It would be only seconds.

Suddenly the green light flashed on—Go! Captain Siegel leaped out and was followed at split-second intervals by his men, each going out the door right on the neck of the trooper in front of him. A one-second delay would mean a huge gap on the ground from the nearest comrade. This could prove fatal—to the trooper and to this mission. Fast . . . fast . . . fast. Out the doorway fast!

Like many others on this night in the thick forests of southern France, Captain Siegel's parachute caught on a tall tree, leaving him swinging fifteen feet off the ground. He cut the harness strands with his trench knife and scrambled down the tree.

Now the black sky behind the Riviera was awash with billowing white parachutes as planeload after planeload of men of the 509th Parachute Infantry bailed out. Private First Class Leon Mims's chute snagged on the top of a towering pine tree, leaving the twenty-five-year-old Georgian dangling forty feet in the air. Seconds later a shell fired by German gunners seeking out the C-47s exploded against the tree, sending Mims tumbling down through the branches and to a jarring landing on the ground.

His leg had been shattered, and Mims was in excruciating pain. The impact had been so hard that the main bone in Mims's leg had been snapped in two, and the jagged tips pushed past each other so that they overlapped.

After what seemed to Mims to be an eternity but was probably only a few minutes, two comrades spotted him after hearing his moaning. They relieved his suffering with morphine injections.

"You'll be okay, Leon," the pair assured him. "We'll stick with you until a medic shows up."

"No, no!" Mims protested through clenched teeth. "You've got a job to do. Now get the hell on your way!"

Reluctantly, the two Five-O-Niners stole off into the night in search of their drop zone. Before leaving, the pair had covered the seriously injured trooper with leaves and other foliage to conceal him from Germans who might happen past.

Less than ten minutes after his comrades had departed, Mims heard a rustling sound in the vegetation. It drew closer. He froze, hardly daring to breathe. Peering intently through the blackness, Mims discerned a column of men heading in his direction and saw the shadowy outline of the coal-bucket-type helmets worn by the Wehrmacht. Eight Feldgrau filed past Mims as he huddled motionless not more than ten feet away, but they failed to see the paratrooper in his cloak of leaves and foliage.

Leon Mims would lie there for three days, racked with pain when his morphine was consumed, hungry and thirsty. A Frenchman finally saw the American and moved him in a wheelbarrow to his house. It was very risky for the Frenchman; he could have been shot by the Germans for harboring an American soldier.

Eighteen-year-old Pvt. Thomas J. Dellaca of Illinois had been "sweating out" his first combat jump and battle action for two weeks. Standing nervously hooked up in his C-47 as it approached the drop zone, Dellaca called out, "Look at those Kraut tracer bullets going by the wing!"

"Hell, those aren't tracers," a veteran of three jumps responded. "Those are sparks from the engine exhaust."

Dellaca bailed out with his stick and was puzzled as to why he couldn't see the sliver of moon and the pall of fog. Only after he had crunched to a heavy landing did he grasp the answer: All the way down he had kept his eyes tightly shut.

Descending under his white canopy, Lt. Solomon Weber, the battalion communications officer, pondered if he would land on or near the DZ this time. On two previous combat jumps he had landed many miles from the target. Weber was a large man, so he came down rapidly, eyes straining for a glimpse of the ground. Suddenly he became aware of an eerie swishing sound below him, and it flashed through his mind that he was plunging to a watery grave in the Mediterranean Sea. Moments later he was crashing through the branches of a huge tree (the swishing noise he thought was the lapping of the waves was actually the wind-driven rustling of leaves and tree limbs).

Weber came to a halt dangling from a branch. As he swung forward in his harness, his toes barely scraped the ground, which he was unable to see due to the darkness. As he swung backward, he could feel nothing. Weber was certain that he was hanging over the edge of a cliff. Tree branches were creaking and groaning in protest of Weber's weight. Gingerly he cut his harness, and as he felt it give, he lunged forward and collapsed on solid ground. His relief was mixed with a tinge of embarrassment—he had not been precariously hanging over a cliff but had come down on the side of a steep hill.

Meanwhile, Capt. Ralph Miller, a company commander in the 509th Parachute Infantry, had been standing in the doorway of a C-47, trying vainly to part the darkness and the fogbank below for a glimpse of the DZ. Only in recent days had the well-liked Miller been promoted to captain and assigned to lead a company into southern France. Suddenly the green light flashed on in the cabin of Miller's aircraft and out the doorway he went, followed at split-second intervals by others in the stick. Neither Captain Miller nor his men were heard from again. They had bailed out over the Mediterranean.

Lieutenant Ted Wallace, a platoon leader in the 509th Battalion, smashed into a stone wall on landing, breaking his leg. Enormous pain surged through his body, but he administered himself morphine shots, which took the edge off his anguish. Gathering his bearings, he listened intently and could hear the faint sounds of a far-off war, like a midwestern Fourth of July of long ago. And he could hear the gentle lapping of the surf on a beach—but that could not be, since the drop zone was twelve miles inland.

Wallace was alone, alone in a land where his command of the language was limited to *merci beaucoup* and *bonsoir*. He stuffed his parachute under some brush and set about fashioning a splint of grapevine and suspension lines from his harness. Pulling himself over the wall and using his Tommy gun as a cane, the lieutenant hobbled up a trail in the woods in search of his men. In his other hand he clutched his pistol—cocked.

A dim figure rose from a nest in the brush beside the trail and brought a rifle to port arms. Wallace whispered the password "Lafayette." The reply was a guttural "Huh?"

As the rifle lowered in the direction of Wallace, a thousand Sunday school "thou shalt nots" flooded the trooper's brain. He was new to combat. Thou shalt not kill! Thou shalt not kill! Thou shalt not kill! Yet when the rifle leveled, Wallace squeezed the trigger of his pistol. The adversary screamed *"Kameraden!"* as he collapsed in a heap.

A sound like that of many men crashing through the forest toward him seized Wallace's attention. He fired off a few bursts from his Tommy gun in the direction of the rustling noise and ran, oblivious to the excruciating pain in his leg. When he could go no farther, the lieutenant hid in a clump of thick bushes. Behind him in the darkness he could hear the excited shouts of German soldiers; undoubtedly they had found the lifeless body of their comrade.

At first light Wallace crawled a few hundred yards toward the sound of lapping waves and, reaching a high sand dune, was startled to see the wide expanse of the beautiful blue Mediterranean. He reclined on a stone bench in a beachhouse. The coolness of the stone felt good on his throbbing leg, which now was swollen and discolored. But he suddenly rose with a start: Within minutes Allied warships would be pounding the shoreline, so as rapidly as he could hobble, Wallace retreated back up the trail into the woods.

A short distance up the hill he heard the roar of mighty warship guns and at a clearing looked back just in time to see the beachhouse he had departed only minutes before blown to pieces by one of the first shells.

At the top of the hill, Wallace came to another clearing and saw a small wooden hut, its door wrenched from its hinges. He stole up to it, poked the muzzle of his Tommy gun through the opening, and sprayed the interior in approved Infantry School fashion. Limping inside, he found that he had killed perhaps a dozen loaves of black bread, several bottles of schnapps, and a German typewriter.

Undoubtedly this had been a local Wehrmacht CP. Wallace moved around to the rear of the structure, and on the ground was the missing door, which apparently had been used as a makeshift litter. On the door lay the body of a youth garbed in an ill-fitting gray-green uniform of the Germany Army. The Feldgrau's sightless eyes were gazing into the sky. His uniform was saturated with blood, and he was very dead.

As though mesmerized, Ted Wallace stood staring down at the corpse of his enemy. Suddenly a curious sensation flooded the trooper—this was the German soldier he had shot in the darkness along the trail only a short time previously. No doubt the man had been carried to this CP by his comrades, then abandoned when he died.

Wallace detected a trace of a smile on the lips of his predawn adversary. He seemed to be mocking the American. "My long months of the agony of war have ended," the dead youth seemed to be telling Wallace. "But you, you poor bastard, must go on. And sooner or later you'll end up just like me—cold and dead!"*

Inland, shrouded by night, Bob Vermillion, the civilian war correspondent, was hunched over on his hands and knees, desperately shaking his head to chase off the cobwebs. Vermillion had billed himself in recent days as "a thirty-minute paratrooper," as that was the length of his "training" for his first parachute jump, this one into southern France. Now he had just crashed to earth after plunging through the branches of a pine tree. Green, red, and yellow lights flashed before his eyes like a high score on a pinball machine.

The intense buzzing in Vermillion's head finally ceased. He deftly reached into his pocket to pull out his eyeglasses; even in daylight he could not identify people without his spectacles. Now in this black situation he certainly would need to see as well as he could. He was careful in putting on the glasses lest the sound attract a lurking German.

It was deathly still. All Vermillion could hear was the chirping of crickets. "Why don't those noisy little bastards shut up?" he reflected. Suddenly he heard the crackling of dry twigs from down the hill. He froze. Then other slight sounds from the same direction. Vermillion started edging softly down the incline. His fear of bumping into an armed German was overcome by a stronger desire to link up with an American.

---

*Four months later, during the Battle of the Bulge, Lt. Ted Wallace was knocked out by the butt of a German rifle. He regained consciousness in a veterans' hospital two years later. In 1984, Wallace was in good health and living in California.

His feet went out from under him. He slipped and rolled six or eight feet, plunging into a large bush with a noise that seemed to echo for great distances in the hills. He lay there, not daring to move. Surely much of the Wehrmacht in southern France was preparing to pounce on him. There was a low whistle farther down the hill. Anxious to contact somebody—anybody—Vermillion whistled back, although he anguished over whether it had been a German whistle or an American whistle he had heard.

The reporter softly called out "Lafayette." There was no immediate answer. Then a low voice was heard, "Down here." Vermillion threw caution to the winds. He skidded noisily down the slope and could discern a dark figure huddled against a rock.

"What in the hell are you trying to do, wake up Adolf Hitler in Berlin?" an irritated American voice with a Southern drawl barked in a hoarse whisper.

It was Capt. Charles C. W. Howland of Tallapoosa, Georgia, a staff officer of the 509th Parachute Infantry, who had followed Vermillion out of the C-47. The reporter sought assurance that he had performed well in his first parachute jump.

"You didn't have to push me, did you?" he asked Howland. At the time the reporter bailed out, he had been so frightened he could not recall what had taken place.

Vermillion could sense the veteran paratrooper grinning in the darkness. "Hell, no," Captain Howland replied. "You went right out like an old pro."*

Howland and Vermillion didn't know where they were, but they began stumbling over rocks and through bushes and in a few minutes ran into Col. Bill Yarborough. The three moved out and soon picked up two more paratroopers, including one youth who was so incoherent from tension and the impact of landing that he could not identify himself.

Yarborough, the battalion commander, led the little file of troopers to a nearby hilltop, and there he began flashing a muted blue light in all directions. Steadily, Five-O-Niners began drifting up to the hilltop, attracted by the blue light signals much as a moth would be drawn to a flame. The veterans of the 509th

---

*Captain Charlie Howland probably had seen as much action as any paratrooper in the war; he had been decorated several times and miraculously escaped being wounded. In the closing days of the Battle of the Bulge, during a lull, an isolated mortar round exploded near him. Howland was killed instantly.

Parachute Infantry Battalion on the hill were puzzled by the lack of coordinated German reaction to their jump. There had been scattered firefights, but that was all. The Five-O-Niners were unaware that much of the German commanders' attention was focused on the paratrooper rubber dummies that had been dropped north of Toulon a few hours previously.

One of those puzzled was M/SGT William W. Sullivan of Galesburg, Illinois, who would soon receive a battlefield commission. "Boy, we sure pulled a sneaky one on the Krauts!" he chortled.

About three miles from his DZ, Capt. Tims Quinn of Louise, Mississippi, was lying stunned alongside a stone wall bordering a large field. The twenty-six-year-old Quinn, operations officer of Colonel Joerg's 551st Parachute Infantry Battalion, had jumped with the 463rd Parachute Field Artillery Battalion, which was attached to the 509th Parachute Infantry, in order to be on the drop zone when Joerg's men bailed out in daylight hours. Captain Quinn had crashed into the stone wall but, other than being dazed, suffered no serious injury.

When he had shaken the cobwebs out of his head, Quinn instinctively began feeling around the dark ground for his personal weapons. Then his woozy mind played a flashback: When his parachute popped open he had received a terrific jolt; his Tommy gun, Colt 45, and musette bag had been ripped from his body by the hurricane blasts that had engulfed him. Now, in enemy-held territory and alone, he was armed only with a trench knife. Silently Captain Quinn cursed the pilot of his C-47; obviously he had flashed the green jump signal while racing at a speed far in excess of the 110 miles per hour orders specified for dropping paratroopers.

Quinn started stealthily slipping through the night in what he thought was the direction of his DZ. In the quiet, he heard a barely restrained, "Pssstttt!" The captain froze. "Pssstttt" certainly was not the password. Then he heard it again, this time louder and more insistent—"Pssssttttt!"

As the battalion operations officer gripped his trench knife tightly, there was a rustling in the bushes and an American paratrooper, clearly overjoyed to discover a friend, edged up to Quinn. The captain, too, was relieved to find a comrade. He said nothing about the "Pssstttt" password, presuming that the trooper had been too excited to remember the real one. The pair trekked off into the night.

The first faint tinges of gray were lightening the sky when the Five-O-Niners on the hill spotted their first Frenchman. He was casually ambling across a field carrying rabbit traps. A soiled black beret clamped on the side of his head and a foul-smelling cigarette dangling from a corner of his mouth, the French farmer was not surprised to see suddenly a group of armed, baggy-pantsed soldiers, many looking like pirate cutthroats with black-painted faces and Mohican haircuts. He knew that the invaders had arrived—two American paratroopers had landed right in his front yard.

Now the beaming Frenchman invited the *libérateurs* to his nearby house for wine.

"Hell, no," snapped Colonel Yarborough. "We're looking for Krauts!"

Mass Confusion in the Dark

Colonel Rupert Graves—the Gray Eagle—was relieved to see the red warning light flash on in the cabin of his C-47. For two hours he had been tightly wedged in a bucket seat and by now was squirming in discomfort. Like others with him, the leader of the 517th Parachute Regimental Combat Team had been wearing his heavy combat gear for the entire flight. Only leg and shoulder straps had been loosened so that the webbing would not cut.

Graves's combat team, some thirty-nine hundred parachutists, was winging close on the heels of Yarborough's 509th Parachute Infantry Battalion and was slated to drop at 4:30 A.M.

The colonel and his men waddled closer to the door and soon were plummeting through the blackness. Just before bailing out, Graves saw the peak of a high hill rising out of the fog. It flashed through his mind: That sight is as comforting as the crest of Mount Ararat must have been to Noah after the Flood. It meant that he and his men were not plunging to their deaths in the Mediterranean.

Nearing the ground in his descent, Graves could discern the dark shapes that looked like trees and knew he was missing the DZ, which was in an open vineyard. Moments later came the jarring impact with the unyielding earth. His carbine, which was tucked under his reserve chute on his chest, swung upward and smashed him violently across the face, momentarily stunning him. His billowing parachute descended over Graves, tangling him in a maze of silk and suspension lines.

He pulled out his pistol and laid it carefully on the ground, in case he should be jumped by lurking Germans, and started hacking at the strands with his knife. It was hard work, and soon he was perspiring profusely. He cursed himself for putting on a heavy undershirt. The cords were tough, but the colonel finally cut himself free. Then he began feeling around on the ground for his pistol—and couldn't locate it.

After ten minutes he gave up the search and moved out through the blackness in search of his men. Several times he fell into deep, rocky gullies, got tangled up in the underbrush, and tripped over fallen trees. He eventually came upon a pair of his troopers, whom he had heard thrashing around.

"Where are we, Colonel?" one man asked.

"I feel reasonably certain that we're somewhere in France," Graves replied. "Other than that, I haven't the faintest notion where we are."

Graves decided that it was futile to continue stumbling through the darkness, and would wait another hour until daylight before heading for his regiment's assembly area—wherever that might be.

Somewhere out there in the murky night were thirty-nine hundred of Colonel Graves's paratroopers. But for the moment the force directly under his command totaled two privates.

Elsewhere, Lt. James A. Reith, a platoon leader in the 1st Battalion of the 517th Parachute Infantry, was crawling out of a water-filled ditch into which he had parachuted moments before. His jump suit was saturated. As he lay on the gravel country road alongside the ditch, Reith could hear excited German voices nearby in the darkness.

Frantically the lieutenant labored to get out of his parachute harness. It seemed to take forever. He heard the rustle of underbrush and of footsteps drawing closer. Now the buckle on his reserve chute was stuck. Just as he freed himself from the harness, Reith looked up from his prone position and discerned the form of a German aiming a machine pistol at him. The trooper whipped out his .45, which had been in the ditch water. Would it fire?

U.S. NAVY

Only a small portion of the mighty Dragoon fleet crowds Naples harbor before sailing for southern France.

Enormous stockpile of vehicles and supplies destined for the invasion of southern France.

U.S. ARMY

A stick of Headquarters, 2nd Battalion, 517th Parachute Infantry, just before taking off for Hitler's Riviera. Identifiable, kneeling from left: S.Sgt. George Backus, Jr., Sgt. William Huffman, Maj. Thomas Cross, Capt. ''Doc'' Reese, and Capt. Harold Migibow (the last two, battalion surgeons).

American gliders lined up in Italy just before takeoff.

Airborne force commander Brig. Gen. Robert B. Frederick (after subsequent promotion).

Maj. Gen. Alexander M. Patch (after subsequent promotion).

Cpl. Milo Huemphner, 551st Parachute Infantry Battalion, snapped this photo just before bailout over southern France.

In textbook-perfect formation, Lt. Col. Wood Joerg's 551st Parachute Infantry Battalion bails out behind the Riviera on the evening of D-Day.

Members of the 509th Parachute Infantry Battalion shortly after landing in southern France.

Men of the 550th Glider Infantry Battalion moments after crash landing.

Wrecked Allied glider.

Follow-up troops of the 45th Infantry Division wade ashore on Camel beach.

A unit of the 3rd Infantry Division marches along Alpha beach.

Rear Admiral H. Kent Hewitt (in backseat) arrives on beachhead on D-Day plus 1.

The German machine-gun crew was wiped out by a grenade tossed by Lt. James Reith, 517th Parachute Infantry. Reith took this photo from one of the bodies.

German defenders of the Riviera in more carefree times. These four photos were removed from the pocket of an enemy grenadier who was killed in action by Sgt. Maj. William L. Sullivan of the 509th Parachute Infantry Battalion.

First Special Force men in southern France. Seated from left: Lt. William Story, Frank Juback, Don Henderson. Standing from left: Ken Lavery, John Kures. All are Canadians.

COURTESY WILLIAM S. STORY

Pvt. W. D. Eason of 509th Parachute Infantry Battalion confers with Marc Rainault, a leader of the Resistance in Saint-Tropez. Nicola Celebo-novitch (center) served as a front-line guide in the capture of the coastal resort city (note pistol in her belt).

COURTESY THOMAS DELACCA

These two rather grainy combat photos show (top) troopers of 551st Parachute Infantry firing in Draguignan, (bottom) Pfc. Joe Cicchinelli (right) and Trooper Ed Schultz with Nazi flag they took down from above door of General Bieringer's headquarters (rear) shortly after the German general was captured by them. This photo was taken with General Bieringer's camera.

Lt. Col. Richard J. Seitz, 517th Parachute Infantry.

Lt. Col. William P. Yarborough, 509th Parachute Infantry.

Lt. Col. Edward Sachs, 550th Glider Infantry.

Lt. Col. Wood G. Joerg, 551st Parachute Infantry.

Col. John F. R. Akehurst, First Special Service Force.

Major Armstrong, 517th Parachute Infantry.

Col. Rupert D. Graves (left) and Lt. Col. Melvin Zais, 517th Parachute Infantry.

Lt. James Reith, 517th Parachute Infantry.

Cpl. Charles E. Pugh, 596th Parachute Engineers.

Cpl. Duffield Matson, Jr., General Frederick's bodyguard.

1st Sgt. William W. Lumsden, 551st Parachute Infantry.

Capt. Tom Cross, 517th Parachute Infantry.

Pfc. Thomas B. Waller, 551st Parachute Infantry.

Capt. Judson Chalkley, 551st Parachute Infantry.

Lt. Glenn E. Rathbun, 3rd Infantry Division.

Men of the 509th Parachute Infantry Battalion stand in the first vehicle to enter Nice. Sgt. A. Haynes Dunlap shields eyes, to the left is Sgt. Ted Fina, and between them is Pfc. Blass.

Troopers of 509th Parachute Infantry move through liberated Nice on a truck.

Reith rapidly rolled over just as the Feldgrau pulled the trigger. The burst of fire struck where the American had been. Reith squeezed off several rounds from his Colt, one of the slugs striking the German in the chest. He toppled over.

Knowing that the firing would alert the German's comrades, Reith hurried off into the night. Soon his attention was attracted by the glowing red light on an equipment bundle, and he headed toward it. He saw the dim outline of a paratrooper standing near the bundle and gazing up at the C-47s that were still flying over. Reith edged up to the figure, who continued to peer upward through the fog.

Moments later the American grew suspicious of his newfound comrade. The man literally had a fishy odor about him, and Reith had heard stories that German soldiers smelled like this from a regular diet of smoked salmon. Casually stooping to gain a better look at the other man's silhouette, Reith's heart skipped a beat when he discerned the coal-bucket-shaped helmet. This was not an American paratrooper he was standing beside, this was a German.

At almost the same second, the German became aware of Reith's identity. His hand flashed toward his pistol, but the American beat him to the draw. Reith stuck his .45's muzzle into the German's stomach and squeezed the trigger. The enemy soldier let out a dying grunt before collapsing in a heap onto the ground.

Less than a mile northeast of Le Muy, Sgt. Theodore J. Van Cleave, Capt. Robert B. Pearce, and another sergeant parachuted directly into a walled enclosure manned by a force of some eighty-five Germans. Alert and waiting, the enemy soldiers loosed a withering burst of fire at the three Americans. Pearce, his leg broken on impact, was in intense pain and unable to get out of his harness. Under a hail of fire, Van Cleave slithered off into a vineyard.

Three Germans began stalking Van Cleave. Hoping to elude the searchers, the sergeant lay stone-still, tightly clutching his trench knife. Moments later he heard a rustling in the vineyard, and one of the Germans leaped on him. A death struggle erupted as the two adversaries grappled on the ground, rolling and thrashing about. The paratrooper worked an arm free, and with a mighty swipe plunged the needle-sharp point of his trench knife deep into the German's stomach. Blood spurted from the Feldgrau's abdomen and mouth, drenching Van Cleave's jump suit.

Attracted by the commotion, the other two searching Germans rushed up to investigate. Sergeant Van Cleave pitched a grenade and in the fiery orange glow of the explosion saw the two enemy soldiers knocked to the ground, their screams piercing the night air. Anguishing over having to leave Captain Pearce behind, Van Cleave made a quick getaway.

At daylight, a force of paratroopers, using mortar and machine-gun fire, stormed over the wall of the German-held enclosure. In the savage hand-to-hand fight that swirled around the fortification, twenty-nine Germans were killed, twenty-one wounded, and thirty-two captured. Several Americans were casualties. Captain Pearce, who had been a prisoner of the Germans inside the enclosure, was freed.

Shortly before dawn, Maj. Tom Cross of Lieutenant Colonel Seitz's 2nd Battalion was hobbling along in severe pain. He had parachuted into a ditch and had broken his leg. He longed to remove the heavy pressure of his jump boot from his throbbing leg but didn't dare do so for fear he would not get the boot back on again and then would not be able to join in the fight.

Cross was leading a company-size group of paratroopers who, alone and in pairs, had joined the major's column. The battalion executive officer was trying to reach his drop zone but was hopelessly lost. In the gathering gray he saw a Frenchman on a bicycle. Speaking in fractured French, Major Cross sought directions to Le Muy. The native remained mute. Irritated, Cross pulled out his pistol, placed the muzzle to the Frenchman's forehead, and barked: "Now start talking! Which way to Le Muy?"

The ashen-faced Frenchman began shaking uncontrollably but made no reply. Then Cross realized the reason for the native's silence: He was petrified with fright. Not only was a gun being pointed at his head, but also the Frenchman was still in shock over unexpectedly being confronted by what appeared to him to be a sinister group of cutthroats with black-painted faces, Mohican Indian hair styles, and loaded with dangling hand grenades, nasty-looking daggers, and other weapons.

"Hell, it's hopeless," Major Cross exclaimed, replacing his pistol. "You can't blame Pierre here. Hell, the way we look, I'd be speechless, too!"

Many miles from the confrontation with the petrified Frenchman, Lt. Col. Melvin Zais, leader of Graves's 3rd Battalion, stomped into a large farmhouse outside the little village of Seillans. Zais was both agitated and concerned. His battalion was to have landed near Le Muy. Then they were to attack southward along Route Nationale 7, the main highway leading to Saint-Raphael and Fréjus on the coast, in order to prevent the Germans from pouncing on the 36th Infantry Division as it stormed the beach. But Zais and most of his headquarters company had been dropped so far from the DZ that the area did not appear on Zais's maps. Only later would the twenty-eight-year-old Zais learn that his battalion had been scattered around the villages of Seillans, Fayence, and Callian, nearly twenty-five miles from the drop zone.*

Inside the house, Capt. Martin J. Fastaia, commander of the headquarters company, and a number of his troopers had already congregated. The structure was serving as an assembly point for Fastaia's men.

"Where in the hell are we?" Colonel Zais asked the captain in an impatient tone.

"As near as I can make out after conducting a hurried survey of the terrain, we're twenty-five miles or so from our DZ," Fastaia replied. A few minutes later two Frenchmen were brought before Zais, and from them he learned his precise location.

By now some 105 paratroopers had assembled in and around the rambling old farmhouse. "Okay, form up the men and we'll head for the DZ," the battalion commander instructed Captain Fastaia. In minutes Fastaia's headquarters company and assorted stragglers from other parachute units were marching toward Saint-Clariers, the first town in the direction of the DZ. Suddenly the gray early dawn was pierced by the roar of low-flying aircraft. The troopers, strung out in approach-march formation, instinctively looked up through the haze and saw a flight of twin-boomed American P-38 Lightnings diving on them.

The men hit the ground just before several bombs exploded around them. Clearly the marching column, cloaked in the early-morning haze and twenty-five miles from where the 517th Combat Team was to have dropped, had been mistaken for a

---

*After the war, Lt. Col. Melvin Zais rose to four-star rank.

German force heading for the scene of the airborne landings.

Above the noise of exploding bombs, Colonel Zais, lying flat on the ground, shouted, "Somebody get some yellow smoke going!" That was the recognition signal to friendly aircraft.

Now the P-38 flight had banked and was coming back at treetop level for a strafing run. A trooper had set out a yellow-smoke pot, which was sighted at the last moment by the American pilots. The P-38s zoomed upward and flew off in search of other prey.

Colonel Zais and his column of some eighty-five paratroopers (nineteen men injured in the jump had to be left back at the Seillans farmhouse) had been trekking over the steep hills and through thick forests for about two hours when, in a nearby valley, they spotted another file of armed men heading in the same direction as the Americans. As Zais was ready to deploy his troopers to attack the other force, someone called out: "Look! Some of them are wearing red berets!"

The maroon headware was the distinctive badge worn by the Red Devils of the British airborne. This was a force of some eighty of Brigadier Pritchard's 2nd Independent Parachute Brigade who had been dropped far off target in the same region as Zais's men. Joining up, the American and British paratroopers continued the tortuous march to Le Muy and their assembly areas. En route they stumbled onto a German convoy heading for the landing beaches, and a violent firefight erupted. The convoy was destroyed, mainly by bazookas and machine guns, and all of the enemy troops were killed or captured.

Much closer to the drop zones, S. Sgt. Clyde V. Hoffman and Cpl. Harold A. Roberts, both of the 596th Parachute Engineer Company, were sprawled facedown against the damp earth. They had landed only thirty yards from a German pillbox, and before they could shuck their chutes they had to duck under machine-gun fire from the concrete structure. For over an hour Hoffman and Roberts lay motionless as streams of bullets periodically whistled past.

When the German machine gun was not chattering, it was deathly quiet. The two Americans could hear the Feldgrau talking inside the concrete bunker. As dawn arrived, Hoffman and Roberts began to slither over the ground from one vineyard row to another, keeping the pillbox gunners guessing where they were hiding. Periodically machine-gun bursts were fired up this row and then that one. This cat-and-mouse game continued for several hours. Apparently the Feldgrau would not emerge from their cover for fear that many more American paratroopers were lurking outside to pounce on them.

Finally, Hoffman and Roberts slipped into a sluiceway; with water up to their necks they began wading along. They had no idea that their route of escape would take them directly through the heart of the key German stronghold of Le Muy. Wading through the town, the pair felt naked, even though only their heads were visible. To either side of the water-filled ditch they caught glimpses of German soldiers manning defensive positions only a few yards away.

When the exhausted Americans felt they could not take another step, they emerged on a riverbank. There they rested for a few minutes, but hearing German voices moving toward them, they began crawling onward. After what seemed like an eternity, they again heard voices—but these were speaking English. Hoffman and Roberts, near collapse from the enormous physical ordeal of wading several miles through neck-deep water, were back among their own.

Not far from Le Muy, Pvt. Frederic Johns of Maj. William J. Boyle's 1st Battalion, and several comrades, were making their way in the direction of their DZ. Suddenly, a German machine gun opened fire, and three bullets ripped into Johns. The tiny group of Americans had stumbled into an ambush.

Johns collapsed on the ground as his comrades deployed and returned the fire. After an intense but brief firefight, the enemy machine gunners melted away into the darkness.

Frederic Johns lay quietly. Blood was streaming from his wounds, saturating his jump suit, a garment he regarded with great pride. Wearing a jump suit signified that he had measured up as an American paratrooper. The dying youth softly uttered some words, but his comrades hovering over him could not understand. One trooper knelt down and placed his ear to the fatally wounded man's mouth. Off in the distance could be heard the rattle of small-arms fire.

"What did you say, Frederic?" the kneeling trooper asked softly.

The youth whispered hoarsely, "I'm sorry I let you fellows down."

Moments later, Frederic Johns was dead.

About two miles west of the drop zone for Lt. Col. Dick Seitz's 2nd Battalion in the vicinity of La Motte, Lt. Albert N.

Robinson, leader of the 517th's machine-gun platoon, and a few of his men were searching in the dark for equipment bundles containing ammunition and parts for their automatic weapons. If the Germans were to counterattack after dawn, this ammo would be essential. Although each equipment bundle had a tiny glowing light attached to it, so vast was the area over which they'd been dropped that Robinson's task was akin to locating the proverbial needle in a haystack.

Lieutenant Robinson was so weak that his legs felt like jelly. Only two days before, he had sneaked out of a Naples hospital (absent without leave, the Army officially termed such actions) to join his comrades in the jump into southern France. It was chilly in the predawn Mediterranean air, but the young officer was perspiring profusely with a fever.

Suddenly from out of the blackness Robinson and his three machine gunners were raked by Schmeisser machine-pistol fire. One of the first bullets ripped into Lieutenant Robinson, who toppled over. He was dead before he hit the ground. Several slugs tore into the body of Pvt. Pat Clark. Under a hail of bullets, a comrade slithered to Clark's aid, but the grievously wounded youth called out weakly, "I'm okay. You guys get the hell out of here while you can."

At daybreak, several paratroopers returned to the site of the ambush and recovered Lieutenant Robinson's body.* Nearby was the lifeless form of Pat Clark, a pool of blood beneath him. Lying beside his stiff hands was his rifle. Clark, although in excruciating pain and his life ebbing away, apparently had shot it out with the German force to permit his surviving comrades to escape. The ammo clip in his rifle was empty.

Meanwhile, Lt. John A. "Boom Boom" Alicki had landed directly on his DZ near Le Muy and was searching in the darkness for other members of his demolition platoon of the 517th Parachute Infantry. They should be nearby, Alicki reasoned, as they had all leaped from the same C-47—or so he thought. But he could not locate a single one of his troopers.

A split second after the twenty-six-year-old Alicki had jumped, the pilot made a sharp L-bank, and the remainder of Alicki's stick parachuted down on top of a German bivouac. A violent firefight erupted as the Feldgrau attacked the trapped

---

*Lieutenant Albert N. Robinson remains today buried with comrades in the American cemetery at Draguignan. A street in Draguignan is named in his honor.

parachutists from all sides. Sizing up the situation in the confusion and darkness, Sgt. William Brown managed to get eight men together, but they were quickly surrounded by thirty to thirty-five Germans. Private Giner was killed instantly by a bullet. The uneven slugging match could have only one ending: Sergeant Brown and his seven remaining comrades were captured and taken to Le Muy.

Unaware of the fate of his missing stick, Lieutenant Alicki was walking along a country road just as dawn was starting to break. Coming toward him was a French farmer, who stared in disbelief at this black-faced apparition weighted down with the accouterments of war. Then the native spotted the tiny American flag each trooper had sewn on the sleeve of his jump jacket at the shoulder. ''Américain! Américain!'' the farmer shouted over and over, literally dancing with joy. As torrents of tears rolled down his leathery cheeks, the Frenchman grabbed Alicki in a bear hug and planted kisses all over his grease-streaked and perspiring face.

SOMEWHERE BETWEEN LE Muy and La Motte, Sgt. Leo Turco of Rochester, New York, had been stumbling through the night for what seemed like hours, desperately seeking a comrade. He could hear the grinding of vehicles and an occasional German voice nearby. Clutching his Tommy gun tightly, Turco kept moving. He was obsessed with the uneasy feeling that he was about to be pounced upon and get his throat cut.

Suddenly Turco froze. Behind him was the unmistakable sound of dry twigs rustling. The sergeant whipped around with his Tommy gun leveled just in time to see a shadowy form crash out of the underbrush. Turco started to squeeze off a burst when the dark figure called out, ''Is that you, Sergeant Turco?''

The wiry chief lowered his Tommy gun and emitted a sigh of relief. He had nearly killed one of his men, Pfc. Dan Rotundo of Bethlehem, Pennsylvania, whose voice he had recognized.

''For God's sake, Rotundo,'' Turco scolded in a hoarse whisper, ''you're supposed to call out the password, not 'Is that you?' ''

CAPTAIN ALFRED J. Guennette looked like any other paratrooper as he parachuted down and crashed hard against the ground. Guennette was husky and peppery; he'd reportedly cleaned up on occasion in crap games with the boys back in Italy. Officers were not supposed to indulge in games of chance involving rolling dice with enlisted men, but Captain Guennette never worried too much about the niceties of Army regulations. Maybe that was why the troopers to a man were so fond of him. He was the Catholic chaplain of the 517th Parachute Infantry Regiment.

Father Guennette heard German voices out in the blackness as he rapidly shucked his parachute. He paused briefly to ponder in which direction he should head when he heard a thrashing in the nearby underbrush. Hoping that these were Americans making so much commotion, he called out "Lafayette" in a stage whisper. There was no reply, but two shadowy figures emerged from the bushes. The priest could discern that they were paratroopers, and he scolded them for not responding with the counterword.

Still the two youngsters said nothing. Then Father Guennette realized that they were too frightened to speak or to recall the counterword.

Protestant Chaplain Charles Brown suffered the fate of numerous other troopers in the mass jump—he broke a leg. Tall, handsome, and well liked, Captain Brown was helped to a French farmhouse, where the family hid him in a hayloft. Captain Brown would remain in his hideaway for nearly twenty-four hours. Peeking through cracks in the barn after daylight, he spotted a German patrol moving past a short distance away.

ELSEWHERE, LT. JIM Reith, the platoon leader in Bill Boyle's 1st Battalion, was relieved to see the dark sky dissolving into gray. The light might reveal him to lurking Germans, but anything would be better than continuing to stumble along virtually blind in the darkness and fog. Reith within the hour had dispatched two Feldgrau, but he had no time to dwell on their fate. There were more urgent matters on his mind: He and fifteen of his troopers had been assigned a special mission. They were to drop just outside Draguignan, slip into that Wehrmacht stronghold before the enemy realized that southern France was under parachute attack, and kidnap General of Infantry Ferdinand Neuling, commander of the LXII Corps. If seizing the enemy general alive were not possible, then Neuling was to be killed and the paratroopers were to get out of

Draguignan as best they could—if they could.

Lieutenant Reith and his men long had been intensely studying plans for the kidnapping. Details of General Neuling's residence, Villa Gladys, a stately old mansion nestled among a stand of towering pines on the outskirts of Draguignan, was well known to them through architect's drawings stolen by the French Underground. The details of Neuling's daily routine and personal habits had been obtained from a middle-aged French woman living next to Villa Gladys. She had gained the wrath of Draguignan townspeople in past months for regularly inviting the tall, courtly, lonely German general into her home for socializing interludes. Afterward she recorded even his casual remarks made while his guard was down. Lieutenant Reith learned such details as Neuling's breakfast routine (he ate at 6:00 A.M. on the dot—two fried eggs, bacon, and toast).

Now on D-Day at a country crossroads in the gathering dawn, Jim Reith glanced at his watch. It was 5:35 A.M. He had been in France for only an hour, but it seemed to be an eternity. How could he conceivably hope to carry out his mission of kidnapping the general in Draguignan? Reith was alone, he had no idea of his location; the Wehrmacht in Draguignan and at points in between was certain to be on full alert by now, aware that thousands of Allied paratroopers had fallen from the black sky and were marauding through the countryside.

A short time later, Lieutenant Reith ran into his mortar sergeant, twenty-one-year-old Joseph Blackwell, who advised his platoon leader, "We're at least twenty miles from Draguignan."

That depressing revelation ended any remote hope that the kidnap plot could be carried out.

"Have you seen anything of Ritchie?" Reith inquired. Ritchie was Reith's platoon sergeant and invaluable right-hand man.

"Yeah, I saw him," Sergeant Blackwell replied matter-of-factly. "He's lying back there about a mile, under a tree."

"What do you mean by 'he's lying under a tree?'"

"Broke both legs in the jump and that's where we put him."

In the meantime, Gen. Bob Frederick, the taciturn leader of the 1st Airborne Task Force, had bailed out wearing a white scarf made of parachute silk and carrying a blue-lensed flashlight for signaling on the ground.

Frederick had had little to say on the long flight from the Rome area. One of his few remarks to those seated near him was, "I hope you boys enjoyed your bread and jelly," referring to a last-minute snack that had been distributed to the troopers. During the flight he checked his map several times. As Frederick's C-47 neared the French coast, there were flashes of light from German ack-ack guns on the ground. The general observed calmly, "It looks like they're expecting us."

Corporal Duff Matson, Frederick's bodyguard, had crashed to earth near where the general came down. Matson landed on a tree stump or stake and "messed up" his left leg. Peering through the darkness, the corporal detected a parachute draped over a pole in a vineyard and concluded that it had to be Frederick; the general's blue-beamed flashlight was glowing there.

Clutching his rifle, Matson hobbled toward the general, recalling the stern words of an officer who had assigned the corporal to be Frederick's bodyguard: "You are to protect the general from harm—even if it costs you your life!"

Nearing Frederick, Matson felt a surge of deep concern. Five or six forms were edging toward the airborne task force commander, and now the bodyguard could detect the dim outlines of their helmets—they were Germans. He shouted a warning to Frederick, who was studying a map by the blue flashlight, then squeezed off several quick shots in the direction of the dark figures. Two of the Germans toppled over, and the others fled.

General Frederick casually looked up, then returned to his map.

Corporal Matson was now in extreme pain from his mangled leg and could not walk, so Frederick set out alone down a fog-covered path through a wooded area and minutes later spotted a dim figure wearing the bowl-like helmet of the German paratroops. The general stealthily edged around behind the dark form and with a catlike leap pounced on the man. The slight Frederick flung his arm around the adversary's throat and began to break his neck, a technique learned in a "killer school."

Moments later the opponent muttered a curse with a British accent. Frederick relaxed his hold; the foe was a Red Devil of

Pritchard's parachute brigade who had lost his weapon in the jump and was searching for comrades.

"I say, old boy," the Red Devil exclaimed, not aware that he had nearly been done in by an American general, "you *are* a bit rough!"*

In the vast sweep of rugged landscape behind Hitler's South Wall, American and British paratroopers jumped the enemy at every opportunity as they picked their way through the darkness en route to DZs. Individually and in tiny groups, the parachutists moved through the countryside, creating fear and confusion among the Germans. Reminiscent of Indian warfare tactics of America's Old West, these stealthy raiders, many wearing war paint and with heads shaved, lay in wait in the darkness along roads, then ambushed German motorcycle couriers rushing orders to Wehrmacht command posts.

Paratroopers shinnied up telephone poles to cut wires linking various German CPs and defensive positions. They blew up bridges, planted mines in roads, and created widespread havoc. Enemy patrols sent out to probe the parachute landings were suddenly sprayed with Tommy-gun and rifle fire and bazooka rockets from the shadows. Survivors of ambushed German patrols spread wild tales of being pounced on by large numbers of parachutists in baggy pants. Usually, these "large numbers" were a handful of troopers manning a roadblock, but the invaders had the advantage of surprise and concealment.

Not knowing where the American and British paratroopers were going to be encountered or how many of them had landed caused near-panic among the Wehrmacht. At General Neuling's LXII Corps headquarters in Draguignan, alarming reports were pouring in from German field commanders. Most were exaggerated; poor visibility abetted the confusion. But the reports caused Neuling to believe that he was facing many times the number of Allied paratroopers than actually was the case.

---

*The British had modeled their paratroop helmets after those of German parachute troops. In the darkness, it was often difficult to distinguish between the two headgears.

Indian Warfare

As dawn broke on D-Day, Lt. Col. Bill Yarborough and most of his veteran 509th Parachute Infantry Battalion were perched on the rugged, rocky high ground outside the key crossroads town of Le Muy. Yarborough was peering through his binoculars down into the valley, and as the haze began to clear on this warm summer morning he had a balcony seat from which to watch a large German force trying to scramble out of town.

Yarborough looked on with satisfaction as the enemy unit hurriedly pulled back from Le Muy. It had run into elements of Brigadier Pritchard's British 2nd Independent Parachute Brigade, who were blocking the principal road.

The 509th Battalion commander had been getting reports from his company and platoon officers during the past hour and was pleasantly surprised. Despite the hilly, wooded, rocky nature of the terrain, relatively few injuries were sustained. One of those limping around the hill but ready for action was Lloyd Bjelland of Milwaukee, Wisconsin, platoon sergeant of the demolition platoon. A battle-tested fighting man since the days of the North Africa invasion in November 1942, Bjelland had landed hard.

Known in the battalion as Mother BJ, the platoon sergeant had fallen victim to his conviction that the best technique for a night parachute jump was to land on one's posterior. Descending into a black, burned-out woods, Sergeant Bjelland crashed down on his buttocks as planned, but directly onto a sharp tree stump. Now he was having difficulty walking.

Bjelland told needling comrades, "I still think it's the best way to land. How the hell did I know the Krauts would put a tree stump there?"

Colonel Yarborough's satisfaction at having the bulk of his battalion rapidly assembled was tempered with the knowledge that one of his companies was missing. At that moment, he had no way of knowing that the company commanded by Capt. Jess H. Walls had been dropped far off target, twelve miles to the south, along the coast at Saint-Tropez.

It was a difficult baptism of fire for Captain Walls, who had joined the battalion only a short time before. Scanning his maps after landing, Walls knew that he and most of his men had come down far from the DZ, south of Saint-Tropez. In the darkness they had heard the lapping of the nearby Mediterranean Sea, and now that it was getting light they could see the beautiful blue, placid body of water off in the distance.

Captain Walls's C Company were not the only troopers to land around the stylish resort town of Saint-Tropez. Nineteen men from B Company and elements of the 463rd Parachute Field Artillery Battalion also dropped in the vicinity. By means of blinking blue lights, paratroopers from mixed units drifted into Walls's hilltop CP, and soon he had more than 250 parachutists in his force.

Added to the normal concern he felt when he learned that his company had dropped twelve miles from the DZ, Captain Walls was beset by an even more ominous predicament: He and his men were directly on the impact area long the coastline, which would be heavily bombed from the air and pounded by the guns of warships lying in the haze offshore.

As senior officer present, Walls took command of the hodgepodge force of paratroopers who had landed around Saint-Tropez. But he was not certain of his next move, since he didn't know the location and strength of the German forces in the area.

As Walls discussed the situation with other officers, a trooper brought two members of the French Underground before him. They both lived in Saint-Tropez and had been expecting to see Allied invaders; they had been advised of the BBC message "Nancy has a stiff neck," the code-phrase alerting the Underground that an assault on the Côte d'Azur was at hand. The excited Resistance men, each wearing a French tricolor armband and carrying an ancient rifle, told Captain Walls that the Germans were preparing to blow up the port facilities in Saint-Tropez to deny them to the invaders.

Hardly had the words been spoken when an enormous roar shook Saint-Tropez, and an orange fireball shot into the sky, illuminated the hazy gray dawn. The Germans in the coastal city had begun demolishing the docks, the long jetty, and other key facilities. The time was 5:50 A.M.

Captain Walls's mind was made up: He would attack Saint-Tropez. If the Germans were blowing up the docks, they must be preparing to pull out. But first he and his men would have to cling to the ground for two hours—while being pounded by "friendly" bombs and shells.

Meanwhile, shortly after daybreak, the leader of Yarborough's pathfinders, Lt. Dan De Leo, was resting briefly in a girls' school a short distance from where he had landed unconscious in a tree after bailing out of a C-47. De Leo, along with Charles McDonald, who had rescued the lieutenant from the tree, had collected a few more men and then had come across an Englishman who operated the girls' school. The English headmaster invited the Americans to his facility, where he fed them a modest breakfast. Serving the black-faced paratroopers were two Wehrmacht soldiers, both Russians, whom the Englishman had talked into surrendering to him.

De Leo and his comrades had nearly finished their meal when a young member of the Underground, wearing the tricolor armband, burst excitedly through the doorway and began speaking rapidly in French to the headmaster.

"What's he saying?" De Leo asked.

The Englishman, as calm as though he were enjoying cricket on the playing fields of Eton, replied, "He says a large patrol of Germans is heading directly toward us."

Lieutenant De Leo knew that the headmaster would be in serious trouble if the enemy found the Americans in the school. "Okay, let's go!" the parachute leader called out. "We'll arrange a little surprise party for the Krauts."

The five parachutists grabbed their weapons, hurried out of the school, and double-timed to a point about three hundred feet away in the direction from which the German patrol was coming. There the Americans took cover alongside the road, and in three minutes De Leo, peeking through a bush, saw the enemy contingent marching toward them. Strung out in two files with a sergeant in the lead, the Germans came closer and closer. The Americans gripped their rifles and Tommy guns tightly.

De Leo saw that the Germans were holding their weapons at the ready and glancing nervously from side to side, obviously fearful of running into an ambush. Now the concealed parachutists could hear the clatter of the hobnailed boots, and moments later the Wehrmacht sergeant in the lead was opposite De Leo. The lieutenant leaped to the side of the bush and in one motion raised his rifle and squeezed the trigger. The German gave a short grunt and toppled over, a neat, red-rimmed hole right between the eyes.

The unexpected development threw the Germans into confusion, and they began dashing helter-skelter for cover. Two Feldgrau tried to flee over a small hill and were riddled by a parachutist with a Tommy gun. Several other Germans went down as the Americans continued to pour fire into their ranks. Now there were calls of *"Kamerad! Kamerad!"* (Comrade! Comrade!) and *"Nicht schiessen!"* (Don't shoot!)

It was all over in one minute. Four Germans were dead, three were wounded, and thirteen were taken prisoner.

CAPTAIN BUD SIEGEL, the company commander in the 509th Parachute Infantry Battalion, who had been the first man to bail out in the main flight of the 1st Airborne Task Force, had assembled his unit amazingly quickly, considering the fog and the darkness. Within a half hour of touching down, Siegel and his troopers were organized and looking for a fight. By dawn Siegel's men had secured a bridge leading into Le Muy and a small patrol had been sent to probe Le Muy itself.

Siegel was feeling pretty smug about the success of his company's mission so far when he sensed someone coming up behind him at his CP on the high hill overlooking Le Muy. He turned to see Lieutenant Colonel Yarborough, looking very dapper, bright-eyed, and bushy-tailed, Siegel reflected. The battalion commander wasted no time on small talk.

"Captain, what are your plans to attack?" he inquired in a formal tone.

Siegel had no plans to attack, not knowing yet where the

Germans were to attack. At that moment the captain received a call over his walkie-talkie from the patrol he had sent to probe Le Muy.

"Captain," a calm voice said over the wireless instrument, "there's a good-sized group of Krauts marching northward into Le Muy."

"There's your answer, sir!" Siegel said to Yarborough. "We're going to trap the bastards."

"Okay, go get 'em!" Yarborough responded.

The Germans apparently were unaware that a large portion of an American paratroop battalion was sitting on a high hill outside the town. Siegel reasoned that his men therefore would have the advantage of surprise. Lieutenant Kenneth Shaker, who as a teenage private had fought in the Spanish Civil War, and his platoon were sent to the northern outskirts of Le Muy. There Shaker set up an OP (observation post) in a small farmhouse a hundred yards from the road running through the town.

During this time, the German column of infantry and a few vehicles had entered Le Muy from the south, marched through the town, and were heading along the road where Shaker's platoon had deployed. Machine guns and mortars were in place to rake the approaching enemy force. Captain Siegel by now had moved his other platoons into ambush position along the road. He ordered his platoons to hold their fire until the order was given; Siegel wanted to make certain the entire German column had entered his iron trap before his troopers began to fire.

As the enemy contingent neared the concealed Five-O-Niners, it suddenly halted. Apparently its commanders had sensed that an ambush had been laid. The Germans quickly deployed and opened a fusillade of machine-gun and rifle fire into the woods where Siegel's men were waiting.

All hell broke loose as the paratroopers returned the fire. The German column scattered for cover, and one machine-gun squad dashed into a farmhouse near Siegel's company CP, where they set up the weapon in the attic. From there the Feldgrau machine gunners sprayed the paratroopers, forcing them to keep their heads down. The roof of the farmhouse was built of red tile; when an American machine gun sent a few bursts into the roof and the tile fell off, the German automatic-weapon crew was left cowering under the bare rafters in plain sight. Paratrooper sharpshooters quickly picked off two of the enemy, and the others scrambled downstairs and fled out the back doorway.

Another group of Germans had deployed into tall grass and were firing heavy bursts just over Captain Siegel's CP, apparently aiming at some target to the rear. Siegel became aware that someone was approaching him from behind, and yelled over his shoulder, "Keep your goddamned head down!" It was Colonel Yarborough, who had dropped by to check on the progress of the heavy firefight.

Under the hail of fire, a Five-O-Niner, twenty-five-year-old Cpl. George W. Stenger, and his machine-gun crew were dashing forward across an open field. Bullets were splattering into the earth all around him but there was no cover, so he and his comrades kept running. Out of breath from the exertion of lugging his heavy gear, the corporal halted and snuggled up to a large tree for protection. He was huffing and perspiring profusely.

Stenger pondered his past few hours. He concluded that so far he had been leading a charmed life and hoped that his good fortune continued. When bailing out of his C-47, Stenger had plunged onto the blossoming parachute of someone who had jumped from another plane, and for moments was tangled in a maze of silk. His own chute by now had popped open, and he fought to get out of the cloth trap before he was seriously hurt or killed on landing. Stenger gave a sigh of relief as he suddenly broke loose and floated to the ground.

Now, after a brief respite, Stenger's squad sergeant, Willie Holtz, waved his men forward, and as he moved out, the corporal began to scratch himself furiously. A large colony of black ants living in the tree behind which he had taken cover had infiltrated Stenger's clothing and were now scampering madly about over his flesh.

Minutes later the machine-gun squad spotted five Germans dashing into a nearby house. Hoping to avoid a bloody shoot-out with the Feldgrau, Sergeant Holtz edged up close to the house and called out an order in fluent German:

"Get back out of that house, you stupid bastards! Are you trying to get yourselves killed?"

Thinking that a German officer had shouted the order, the five Feldgrau dashed back out of the house and into the leveled guns of Sergeant Holtz and his squad.

For nearly two hours, elements of the 509th Parachute Infantry Battalion fought the Wehrmacht outside Le Muy before the enemy force pulled back into the town, leaving scores of dead and wounded comrades sprawled about the fields. Sixty Germans were taken prisoner.

Despite the little victory by the American paratroopers, the key initial objective of the 1st Airborne Task Force, Le Muy, remained in German hands.

AT DAYBREAK, MAJ. Forrest Paxton, operations officer of Graves's 517th Parachute Infantry Regiment, had gathered a force of some seventy-five troopers and was leading them toward the DZ by way of the village of La Motte. Twenty minutes after moving out, Paxton heard the faint hum of motors and waved his men to both sides of the road. Moments later, two Germans on a pair of motorcycles came racing down the road toward the concealed paratroopers. At the last second the enemy couriers spotted the Americans and made desperate efforts to slam on brakes. A roar of small-arms fire erupted, and the enemy motorcyclists toppled from their mounts.

After the bodies of the hapless Feldgrau were dragged into nearby woods, the urgent orders they were carrying removed from pouches, and the battered two-wheeled vehicles hidden from view, Major Paxton and his men marched onward and entered La Motte at 8:55 A.M. No Germans were encountered in the town. La Motte may have been the first community in the southern two thirds of France to be liberated from the Wehrmacht.

Meanwhile, Lt. Jim Reith had managed to assemble a company-size force of men from several 517th Parachute Combat Team units and was trekking toward the DZ. As the column rounded a bend in a country road, it was suddenly raked with machine-gun fire. The troopers flopped to the ground and began firing back. Reith motioned to three men to follow him and began crawling off to the right to outflank the automatic weapon. A half hour later, Lieutenant Reith and his three troopers had slipped up unseen to one side of the German machine-gun crew. On signal, each parachutist tossed a grenade in unison, and the enemy gun was blown into the air. Lying mangled and dead beside the twisted machine gun was its three-man crew.

Moving out again in the direction of the DZ, Reith's group

reached a small German gasoline dump. Two Feldgrau raced off under a hail of fire, and one of the troopers tossed a grenade into the dump, causing it to explode and shoot an orange fireball into the sky. The man who had thrown the grenade was seriously burned about the face when flaming gasoline struck him. He insisted on continuing toward the DZ, although in severe shock. Strips of burned skin dangled from his face, but he marched along without a whimper all the way to the assembly area.

AS DAYLIGHT ARRIVED, Col. Rupert Graves, still in command of a force of two privates, could hear heavy firing toward the bottom of the forested hill. Graves moved out and began picking up more troopers wandering around in search of comrades. He could see a town down in the valley, and after studying the pattern of roads concluded that it must be Le Muy. He could hear a lot of shooting in the direction of Le Muy, probably Capt. Bud Siegel's Five-O-Niners tangling with the German column that had marched out of the town. Since Le Muy was scheduled to be captured by Pritchard's British Red Devils, Graves bypassed the town.

Marching along over the rugged terrain, Colonel Graves's group halted briefly for skirmishes with concealed bands of Germans, who by now were also engaged in the hit-and-run tactics of Indian warfare. One German, who could not be seen in the thick brush, kept firing his Schmeisser machine pistol at the colonel and his men, all the time shouting, *"Kamerad! Nicht schiessen!"*

A leather-lunged paratrooper called out from his prone position, *"Nicht schiessen* yourself, you son-of-a-bitch!" The trooper wiggled forward through the thick brush and pulled his arm back to pitch a grenade at the German in the woods. Just then an American voice to his front yelled, "Don't throw that goddamned grenade—I'm right in front of you!"

The shouting German in the woods was not heard from again. Apparently he had been covering the withdrawal of his force, then had drifted back through the woods.

Colonel Graves and his marching column moved down into a valley where they continued to pick up a few individual troopers who had been hiding from German patrols. One excited youngster scrambled out of bushes and dashed up to the regimental commander. "What kept you so goddamned long?"

he demanded of Graves. The colonel overlooked the tone. The youth had been alone and dodging a German patrol that had spotted him on landing and had been chasing him.

Nearing La Motte, Graves sent out a patrol to probe the town. It quickly returned with word that elements of Dick Seitz's 2nd Battalion had secured La Motte and were now advancing along the road toward Draguignan, four miles northwest of La Motte. It was in Draguignan that the leader of the German LXII Corps was issuing orders to blunt the invasion, unaware that he had been earmarked as the target of an American kidnap plot that had gone awry.

At 7:45 A.M. Capt. Jess Walls launched an attack against Saint-Tropez with his mixed bag of paratroopers. Explosions still rocked the resort city as efficient German engineers blew up crucial facilities. A death pallor of haze and smoke shrouded the white buildings, the pink houses, and the once-bustling harbor. Guided by members of the Underground, Walls's leading elements pushed steadily ahead. The Resistance guides were vital, as Walls had no maps of the region.

In the mile trek over hilly, forested terrain, Captain Walls's troopers met surprisingly weak opposition. Only later would he learn that the main enemy force had pulled back into the center of Saint-Tropez and would make its stand there. Wehrmacht soldiers, mainly Poles, Russians, and Armenians left behind as last-ditch defenders of the approaches to the coastal city, filed out of thick-walled bunkers and pillboxes carrying white flags. They hadn't fired a round. Two coastal batteries, which could have played havoc with incoming American assault boats, fell in rapid fashion.

Now Walls was advancing toward Saint-Tropez with some five hundred men—half of them American paratroopers, the other half German prisoners.

AS CAPTAIN WALLS and his paratroopers were hacking their way into Saint-Tropez, twelve miles to the northwest, Maj. Wild Bill Boyle, commander of the 1st Battalion of the 517th Parachute Infantry, and fifty of his men were fighting for their lives inside the key town of Les Arcs. Nestled in a valley with steep hills on both sides, Les Arcs was the gateway through which German troops would have to funnel to reach the coastal beaches in order to attack the American assault divisions when they came ashore at 8:00 A.M.

Shortly after dropping in the darkness, a platoon-strength group of Boyle's men under a captain had edged into Les Arcs and exchanged sporadic small-arms fire with a German force holding the town. Until daylight it had been relatively quiet, as neither adversary knew the strength of the other in the darkness and general confusion. At daybreak, Major Boyle inspected his positions and found that his little band was astride a railroad track. Standing tall and refusing to duck when bursts of enemy machine-gun fire hissed past, Wild Bill peered down the track through the early-morning haze and could see German soldiers —plenty of them. Boyle had no way of knowing at the time that his fifty men were confronted by nearly a battalion of Germans.

Suddenly a torrent of automatic-weapons and rifle fire poured into the ranks of the paratroopers, and the Americans could see swarms of Feldgrau coming down the tracks toward them and fanning out into side streets to assault the GIs from each flank. A savage fight raged for an hour as Boyle's besieged little band struggled to prevent the much larger German force from circling behind and trapping them.

It was nearing 9:00 A.M. when Major Boyle realized that he and his men were about to be cut off and surrounded. He could hear heavy firing on three sides. "Okay," he told an officer, "we've got to pull out. Pass the word to the men."

As the officer started off, Wild Bill called out, "And tell them to be goddamned sure that not a single wounded man is left behind!" Boyle, like other parachute officers, refused to abandon his wounded, no matter what the situation.

Leaving a couple of BAR men to cover the withdrawal, Boyle's force, one by one, began slipping out of their cover and moving back. Major Boyle was the last man to depart. When nearly all of his men had crawled away toward the rear under a hail of bullets from three sides, the battalion commander strode around the abandoned positions, making certain that no wounded trooper would be left behind. Again he stood upright, his tall form making an ideal target, as bullets whizzed past his head.

"For chrissake, get down, Major!" one of the last men to leave shouted, "You'll get your head shot off!"

Satisfied that all of his men were accounted for, Major Boyle spun on his heel and headed back down the tracks where his makeshift unit was reassembling. Minutes later the paratroopers formed into a column and began the trek out of Les Arcs. Wounded troopers were being carried over the shoulders of able-bodied men, and those injured more seriously were being lugged on improvised litters.

Rounding a bend in the road, Boyle and his men heard the harsh chatter of a machine gun to their front, and streams of bullets poured into the marching column. A few men were hit; a couple of the wounded again had slugs rip into their bodies. The paratroopers dropped face downward, and wounded men lay helpless on litters as bullets hissed overhead.

Apparently Major Boyle and his men were trapped. Behind them the Germans could be heard pressing hard on the withdrawing band's heels, and on both sides there was intense firing as the Feldgrau closed in. Now a machine gun to their front had the parachutists pinned down.

"We sure as hell can't stay here!" Boyle called out above the noisy din of small-arms fire. "Let's head in that direction!" He pointed off to the left, where there seemed to be less enemy firing. Picking up the wounded, the troopers began edging onward. Although swarms of bullets continued to seek them out, Boyle and his men slipped through the closing German trap and about a mile farther along reached a rambling, sturdy old farmhouse. There the battalion CP was set up, outposts established, and the wounded brought inside. Little effort was required in setting up the CP—it consisted of Major Boyle sitting down on a rickety kitchen chair. He had no staff or contact with other units.

As the battalion commander pondered his next move, he asked one of his officers, "How many men do we have left who are able to fight?"

"Counting our walking wounded, about forty," was the reply.

"And how many Krauts would you say are attacking us?"

"It looked like there're about four hundred of them."

Wild Bill Boyle thrust his chin out. "Well, that makes it a pretty even fight. We're outnumbered only ten to one."

In his heart, Major Boyle no doubt believed that one American paratrooper was a match for ten German soldiers. In his mind, he knew that unless help were to come soon, his lightly armed parachutists stood an excellent chance of being wiped out.*

IT WAS 7:00 a.m. when Gen. Bob Frederick, commander of the 1st Airborne Task Force, arrived at the sprawling farm outside Le Mitan, a few miles north of Le Muy. He had selected the farm as his initial CP from aerial photographs he'd studied back in Italy. Like Colonel Graves and his force of a few men, Frederick reached his destination accompanied by his aide, Capt. George McCall, and a handful of stragglers collected during his trek.

It was just past 8:00 A.M. when a flight of thirty-five C-47s of the 435th Troop Carrier Group towing Horsa gliders (with British pilots) was winging to France after passing over the northern tip of Corsica. Code-named Operation Bluebird, the glider mission was to bring artillery support to Brigadier Pritchard's British 2nd Independent Parachute Brigade near Le Muy. Trailing by eight minutes was a flight of forty aircraft of the 436th Troop Carrier Group tugging American Wacos. Radio reports from the Riviera indicated that the landing zones were still blanketed by fog, haze, and the smoke of battle, making it impossible for the C-47 pilots to locate their LZs.

At his ground headquarters, Brig. Gen. Paul L. Williams, commander of the Provisional Troop Carrier Air Division, was growing concerned. The huge Horsas were so heavy that if there was a delay in releasing the gliders over the LZ due to the smog, the aircraft might not have enough fuel to make the return trip. He signaled the leader of the Horsa flight: "Mission postponed. If fuel is low, land in Corsica. Otherwise return to home bases [in Italy]."

Meanwhile, the 436th Group flight towing the much lighter Wacos burrowed on through the Mediterranean skies. Halfway between Corsica and the Côte d'Azur one Waco disintegrated and was scattered over the seascape. Another glider broke loose from its tug, soared downward, and landed in the water, where a Navy ship rescued those aboard. Reaching the landing zones, the leader of the 436th Group serial decided to circle the Argens Valley and wait for the haze and smoke to clear. It was a

---

*Major William J. Boyle was seriously wounded a few months later in the Battle of the Bulge. He was again critically wounded in the Korean War and received a medical discharge with the rank of colonel.

situation fraught with peril, for had the Luftwaffe made an appearance, the lumbering C-47s and their gliders would have provided a turkey shoot for eager German fighter pilots.

It was nearing 9:30 A.M., and the forty tug-Waco combinations had been circling Le Muy for nearly an hour. The C-47s were running perilously low on fuel, and the flight leader was about to give the order to return to Corsica or Italy. Just then the overcast broke slightly, and instructions were given to cast off the gliders. Thirty-seven of the Wacos crash-landed in relatively routine fashion, bringing in the 64th Light Artillery Battalion and elements of the British brigade's headquarters unit, plus numerous guns and a large quantity of ammunition. Seven Wacos landed a considerable distance from the LZ.

Bluebird was now half complete, and General Williams had to make a crucial decision: what to do with the thirty-seven Horsas that had returned to Corsica and to airfields in the Rome region. He huddled with Col. Frank J. McNees, leader of the 435th Group, and with liaison officers of Gen. Bob Frederick's airborne task force. A quick decision was reached: The Horsas would be returned to France that afternoon.

ON THE GROUND that morning, mass confusion prevailed on both sides. It was what the military calls a "fluid situation." One group from Colonel Graves's 517th Parachute Infantry landed near Draguignan. They ambushed two German trucks carrying troops to the coast, and in the ensuing firefight the paratroopers captured three enemy officers and twenty-five men. A patrol was sent to probe Draguignan, but the patrol was ambushed and captured by 250 Germans. The German unit in turn was surrounded by an even larger force of French Underground fighters. Fearful of falling into the hands of the vengeful Frenchmen thirsting for blood after years under the Nazi yoke, the German commander summoned Pfc. William Gray, leader of the American paratrooper patrol, and announced: "I am surrendering my unit to you, not to the French terrorists."

Gray promptly accepted the capitulation, ordered each German to destroy his weapon, then turned over his 250 captives to the French Partisans.

"We haven't got time to be your nursemaids," Gray told the flustered Wehrmacht commander.

NOT FAR FROM Le Muy, Pvt. Henry Wikins of the 596th Parachute Combat Engineer Company was lying in anguish near a dusty road. He had broken his leg in the jump and was made as comfortable as possible by his comrades, who then proceeded to their DZ. Eighteen-year-old Wikins was the son of German-Jewish immigrants who had fled the Third Reich. The teenager had volunteered for the paratroops as a seventeen-year-old, and had changed his name from Wikinski so that, in the event he was captured, he might not be identified as a Jew by the Germans and perhaps mistreated.

Later that morning, some of Wikins's comrades returned to the scene. They were stupefied and infuriated at what they saw: Private Wikins had been riddled with bullets, hanged from a tree limb, and his penis had been amputated and shoved into his mouth.

Man-Made Hurricane Strikes Coast

A ghostly bank of mist hovered over a thirty-mile stretch of the Côte d'Azur between Antheor and Cavalaire in the predawn period before H-Hour. It was refreshingly cool, and only a hint of a breeze played over the mirrorlike waters of the Mediterranean. Along these beaches of golden sand and tangled piles of rock, three of the U.S. Army's finest infantry divisions would storm ashore at 8:00 A.M. on sectors unromantically labeled by Allied planners as Alpha, Delta, and Camel.*

All over this region of the Mediterranean, the enormous Allied war machine that would smash into the Riviera was starting to uncoil. In wardrooms of British Rear Adm. T. H. Troubridge's task force of nine aircraft carriers, drowsy fliers were gulping down long slugs of hot coffee as they listened intently to last-minute briefings. At airfields on Corsica and Sardinia, fighter-bomber pilots were crawling from their bunks and shivering slightly in the predawn chill. Along the southern boot of Italy, ground crews were swarming over big four-motored bombers like colonies of gigantic ants, loading bomb bays and warming up the powerful engines.

---

*Double daylight saving time, two hours later than Greenwich, was used by the Allies in the Mediterranean.

158

Ten to twelve miles off the coastline, the silhouetted hulks of hundreds of Allied ships were lying mute in the calm waters. Hazily outlined were the sleek configurations of cruisers and destroyers. Command ships bristled with a maze of antennae jabbing slender fingers into the dark summer sky. Smaller vessels carrying messages darted to and fro among the larger ships, much like waterbugs scurrying about in a farm pond.

Belowdecks in the cramped, dingy holds of bulky transport ships, assault troops waited, nervous and tense. Grim-faced, they checked their rifles. Many prayed.

On the flagship *Catoctin*, Adm. Kent Hewitt, Gen. Sandy Patch, and Gen. Lucian Truscott were straining to appear confident and relaxed. Yet their minds were awhirl. Had everything humanly possible been done to assure the success of the amphibious assault at the least cost in lives? Were entrenched Germans on the shoreline alert and ready to pour a murderous fire into the ranks of infantrymen storming the beaches? Perhaps at that very moment, Wehrmacht reinforcements were racing for the landing beaches. Would the Luftwaffe be out in force?

In the wheelhouse of LSTs (landing ship, tank), Navy officers were carefully maneuvering through the darkness into their final positions, the magic of radar preventing them from crashing into other vessels. On the warships, gunnery officers checked fire plans—and checked them again. There were last-minute inspections of guns, ammunition, and fire tables.

The clock ticked inexorably toward H-Hour.

At 5:15 A.M., shortly before first light, scores of small Allied mine sweeping vessels headed for the beaches at Saint-Raphael and Sainte-Maxime and Pampelonne and Cavalaire. They began clearing lanes through which hundreds of LCVPs (landing craft, vehicle personnel), crammed with heavily burdened assault troops, would soon be plowing. Some of the mine craft, with guns barking, boldly pushed to within 150 yards of the shore. These were met by machine-gun fire from out of the haze ashore, but the Allied gunners on board the little craft returned the fusillades and soon the German automatic weapons fell silent.

Hard on the heels of the sweepers, the Apex drone boats churned toward the shoreline to explode underwater obstacles. These were the newly developed devices that had been tried and found wanting during a rehearsal back in Italy. At that time, the drone boats had been ridiculed as Rube Goldberg creations and all but written off. Now some drones performed with amazing effectiveness; they took out nine underwater obstacles at the Cavalaire beach and six at Pampelonne.

One Apex boat released its drone, which continued on toward the shore to blow up the submerged obstacles. The drone suddenly altered its course, went out of control, and dashed wildly up and down the beach. Then the berserk robot headed back out to sea, but turned toward the shore once again before exploding—right next to an Allied subchaser whose skipper was maneuvering desperately to evade the maverick drone. The explosion rendered the subchaser *hors de combat*.

Along the thirty miles of beaches between Cavalaire and Antheor, German soldiers manned blockhouses, casemated gun positions, and machine-gun posts. Terrified French civilians huddled in cellars in Fréjus, Sainte-Maxime, Saint-Raphael, and points between. All of them heard a faint humming noise in the early-morning hazy and gray Mediterranean sky. It was 5:50 A.M. Wehrmacht veterans promptly recognized the ominous sound off in the distance—a mighty Allied bomber stream was approaching.

The humming noise grew louder and developed into a roar. Moments later there was the whine and whistle of thousands of bombs plunging through space. All up and down the thirty miles of beaches and for several miles inland, the ground shook and shivered and thrashed about under the enormous pounding. Gigantic orange balls of fire and gushers of earth shot into the air. Countless forest fires broke out. Wooden buildings were turned into splinters and stone structures into powder.

German soldiers in pillboxes, nearly driven out of their minds by the drumfire of explosives, bled profusely from the nose, mouth, and eyes from the concussion of blockbuster bombs hitting on or near their thick-ceilinged concrete structures.

For ninety minutes, thirteen hundred big bombers blasted Hitler's South Wall as hundreds of escorting Thunderbirds, Mustangs, Spitfires, and Lightnings darted about like protective mother hens watching over their broods. On this calm, hazy morning, the sky bombardment raised a tremendous cloud of dust and smoke that hung like a death pallor along the Côte d'Azur.

At 7:30 A.M. the last of the big birds flew home to allow the warships to get in their licks.* The British cruiser *Ajax* had fired the first naval shell, at 6:06 A.M., and other warships followed with an occasional round. But now there was a mighty roar over the blue seascape as scores of Allied vessels began pounding the pockmarked beaches and key targets inland. Eerie swooshing noises erupted from specially equipped LCTs as thousands of rockets arched high into the haze-filled sky and drenched the beach, the enormous cracks on impact sounding as though huge whips were lashing the terrain.

A few thousand yards offshore, Allied brass on the bridge of the *Catoctin* gaped in awe at this man-made hurricane of steel and explosives. "How can anything live under such a bombardment?" Gen. Lucian Truscott exclaimed.

Next to Truscott, Adm. André Lemonnier, chief of staff of the French Navy, had been watching the two-hour bombardment of his homeland in total silence, too emotional to speak. Soon he would set foot on the sacred soil of France after four years in exile.

ON THE DESTROYER *Kimberley,* lying off Saint-Tropez, Winston Churchill, a long cigar clamped in his teeth, was staring avidly through binoculars at the military extravaganza unfolding before him. British Adm. Sir John Cunningham, long aware of the doughty prime minister's penchant for injecting himself into the thick of the action, had appointed a trusted naval officer to stand at Churchill's elbow at all times. The escort's orders from Cunningham had been terse and stern: "Don't let the prime minister out of your sight for one minute!"

The protective measures for the head of the British government soon proved to be well advised. Almost immediately Churchill demanded that the *Kimberley* move closer to shore "to get a better look at things." Told that there were strict orders forbidding the *Kimberley* to approach no nearer than seven miles to the beaches because of hundreds of floating mines, the prime minister was unmoved. Unfurling his renowned powers of persuasion and the same bulldog tenacity with which he opposed Operation Dragoon for many months, Churchill, before the morning was out, would coerce the

---

*On Dragoon's D-Day alone, Allied warplanes flew more than forty-two hundred sorties in direct support of the amphibious assault.

Kimberley's skipper into approaching to within four miles of the battered beaches.

Meanwhile, tension was thick on the bulky, drab transports lying ten to twelve miles offshore and holding assault troops of O'Daniel's 3rd, Dahlquist's 36th, and Eagles's 45th Infantry divisions spread out along thirty miles of the Côte d'Azur. At 5:55 A.M., loudspeakers blared out: "Lower landing boats!"

The seascape was alive with the sound of windlasses whirling as booms on the transports swung out LCVPs and lowered them gingerly into the placid, blue waters of the Mediterranean.

Belowdecks in the stuffy holds, grim-faced fighting men were getting more nervous by the minute. The moment of truth was at hand. Soon intercoms in the troop compartments called out a chilling message: "Assault troops to your boarding stations!"

American infantrymen, some to take part in their fourth amphibious invasion and others who had never heard a shot fired in anger, scrambled up steel ladders and onto the decks, then to their assigned positions along the railings just above the LCVPs resting quietly thirty feet below.

Burdened with heavy combat gear, the men were tense. It was cool, but perspiration dotted foreheads. Palms sweated. Stomachs churned. A few men vomited on deck. Old friends grimly shook hands. There were solemn calls of "Good luck!" and "See you on the beach!"

As the troops stood silently along the railings, loudspeakers blared again: "Now hear this. Board your landing boats!"

It was the dreaded order most did not want to hear. Yet each knew it had to come.

With a heavy rustling of equipment, the assault troops climbed over railings and began the arduous descent down slippery rope ladders and into landing craft. Curses rang out as men lost their footing in the tangled webbing or were struck heavy blows in the face by the rifle barrels of struggling comrades climbing down alongside.

As each assault boat was loaded, it circled its mother ship until all LCVPs were filled. A final order echoed over the water: "Away all boats!"

There was a raucous revving of motors, the LCVPs maneuvered abreast, and the long run to the beaches of Adolf Hitler's Riviera commenced. General Bob Frederick's paratroopers had already jumped behind the South Wall of Fortress Europe; now Lucian Truscott's seaborne troops were ready to smash into it. The men of the 36th Infantry Division were going in on the right, the 45th Division in the middle, and the 3rd Division on the left. If all went according to plan, leading elements of each division would hit the beaches simultaneously.

Crammed into LCVPs and heading for a strip of the Riviera code-named Camel were men of General Dahlquist's 36th Infantry Division—the Texas Army, its members liked to call themselves. Maj. Carthel N. "Red" Morgan of Amarillo, Texas, commander of the 3rd Battalion, 141st Infantry Regiment, was peering from his assault craft at the hazy coast of France, which was rapidly drawing closer. Red Morgan knew firsthand that landing on a hostile shore was a perilous task. He had survived the amphibious assault at Salerno the previous September and was aware that many comrades in the Texas National Guard division lay quietly in two Italian cemeteries.

This assault could be another rough one. Aerial photos had disclosed the presence of blockhouses, bunkers, and casemated artillery batteries. And, of course, the Texans could expect the usual Wehrmacht array of heavily fortified positions, including trench networks, dugouts, barbed wire, minefields, booby traps, and interlocking machine-gun fire.

There was a grinding crunch as the coxswain beached Major Morgan's LCVP. A curious thought flashed through the battalion commander's mind: "My God, is this pile of rocks a Riviera beach?"

That it was. On Morgan's map it was identified as Green Beach, and at Truscott's VI Corps headquarters it was known as Beach 264B.

Some of Capt. Roy F. Sentilles' men were already scrambling up the rocky slope. A German shell whistled just overhead and crashed into the rocks a short distance down the beach. Morgan glanced at his watch: 8:03 A.M.

Major Morgan could scarcely believe his eyes and ears. Instead of the expected grating chatter of enemy machine guns on Camel Green Beach, there was nothing. Next to Morgan a sergeant raised his arms as though praising God for the miracle. "What do you want to do now, Major?" the sergeant inquired.

"Get the hell on inland as fast as we can and while we can!" Morgan exclaimed.

Off to the right, Red Morgan heard the crash of artillery and the staccato bark of German automatic weapons. He knew that Lt. Col. William A. Bird's 1st Battalion was being heavily engaged at Camel Blue Beach, a strip of coastline only eighty yards long lying near Antheor. The Corniche coastal road skirted Blue Beach, and just inland was a high railroad viaduct that Allied pilots had done their best to destroy. More bombs had been dropped and shells fired into this small area at Blue Beach than in any other sector along the Riviera. But as Bird's LCVPs approached the shoreline they were raked with murderous fire from several German antitank guns on top of Pointe d'Antheor.

As the Texans scrambled from landing craft onto Blue Beach, they were greeted by bursts from automatic weapons. Pulling back from the shore after discharging passengers, three landing craft were sunk by sharp-eyed German gunners looking down from Pointe d'Azur.

Blue Beach was protected by an elaborate system of trenches, which were connected with underground shelters and ammunition dumps. But the enemy manning the fortifications had been stunned by the prodigious weight of bombs, shells, and rockets that had rained down on them for two hours. In their gray-green uniforms covered with masonry powder and looking as though sacks of flour had been dumped onto them, bleeding from mouths and eyes, the dazed defenders of Blue Beach began staggering out of dugouts and bunkers with hands raised.

Colonel Bird's battalion promptly began pushing eastward toward Cannes along the Corniche road, supported by warship guns offshore. Two German tanks were spotted clanking toward Bird's lightly armed leading elements, but the destroyer *Woolsey* blasted one of the panzers, and the other spun around and fled.

Beginning at 9:45 A.M., Col. Paul D. Adams's 143rd Regimental Combat Team came ashore on five-hundred-yard-long Camel Green Beach. Adams's 1st Battalion, led by Lt. Col. David M. Frazior, quickly pushed inland and seized the high ground to the northwest. Frazior and his operations officer, Maj. Marion P. Bowden, were inspecting forward positions when they walked over the crest of a hill and suddenly came face to face with several Germans. Both adversaries were startled by the unexpected confrontation and for moments stood motionless and staring at each other.

One German rapidly raised his rifle and fired a shot at Major Bowden, who was less than fifty feet away. Bowden felt a searing pain as a slug ripped into his shoulder, so near the neck that his metal major's leaf insignia partially deflected the bullet. Had the pellet not been deflected, it could have severed Bowden's jugular vein, resulting in his bleeding to death.

Major Bowden fell to the ground. Despite the intense pain, he was able to pitch three grenades, one of which killed the German who had shot him. Then Bowden blacked out.

At 10:35 A.M. General Dahlquist and a small command group came ashore over Camel Green Beach, which was still being pounded by an occasional artillery or mortar shell. As the 36th Infantry Division commander and his operations officer, Lt. Col. Fred W. Sladen, scrambled up the rocky slope, they were fired on at close range several times by concealed snipers. Dahlquist headed for a high cliff behind Green Beach, from where he would watch the landing that afternoon of his 142nd Regimental Combat Team on Camel Red Beach near Saint-Raphael.

General Dahlquist had no way of knowing at the time that isolating himself on the cliff observation post would soon help to precipitate an intense controversy among Dragoon commanders.

Camel Red Beach, around which the controversy would be centered, was located at the head of the Gulf of Fréjus. It had been heavily mined by the Germans and was strongly defended by coastal gun batteries, some of them masquerading as Saint-Raphael waterfront bars, kiosks, and bathhouses. H-Hour for Red Beach was 2:00 P.M., as sufficient time was needed for bombers, warships, and minesweepers to demolish the defenses. Some sixteen American and British minesweeping vessels had swept boat channels to within five hundred yards of Red Beach by 11:15 A.M., but they were met by a torrent of enemy fire and forced to beat a hasty retreat.

Several destroyers began dueling with the big German coastal guns along the Gulf of Fréjus, and ninety-three four-motored Liberator bombers blasted the shoreline. This massive pounding of Red Beach and adjacent areas failed to silence the enemy guns.

Next, Apex drone boats were sent in to explode underwater obstacles, but the drones went completely haywire, running around in circles. One of the berserk drones headed for the destroyer *Ordronaux,* whose skipper ordered his guns to open fire on the explosive-laden robot to keep it from ramming her. Two of the wildly gyrating drones ran aground, two others were boarded (in a perilous task) and defused, and three exploded according to plan over submerged obstacles.*

Half an hour later, gunfire support was again called for, and the *Arkansas, Tuscaloosa, Émile Bertin,* and four destroyers began to bombard German strongpoints along the Gulf of Fréjus. Still the German batteries fired away, and many of the underwater obstacles as well as most of the shore mines had not been cleared.

H-Hour was fast approaching. A crisis was looming. On the *Bayfield,* flagship for Camel Force, U.S. Rear Adm. Spencer S. Lewis was urgently discussing the situation with Rear Adm. Morton L. Deyo, who was in charge of Camel's bombardment warships. Lewis was in command of Camel operations until the 36th Division was put ashore. Lewis and Deyo quickly arrived at a firm conclusion: Without additional minesweeping, bombing, and shelling, the lanes to Red Beach would be bloody ones.

LCVPs carrying assault troops of Lt. Col. Elliott W. Amick's 1st Battalion of the 142nd Regiment were circling mother ships, waiting for the signal to make the run into Red Beach. At 2:05 A.M. (five minutes after H-Hour for Camel Red Beach), the deputy commander of the assault group, Navy Capt. L. B. Schulten, fired off an urgent signal to Admiral Lewis: "Wave being held back. Request instructions."

Admiral Lewis tried frantically to contact General John Dahlquist. The 36th Division commander could not be reached; he was on top of the Green Beach cliff to watch the landing in the Gulf of Fréjus.

Admiral Lewis found himself skewered on the horns of a dilemma. What to do in this unforeseen situation? General Dahlquist could not be reached. Dragoon's entire tactical plan might be torn asunder if Col. George E. Lynch's 142nd Infantry Regiment did not hit Red Beach as long planned. But could he, Admiral Lewis, idly stand by and do nothing when his professional expertise told him that the Texas battalion would be

---

*The weird conduct of the drone boats in the Gulf of Fréjus later resulted in American Navy engineers stating that German radio operators had "stolen" the radio direction of the "female" or explosive drone units from the "male" Apex directing boats.

heading into a bloody disaster at Red Beach?

Lewis arrived at a crucial decision: He signaled for the Red Beach boat waves to go ashore at already secured Green Beach.

In the meantime, the scores of LCVPs carrying Lieutenant Colonel Amick's battalion had lined up abreast and were knifing through the calm blue waters toward Red Beach. Could a halt signal reach the assault group in time?

A few thousand yards offshore from Saint-Raphael, General Lucian Truscott, the VI Corps commander, had a grandstand seat for the assault on Red Beach. Peering through binoculars, Truscott was delighted with the precision of the unfolding invasion, which clearly was going much smoother than anticipated. These were exciting moments on the *Catoctin* for the hell-for-leather cavalryman and other Dragoon leaders.

Suddenly the entire Red Beach flotilla of LCVPs halted a few thousand yards from shore. Truscott could not believe his eyes. What had gone wrong? Had the berserk drones cavorting around the Gulf of Fréjus held up the entire seaborne assault? Truscott, Admiral Hewitt, and General Patch were furious.

Minutes later, the sophisticated communications center on the *Catoctin* intercepted a signal from Admiral Lewis stating that, due to the uncleared water obstacles and mines before Red Beach, he had ordered the alternate landing for Lynch's 142nd Regimental Combat Team. It was strictly a Navy decision. Truscott grew more furious. Apparently General Dahlquist had not even been consulted. Nor had the corps commander, Truscott.

Admiral Kent Hewitt also joined in the mass temper tantrum on the bridge of the *Catoctin*. He promised an immediate investigation of the entire affair in the Gulf of Fréjus.

Accompanied by two aides, General Truscott climbed huffily into an LCVP and raced for Green Beach to find the commander of the 36th Infantry Division, John Dahlquist. Nearly an hour later, the VI Corps commander caught up with Dahlquist.

Truscott's fury over the last-minute switch of landing beaches had not abated. "Dahlquist," exploded Truscott, "if you ordered that change I will relieve you, and if Colonel Lynch ordered it, I will try him by general court-martial!"

General Truscott felt that the beach switch had set back his tactical timetable and had not been necessary. Back in the Blockhouse in Naples during planning days, Col. George Lynch had tried to get his regiment's landing shifted from Red Beach to one less heavily defended, but at that time Truscott told him: "Any determined regiment can force a landing [on Red Beach]!"

Later Lucian Truscott would explode anew when shown an intercepted signal of congratulations sent by General Dahlquist to Admiral Lewis:

"Appreciate your prompt action in changing plan when obstacles could not be breached. Expect to take Red Beach tonight [by land attack]."*

JAMMED INTO AN LCVP with thirty-one other men of O'Daniel's battle-tested 3rd Infantry Division was Lt. Glenn Rathbun, the young officer who had cleaned up at poker against two doctors as his ship was pulling out of Naples Harbor a few days before. Rathbun's little craft and scores more like it were heading for the Alpha beaches on the left flank of the Dragoon landings. Peering over the side of his LCVP with a fine spray of sea dousing his face, Rathbun instinctively pulled back his head as he heard an approaching shell. The projectile plowed into the water only twenty yards to one side. Moments later a second shell screamed in, this one sending up a geyser twenty yards to the other side.

"Good God, they've got us bracketed!" a shaky voice in Rathbun's LCVP called out. "The next one is going to drop right on top of us!" Silent praying, already intense, in the little landing craft grew more fervent. But the third and crucial German shell never arrived. Perhaps a warship had smashed the enemy gun before it could register a bull's-eye, Rathbun reflected.

THE 3RD INFANTRY Division fighting men were storming ashore at two beaches in the Alpha sector. The landing sites were thirteen miles apart, Red Beach on the Bay of Cavalaire and Yellow Beach on the Bay of Pampelonne. Both locations were on the Presqu'île de Saint-Tropez, a rugged little peninsula measuring six miles in each direction. Except for the areas directly behind Red and Yellow beaches, it is a region of rocky, pine-clad hills dotted with olive groves and tiny vineyards.

As hostile Red Beach drew closer, Lieutenant Rathbun, through the slowly evaporating haze, caught a glimpse of the

---

*After the war John E. Dahlquist rose to four-star rank.

ancient hill town of Ramatuelle in the center of the Presqu'île de
Saint-Tropez. Off to the west he could discern the twin islands
of Port-Cross and Île du Levant, looking like floating clouds
suspended majestically between sea and sky.

Rathbun recalled that Col. Edwin Walker's 1st Special
Service Force was to seize the pair of islands. He wondered if
the American and Canadian commandos had succeeded. Probably so, he reflected, or else the big German guns there would be
firing at his boat wave.

As two battalions of Col. Wiley H. O'Mahondro's 7th
Infantry Regiment were nearing Red Beach at Cavalaire, three
"swimming tanks" joined the assault. The iron monsters had
been lifted into the sea a mile and a half offshore. These DD
(dual-drive) tanks floated by means of watertight, air-filled
"bubbles."

Belonging to the 756th Tank Battalion, the three tanks
"swam" steadily toward shore as rockets fired from LSTs to the
rear arched over them. Suddenly there was an enormous grating
sound. An errant rocket had scored a direct hit on a swimming
tank, killing its commander and wounding the other two crew
members. Bleeding profusely and in extreme pain, the driver
righted the bobbing mass of floating iron and managed to steer it
toward the shoreline. Just before reaching the beach there was an
explosion; the ill-fated tank had struck an underwater mine. The
tracked vehicle and its crew plunged to the bottom.

Promptly at 8:00 A.M., the leading troops hopped out of
LCVPs at Alpha Red Beach and began moving inland. The
terrain resembled the cratered surface of the moon they had
seen in photographs, mute testimony to the thousands of
bombs, shells, and rockets that had plastered Red Beach. Trees
had been knocked down and splintered into toothpick size.
Only a shabby little seaside restaurant had escaped destruction.

Defensive fortifications at Red Beach were extensive, deep
—and unmanned. Not a shot was fired, and no Germans were
discovered in the immediate vicinity. But death still lurked
with every footstep. Rockets were supposed to have saturated
the shoreline, exploding all mines. But due to duds and faulty
aiming, the eastern portion of Alpha Red Beach still had many
active mines.

At 8:25 A.M.—twenty-five minutes after H-Hour—some
Germans, stunned by the heavy bombardment, began fighting
back with machine guns and mortars, shattering the silence

that had fallen over the Bay of Cavalaire. But by 8:50 A.M., ships lying offshore glimpsed the violet-colored smoke rockets fired into the air by Colonel O'Mahondro's men—Red Beach had been secured.

At Alpha Yellow Beach near Pampelonne, the 15th Infantry Regiment splashed ashore at a place dotted with bathhouses and locally known as Le Tahiti. There were elaborate fortifications, but all resistance was wiped out in less than an hour. Polish "volunteers" manning this sector showed little inclination to fight. At 8:40 A.M. the violet-colored smoke signals rocketed into the clearing blue summer sky over Le Tahiti.

On the bridge of his flagship *Biscayne*, a converted seaplane tender, U.S. Rear Adm. Bertram J. Rodgers was intently scouring the nine-mile strip of the Riviera code-named Delta, which was sandwiched between Alpha on the left and Camel on the right. It was Rodgers's responsibility to put Eagles's veteran 45th Infantry Division—the Thunderbirds—onto the beaches. Now he was watching scores of LCVPs carrying Eagles's olive-drab-clothed warriors plowing through the calm blue waters toward the shoreline.

Admiral Rodgers was beset with deep concerns other than the normal anxieties of a commander launching a crucial operation. Because his Delta sector was compressed between Alpha and Camel, it had been necessary for Rodgers to concentrate several bulky troop transports and fourteen battleships, cruisers, and destroyers into two narrow sea lanes, and he feared a disastrous collision. To complicate matters, these lanes intersected the ones that scores of LCVPs were now using to take Eagles's Thunderbirds ashore. Earlier, Rodgers had told his staff, "It will take a miracle for no collision to occur."

Delta sector included the beautiful Gulf of Saint-Tropez and the once-fashionable resort town of Sainte-Maxime. But the assault would take place along a five-thousand-yard beach on the adjoining Bay of Bougnan, where there were numerous stucco villas once painted in bright yellows, greens, and pinks but now rundown and shabby. Overlooking the Riviera beaches, these villas had been converted by the Germans into strongpoints.

At the eastern end of the Bay of Bougnan loomed the Pointe des Issambres, and atop it was a huge 220mm gun camouflaged to look like the garden of a nearby villa. It had beautiful rose bushes painted on the concrete. The Pointe de la Garonne, between the Delta beaches and Issambres, had a 75mm gun and numerous machine-gun emplacements. Delta could prove to be a bloodbath for the Thunderbirds.

Shells from warships were still screaming into the beaches as the LCVPs carrying the first wave to Delta plunged into a thick blanket of dirty gray smoke and dust and crunched onto the sand. As the 45th Division men scrambled from the craft, they were greeted with sporadic machine-gun and rifle fire, and an occasional shell exploded. The veteran Thunderbirds knew their business and methodically blasted stubborn Germans out of pillboxes and bunkers with grenades and dynamite charges.

As Thunderbird infantrymen were mopping up the concrete structures, four amphibious tanks waddled abreast up Blue Beach. There were four loud explosions, and the iron-plated "swimming tanks" appeared to leap several inches off the ground. They had rolled into a minefield.

By 9:10 A.M., the first seven waves were ashore on three Delta beaches.

A few miles offshore on the *Biscayne*, Delta Task Force commander Adm. Bertram Rodgers heaved a sigh of relief. He had predicted that a miracle would be necessary to prevent disastrous collisions in the compressed water lanes. That miracle had been granted.

Forward elements of the 45th Division charged into Sainte-Maxime, which had been heavily battered by the bombing and shelling. These troops were raked by German machine-gun fire. For two hours a bitter house-to-house fight raged with rifle, bayonet, and grenade before the last enemy soldier was killed, captured, or driven out.

While bullets were still hissing through the streets, two Thunderbirds shinnied up the Sainte-Maxime railroad signal tower, atop which the Nazi swastika-emblazoned flag had long flown. The banner of the Third Reich was ripped off and in its place the pair of American riflemen unfurled the Stars and Stripes. Down below, grimy, perspiring Thunderbirds cheered lustily as Old Glory waved majestically in the breeze over Adolf Hitler's Riviera.

"Dig the Bastards Out by Hand"

At 10:00 A.M. on D-Day, Lt. Comdr. Douglas Fairbanks, the Hollywood matinee idol and a man's man, was tuned in to Radio Berlin. Fairbanks's boat was lying off Cannes, which was being heavily pounded by warships.

Fairbanks and his comrades were anxious to learn how effective their Operation Rosie *ruse de guerre* had been— whether the stiff price in lives and prisoners paid by the French Navy men was worth it. To his delight, Commander Fairbanks learned from Radio Berlin that Rosie had totally bamboozled his opponents. A Nazi radio commentator told listeners in the Reich:

"A major Allied force [the sixty-seven French Navy men] attacked Cannes during the night and was repulsed with heavy losses. Antibes and Nice were bombarded by four or five large battleships [the small deck guns of Fairbanks's craft that fired four rounds inland]."

At the same time Josef Goebbels's radio announcers were telling of the southern France assault, French Underground fighters and men and women all over the nation were listening to the Allied commander in the Mediterranean, Gen. Jumbo Wilson, speak to them over BBC radio from London:

172

"The Army of France," the hulking Wilson said, "is in being again, fighting on its own soil for the liberation of its country, with all its traditions of victory behind it. . . . Remember 1918! All Frenchmen, civilians as well as military, have their part to play in the campaign in the south [of France].

"Your duty," he continued, "will be clear to you. Listen to the Allied radio, read notices and leaflets, pass on all instructions from one man and woman to another.

"Let us end the struggle as quickly as possible so that all France may resume again her free life under conditions of peace and security.

"Victory is certain! Long live the spirit of France and all that it stands for!"

SEVERAL HUNDRED MILES from the flaming Riviera coast that morning, an American paratrooper was placed under arrest by military police at an airfield outside Rome. The trooper had been in a C-47 piloted by Capt. Joseph McGloin, with Lt. Max Demuth as navigator. As the aircraft neared the Riviera, the parachutist shot himself through the palm of his hand.

Accident or otherwise, the paratroop jumpmaster insisted that the wounded trooper bail out with the stick. An argument ensued between the parachute officer and the copilot, Maj. Lester Ferguson, who insisted that the injured man return to Italy for treatment. Soon the green light flashed on in the C-47 and the stick leaped into the black unknown, leaving the wounded comrade in the plane. Now the trooper would be brought before a court-martial on a variety of charges.

Even as once-glittering Cannes was being shelled and bombed that morning, Hellmuth Heinz was nervously trying to contact French comrades. Heinz was a German civilian who worked for the German Economic Warfare Section along the Riviera. But his true job was that of a spy for the Abwehr. For months he had been spying on the French to root out leaders of the Underground, and he had built up a formidable network of civilians who were willing to denounce their countrymen for money.

Heinz was barely over five feet in height and so slim he looked as though he had not eaten in weeks. His thin brown hair did nothing to compensate for his sharp facial features, which reminded others of those of a rat.

But now, on the morning of D-Day, Heinz was unable to contact any of his many agents. Either they had gone into hiding, or the Cannes telephone system had been disrupted by the heavy bombardment.*

ALL UP AND down the vast sweep of the Côte d'Azur landing beaches, reinforcements, artillery, tanks, and supplies were pouring ashore, and assault troops were fighting their way inland. A battle patrol from Colonel O'Mahondro's 7th Regiment of the 3rd Infantry Division headed west through the thick pine forests with the mission of seizing the town of Cavalaire, nestled on a small peninsula a mile and a half away from Alpha Red Beach. The rugged peninsula overlooked the entire shoreline where 3rd Division landings were being made, and furnished an excellent observation point for the Germans to rain accurate artillery and mortar fire on the invaders.

Starting inland from the beach, S. Sgt. Herman F. Nevers, leader of the point squad, instinctively glanced over his shoulder just in time to see a mine hanging from a tree explode, cutting a lieutenant into ribbons and killing him instantly. The force of the explosion hurled S. Sgt. James P. Connor back ten feet and knocked him down. He bled profusely from a sliver of jagged shrapnel in his neck. Ordered by Lt. William K. Dieleman, the patrol leader, to return to the beach for treatment, Connor refused to obey. He struggled to his feet, recovered his rifle, and continued onward.

As the leading squad neared a small bridge, a German leaped out and fired a burst from his Schmeisser machine pistol. Sergeant Connor shot the Feldgrau through the head. Minutes later the advancing patrol was struck by a heavy mortar barrage and became disorganized. Connor got to his feet and in the midst of the explosions urged his twenty remaining men forward. Moments later the young sergeant was shot in the left shoulder, the bullet penetrating to his back, and he collapsed on the ground.

His friend Sergeant Nevers hurriedly crawled over to the

*Heinz was ordered by his masters in Berlin to remain behind and spy on the Allies. He was taken into custody by the U.S. Army's spy-catchers, the CIC (Counterintelligence Corps) and was promptly dubbed Rat Face. That was partially due to his facial features and partly to the fact that, in an effort to save his skin, he freely "ratted" on every one of his agents along the Riviera.

badly injured man and admonished him: "For chrissake, Connor, what in the hell are you trying to prove? Stop and go back and get some medical help!"

Grimacing in extreme pain, Connor replied softly, "No, they can hit me, but they can't stop me. I'll keep going until I can't go any farther."

As blood flowed from his wounds, Sergeant Connor began issuing terse orders. "Nevers, get out there on the right flank and get those men moving!" the twice-wounded sergeant exclaimed. "We've got to clean out those Krauts so we can push on to Cavalaire!"

Connor managed to pull himself upright and called out to his platoon: "If there's only one of us left, we're going to get there [to Cavalaire] and take it!"

With Sergeant Connor in the lead, the platoon moved forward again. A German suddenly popped out of a foxhole some thirty feet to Connor's front and shot the American in the leg. For the third time in an hour, Connor fell to the ground, wounded. Sergeant Nevers fired over Connor as he went down, killing the German.

Connor called to Nevers to help him up so he could continue, but the injured man could not stand, and collapsed. Nevers tried to give him first-aid treatment, but Connor wouldn't allow him to look at his wounds.

"There isn't time for that," he admonished Sergeant Nevers. "Take the rest of the men and go ahead." There were about fifteen Texans remaining.

Connor's voice was growing weaker. "If you have to dig the bastards out with your bare hands, then go ahead and dig them out!"

Reluctant to abandon his badly wounded friend, Nevers prepared to move out as bullets hissed overhead. Above the din of gunfire, he heard Connor whisper hoarsely: "I'll see you sometime."*

After advancing a short distance, Nevers glanced back over his shoulder and saw Jim Connor, pain etched in his face and uniform saturated with blood, smile weakly and feebly lift an arm in an effort to wave.

---

*To the astonishment of his comrades, the thrice-wounded Sgt. James Connor recovered. The battle surgeon who treated him declared, "The slightest movement must have caused him excruciating pain."

Following Sergeant Connor's instructions, the fifteen men remaining in the patrol tore into the German force, killing four of them and capturing forty. Along with other elements of the 7th Infantry that had caught up with them, the survivors of Lieutenant Dieleman's battle patrol, inspired by the exhortation of Jim Connor "If you have to dig the bastards out with your bare hands, then go ahead and dig them out!" fought their way into Cavalaire and by 11:30 A.M. had seized that key coastal town overlooking Alpha Red Beach.

MEANWHILE, A SHORT distance outside German-held Le Muy, Capt. Pete Baker, Lt. T. W. "Dumbo" Williams, and other members of the British pathfinder platoon were feverishly working to clear obstacles from the glider landing zone. Scores of the motorless craft were to bring in artillery to support the Red Devils in their attack to seize Le Muy. The principal obstacles were scores of thick, sturdy poles, each eight to ten feet long.

It had been the German pattern to place mines on each of these poles, but this had not been done on this LZ, so it was principally a matter of hard work for the pathfinders. And they knew their task would be a futile one; it would be impossible to remove all the poles before the first wave of gliders came in.

Perspiring profusely as she joined in the pole-chopping function was a pretty French girl of nineteen who lived on the farm on which the LZ was located. As she labored until collapsing from exhaustion, her father milked the family cows nearby.

At headquarters of the German LXII Corps in Draguignan, Gen. Ferdinand Neuling by midmorning had been nearly buried with reports from field commanders. Most of the signals were desperate, contradictory, and reflected the bewilderment of leaders suddenly finding themselves under attack from sky, sea, and land. To add to Neuling's woes, the Luftwaffe had vanished, his foreign troops were proving unreliable (as Neuling had known they would be), and communications between various headquarters and battle units had virtually been severed. Bob Frederick's marauding parachutists, eager French Resistance fighters, plus sea and air bombardments had wiped out most of the Wehrmacht's telephone lines, and the airborne men had ambushed most of the motorcycle couriers dispatched by frantic German commanders.

With the Riviera roof figuratively caving in on him, General Neuling, always imperturbable under stress, refused to panic. Clean-shaven, hair neatly combed, and uniform immaculate as always on this cataclysmic summer morning, the LXII Corps commander tried desperately to contact his scattered regiments in order to launch a coordinated counterattack. The effort proved hopeless; Neuling's only link with the outside world was a telephone line to Gen. Freidrich Wiese at Nineteenth Army headquarters, more than 120 miles away in Avignon.

Wiese, a disciplined soldier and experienced battle commander, was likewise cool and collected. Whatever his feelings about the Allied hurricane that had struck his army along the Riviera, to his staff Wiese appeared to be undergoing just another routine day at the office. Charged by the Führer with defending the French coastline for three hundred miles between Italy and Spain "to the last man and the last bullet," General Wiese knew that the situation was hopeless, yet he was determined to implement Hitler's order as long as he had the power to function.

Since the first Allied paratrooper dropped in the predawn hours, Wiese had been in continual contact with his superior, General Johannes Blaskowitz, whose Army Group G headquarters was at Rouffiac, near Toulouse. But late in the morning the wire went dead, apparently cut by the French Resistance or Allied paratroopers. Blaskowitz, however, felt that he had received sufficient information to pinpoint the invaders' primary objectives—the major ports of Toulon and Marseilles. A skilled tactician, Blaskowitz also felt confident that the Allies intended to thrust northward up the Rhône River valley and link up with rampaging Normandy armies under General Eisenhower that were racing hell-bent eastward toward Paris and the border of the Reich. If this catastrophic junction were to occur, Blaskowitz and his Army Group G headquarters would be cut off west of the Rhône River.

At 11:00 A.M. Blaskowitz called a hurried staff conference to discuss events of the past few hours. Convinced of Allied intentions, he ordered his staff to move the army group headquarters eastward to Avignon—immediately, before it was too late.

General Blaskowitz still clung to one faint hope for turning the tables on the invaders. If General Wend von Wietersheim's crack 11th Panzer Division, which had rushed out of Bordeaux far to the west two and a half days previously, were to reach the Riviera, it could play havoc with American assault divisions still scrambling ashore.

MEANWHILE, CAPTAIN JESS Walls of the 509th Parachute Infantry Battalion and his hodgepodge collection of some 250 paratroopers had run into a buzzsaw in their attack to seize Saint-Tropez. A good-sized German force had holed up in an ancient, thick-walled citadel in the center of the city and were defying the Americans to root them out. Walls's paratroopers were reinforced by about 50 armed members of the French Resistance, who fought valiantly alongside the Americans.

But the attacking force was lightly armed and lacked the firepower to blast the stubborn Germans out of the citadel. At about 3:00 P.M., a company of Eagles's 45th Infantry Division, which had landed on beaches three miles south of Saint-Tropez, plunged into the fight, and its bazookas and heavy machine guns peppered the sturdy old stone structure. At 3:30 P.M., a white flag was unfurled over the ramparts of the citadel, but it took several more hours of house-to-house fighting to wipe out the final German pockets. One hundred thirty Feldgrau were killed or captured in the citadel alone.

INLAND FROM THE 36th Infantry Division beaches at Saint-Raphael, Lt. Col. Gaulden M. Watkins, commander of the 2nd Battalion of the 143rd Infantry, was in a roadside ditch at about 5:00 P.M. when a German tank approached and two enemy soldiers got out to surrender. Watkins left his cover to accept the capitulation, and moments later the panzer's machine gun opened fire. One of the slugs struck Colonel Watkins in the chest. He was replaced by his executive officer, flamboyant, forty-year-old Maj. James C. Gentle, who had been assigned to the 36th Division only five days previously, from a cavalry outfit. Now Gentle suddenly found himself in command of an infantry battalion in a crucial action, and he knew the names of only a handful of his officers.

AT ABOUT THE same time Lieutenant Colonel Watkins was shot, Gen. Lucian Truscott was climbing down the side of the command ship *Catoctin*. The VI Corps commander had returned to the vessel, nerve center for the entire invasion, to report to General Patch and Admiral Hewitt on conditions ashore. With Truscott as he headed for the Sainte-Maxime beaches in an LCVP was his French liaison officer, Col. Jean Petit. Landing on the shore, Truscott scooped up a handful of sand, turned to Petit, and asked: "Well, Jean, how does the soil of France feel to an exile?"

Colonel Petit's eyes were filled with tears, and he was too choked with emotion to reply.

General Truscott located Gen. Bill Eagles of the 45th Infantry Division at the Thunderbird CP a short distance outside Sainte-Maxime. "Well, Bill, how are you doing?" the corps leader inquired.

The soft-spoken Eagles said that his reconnaissance elements had made contact with scattered groups of Bob Frederick's 1st Airborne Task Force south of Le Muy but that he had not yet established communication with Frederick's CP.

Back at his own CP, Truscott quickly pored over reports from O'Daniel's 3rd and Dahlquist's 36th Infantry divisions. Truscott was elated to learn that except for Fréjus and a short strip of beach, all objectives had been taken, and his three assault divisions were pushing steadily inland.

Lucian Truscott turned to an aide and remarked, "I guess this is a fitting celebration of the twenty-seventh anniversary of my original commission as an officer in the United States Army."

INSIDE THE GESTAPO prison in Nice, a battered Helene Vagliano was huddled on a filthy mattress in her rat-infested cell. So distorted were the once beautiful young woman's features that her friends in the French Underground would not have recognized her. It was 2:00 P.M. Suddenly there was a shout from outside under her window: "The Allies have landed at Fréjus! The Allies have landed at Fréjus!"

There were scuffling sounds, then the unknown voice fell silent. Helene Vagliano was electrified by the news, but she knew that the invasion had come too late to save her. She was doomed.

Shouts of joy rang out from tortured souls throughout the stifling, hot prison. Then a voice from its gray depths began singing the "Marseillaise," and other voices joined in. Soon the drab old stone structure reverberated with the vocal strains of the French national anthem.

A short time later, Helene Vagliano, who for months had risked her life as a courier for the Underground, heard the familiar clanking noises as the massive door to her cell was being opened. She knew that this was not yet another brutal interrogation by her Gestapo captors. Her time had come.

Helene, her once silken black hair now a tangled mass of matted blood, was herded into a van, along with a French priest, a nurse, and several other condemned men and women of the Underground. They were driven to an open field outside Nice and lined up before two machine guns. Off in the distance, the doomed patriots could see a flight of American fighterbombers pouncing on the hated Boche. As the Germans prepared to fire, the Resistance fighters held hands and began singing the "Marseillaise." The machine guns chattered angrily, and the voices were stilled forever.

AT ABOUT THE same time the French patriots were dying at the hands of a Gestapo firing squad, Lt. Jim Reith, the platoon leader in the 517th Parachute Infantry Regiment, was moving cross-country with his men when he spotted several curious-looking forms sprawled in a field. He went to investigate and as he drew closer recognized that these were British paratroopers. There were ten of them, and they obviously had plunged to their deaths when their parachutes had failed to open.

The sight sickened the Americans. The Red Devils were in various distorted positions. Legs were driven through shoulders, eyeballs had popped out of sockets, arms had snapped off. Reith and his men were puzzled over their macabre discovery. They could understand how one man's chute could have failed to open, or even two men's chutes in the same stick. But ten failures? It would be one of war's multitude of unexplainable riddles.

Lieutenant Reith had lost his raincoat, so he took one from a Red Devil with the fighting man's customary declaration of truth, "He won't be needing it any longer."

Reith's platoon continued on its mission, which was to establish a roadblock at a key bridge. Hardly had the troopers gotten into position than they heard the purr of an approaching vehicle, and moments later a camouflaged German truck rounded a sharp curve in the road just in front of the bridge. The unfortunate driver was greeted by a fusillade of machine-gun and rifle fire and slumped over dead, riddled by bullets.

Reith's men hid the truck in nearby woods. Minutes later another enemy truck carrying supplies whipped around the bend in the road, and the driver met the same fate as his predecessor. Then another German truck, with identical results.

A short time later yet another vehicle approached the bridge, and as it sped around the curve, the troopers peppered it and its driver with heavy bursts of fire. When the smoke had cleared, Reith and his men were astonished to see that they had bagged a stylish luxury convertible car. As they inspected their handiwork, Reith and his men were in for another surprise: The driver was not a German but a French civilian.

Looking at the Frenchman's bloody corpse, one trooper shrugged his shoulders and exclaimed, *"C'est la guerre!"*

EARLIER THAT SAME day, not long after dawn, General Blaskowitz's faint hope for smashing the invasion—von Wietersheim's 11th Panzer Division—clanked up to the Rhône River at Avignon. Under the lash of its hard-driving leader, the 11th Panzer had been moving steadily along the roads for more than fifty-eight hours, hardly pausing for a rest break. It had been a desperate race between von Wietersheim's low-slung panzers and the Allied invasion force to see which one reached the Riviera first. Only hours before pulling into Avignon, von Wietersheim had learned by radio signal that he had lost the contest—the Allies had struck along the Côte d'Azur.

Yet the panzer leader had hopes of inflicting a severe bloody nose on the invaders. Even though his men had been running a gauntlet of Jabo (fighter-bomber) attacks all the way from the Atlantic coast, von Wietersheim promptly issued orders to his exhausted tankers: Head for the Allied landing beaches, some ninety miles to the southeast. But first he had to get across the Rhône, and all bridges between the Mediterranean and Avignon had been destroyed by Allied aircraft. Von Wietersheim learned that the last bridge had been blasted only that morning.

Now von Wietersheim ordered the division to cross the Rhône on barges, or anything else that would float. Overhead, swarms of Jabos circled, then pounced on the massed panzers, mobile guns, trucks, Volkswagens, and grenadiers, strafing and bombing the loaded barges in midstream and on both banks.

General von Wietersheim was close to tears from frustration. Under the constant pounding by the Jabos, the Rhône crossing was agonizingly slow and costly in men and equipment. It would be four days before the 11th Panzer Division could reform as a fighting unit east of the broad Rhône, too late—far too late—to affect the struggle for the Riviera.

Carnage on the Landing Zone

At noon on D-Day, Montalto Airfield, a hundred miles north of Rome, was a beehive of activity. The 796 men and 46 officers of the green but keenly trained and eager 551st Parachute Infantry Battalion were feverishly preparing for Operation Canary, the second paratroop mission of the day into southern France. If all went according to plan, the Goyas, as they were called, would parachute behind the Riviera at about 6:00 P.M.*

In his CP at the airfield, twenty-nine-year-old Lt. Col. Wood G. Joerg was intently studying late aerial photos of the drop zone while hurriedly issuing last-minute instructions to officers dashing in and out of his office. Wood Joerg was a Southerner. He claimed Texas as his home state, and "The Yellow Rose of Texas" was his favorite song, but he had been born in Eufala, Alabama. Joerg's father was Regular Army.

At West Point, where he was known as Tiger, Wood Joerg was a welterweight on the boxing team and starred in varsity lacrosse. Cheerful and personable, Colonel Joerg nevertheless was an enigma to his officers; they respected, even admired him, but thought him to be aloof. The enlisted men were quite fond of

---

*Goya was an acronym for *Get Off Your Ass*, reflecting the boldness of the paratrooper battalion.

their leader and considered him especially sensitive to their needs. The colonel had won their hearts months before when the 551st Parachute Infantry Battalion was aboard a troop transport en route from Panama to San Francisco. An officious, high-ranking Navy officer had discovered that Furlough, the Goyas' dog mascot, had been smuggled aboard. The Navy officer threatened to have Furlough thrown overboard at sea, but Colonel Joerg intervened, and after a heated dispute the pooch was allowed to continue the journey.

"The colonel knew what Furlough meant to all of us," the Goyas told each other. "He could have been court-martialed for telling off that goddamned gold-braided swabbie!"*

On the threshhold of leading his men into battle for the first time, Joerg patted his jump-suit pocket to see if the prayer he had written was still in place:

Oh God, Commander of all men, we stand before Thee asking Thy help in the execution of the many tasks which confront us. Give us the strength, courage, daring, intelligence and devotion to duty, so that we may perfect ourselves as fighting men. . . .

And, Oh God, if the price we must pay for eternal freedom of man be great, give us strength so that we will not hesitate to sacrifice ourselves for a cause so sacred. All of this we ask in Thy name. Amen.

Elsewhere on the hot, dusty airfield at Montalto, spirits were high among the paratroopers, but tension began to build as the clock ticked onward and time for boarding the drab, squat C-47s neared. Sergeant Donald C. Garrigues of Carthage, Missouri, began steadily to shed what he considered excess equipment. He pitched away his gas mask, musette bag, shelter half, blanket, raincoat, and wire cutters. Yet he and his comrades would still be burdened with a hundred pounds or more of weapons, ammunition, and equipment when they bailed out over southern France.

Seated in the shade of a C-47's wing, Jim Stevens, a rifle company platoon sergeant, was checking his Garand and idly glanced up to see one of his men stroll past in combat gear and

---

*Lieutenant Colonel Wood Joerg was killed six months later, in the Battle of the Bulge.

with a guitar strapped over his shoulder. Stevens shook his head from side to side in resignation, then went back to inspecting his rifle. The previous day several men in Stevens's platoon had pleaded with him to allow the trooper to jump with the guitar. "Hell, no!" was the reply. "He'll get stuck in the door [of the plane]." They persisted, and Sergeant Stevens relented— "against my better judgment."

Most of the 551st troopers had finished their noon meal and marched to a large barn to pick up their parachutes. A few of the men had eaten their food, but the majority had only picked at it. Only hours away from takeoff and a jump into the unknown, few were hungry. Staff Sergeant Charles S. Fairlamb was reaching for a chute when he heard a series of strident shrieks outside the barn. He rushed to the door and saw three husky troopers laboring to subdue one of Fairlamb's mortarmen, who had gone berserk.

The trooper's screams and shouts echoed across the bleak airfield, and he continued to struggle with superhuman effort. Finally his three comrades muscled him into a jeep, and he was rushed to the airfield's aid station. A thick pall of gloom enveloped the paratroopers as the result of the berserk man's actions.

Captain James "Jungle Jim" Evans, a company commander, hurriedly conferred with one of the battalion's two surgeons, Capt. Judson I. Chalkley. "I hope the guy will straighten out so we can take him along," Evans told Chalkley. "He's the best man I have on mortars." Yet Evans had mixed feelings; if the man went berserk again in flight, disaster could ensue.

Dr. Chalkley, who would himself be going on the combat jump, replied drily: "Well, you can try taking him along, but this one is on you." Evans changed his mind; he could not risk a berserk trooper tearing up a C-47 in flight and possibly causing it to plunge into the sea.

Soon—too soon for many troopers—a loud roar echoed across the parched Montalto Airfield as swarms of C-47s started their motors. Minutes later there were the spine-tingling calls: "Load 'em up!" The Goyas lined up in single file and one by one began waddling toward their C-47s. Twenty-year-old Pfc. Joe M. Cicchinelli, stocky and muscular, who had been a boxer and a football player, could hardly walk. With his normal gear, Cicchinelli was also carrying bazooka rockets and mortar shells—150 extra pounds in all, only 15 pounds less than his own weight. He was thankful that two men had been posted at each side of the short steel ladder leading to the doorway to help the troopers into the aircraft.

As he squeezed himself into a bucket seat and awaited takeoff, Cicchinelli glanced up and down the aisle at his comrades. He wondered if his face were as ashen and stonelike as theirs. He concluded that it was. Cicchinelli had a particularly hazardous job—first scout. And as he looked at his comrades he asked Providence: Which of us will come out of this alive, and which of us will die?

His reverie was shattered when powerful engines were revved and the C-47 shivered and shook. One after the other, the forty-one airplanes, each trailing a towering plume of dust, raced down the runway and lifted off for southern France, already a flaming battleground.

As the C-47 flight neared the French coastline, Maj. Joseph C. Antrim, operations officer for the 85th Squadron of the 437th Troop Carrier Group, had a feeling that he had been there before. And he had been. This was the second combat operation of the day for his squadron; earlier Antrim and his fellow pilots had flown in the 460th Parachute Artillery Battalion.

It was dark then, but now he was fascinated to gaze down and view the mammoth invasion apparatus unfolding before his eyes. Great concentrations of shipping could be seen, either anchored offshore or cruising along the coast. Little assault boats, bringing in troop reinforcements and looking for all the world like water bugs, disappeared into smoke screens laid to protect the invaders' entry into France. Antrim could see that the entire region was covered with smoke, and scores of brush and forest fires were blazing brightly. On the major's right was the once-stylish resort city of Cannes; naval shells were exploding along its waterfront, sending gushers of water soaring into the sky.

Antrim's flight knifed over the Côte d'Azur, and minutes later the green lights flashed in forty-one C-47s and the sky was awash with billowing white parachutes. "What a magnificent sight!" the major enthused to his copilot. He said a silent prayer for the hundreds of American paratroopers floating earthward, then banked and headed back to Italy.

Lieutenant Marshall Dalton, a company commander, was floating earthward, still about five hundred feet from the ground, when a parachute carrying an equipment bundle collided with him and collapsed his chute. Thinking quickly, Dalton saved his life by grabbing the equipment bundle and riding it to the ground.

Landing in a vineyard, Cpl. Mel Clark quickly shucked his parachute and began slipping along a row of vines, keeping low. He mentally reviewed the 551st Battalion password and counter-word, and recalled that if any trooper forgot them he was to call out "Billy the Kid," named after a dashing figure of the Old West. Clark heard an ominous rustling noise and knew that someone was moving toward him. Tension built. He gripped his rifle and called out "Liberty!" There was no response of the counterword "France." Once more Clark shouted "Liberty!" Still no reply. The trooper clicked off the safety on his Garand and promptly heard a voice with a thick British accent call out from concealment in the underbrush: "Jesse James, Tom Mix—oh, some bloody American cowboy!"

Sergeant Bill Dean of the light-machine-gun platoon crashed through a tree and was jolted to a halt just above the ground. He looked downward to see that he was dangling just above several foxholes. In each hole was a German soldier—each quite dead—and all covered with swarms of flies.

A short time later, Sergeant Dean was shot in the hip. His comrades heard him howling and cussing. "Some son-of-a-bitch shot me!" he yelled. He would be lugged to a barn, where Dean and five others would remain for two days and nights until located by advancing seaborne troops.*

Private First Class Thomas B. Waller plunged through a tree on the jump and landed hard in a dry creekbed. On the way down, he and others around him were being shot at by Germans in a wooded area. Waller cut his way out of his harness, assembled his rifle, and scrambled out of the creekbed. He promptly came into contact with the first two German soldiers he had seen—both dead, lying on their backs and staring sightlessly into the sky. Waller stared at the corpses for several moments, then stepped over them and hurried off to his company's assembly area.

Just as Waller was approaching the site, he spotted several

---

*Sergeant Bill Dean spent the entire time in the barn with no morphine and in agony. His wound became infected and he nearly died when it spread to his stomach. In Italy Dean was visited by a hospital chaplain who asked, "Are you ready to die, my son?" "Like the devil I am!" the trooper responded. He recovered.

figures emerging from a thickly wooded area. They were wearing the gray-green of the German Wehrmacht. The trooper started to raise his rifle, then lowered it and sighed with relief. Behind the six Feldgrau was Waller's company commander, Lieutenant Dalton, who had ridden down on the equipment bundle minutes before, landed in the woods, and captured the six surprised Germans.

Lieutenant Dick Goins, a platoon leader, landed in a cornfield, and while getting out of his harness looked up to see five Germans coming toward him. Goins felt a surge of fear and whipped up his Tommy gun. Just as he was ready to squeeze off a burst, the enemy soldiers spotted him and threw up their hands in surrender. They tried to give watches and rings to Lieutenant Goins, apparently in an effort to save their lives. These were Russian "volunteers" who had been told that American paratroopers were thugs, murderers, and rapists who would promptly kill any Wehrmacht soldier unfortunate enough to fall into their clutches.

Crashing to earth, Cpl. Charlie Fairlamb felt his leg pockets to see that the five German rifle grenades he had stashed there were still in place and had not been jolted loose in the shock of his parachute's opening. Fairlamb badly injured his back when he struck the ground with great impact, but he pulled himself to his feet and staggered off in search of his company. Only later would he learn that the German grenades were constructed to go off on impact as well as by pulling detonating cords.

As he moved toward the assembly area, Fairlamb spotted Capt. Jud Chalkley, one of the two battalion surgeons, seated alongside the road and sewing up the badly gashed posterior of a comrade, Russell H. Conley. The trooper had landed on a pole and now the surgeon had him over his lap and was using some thread and a large needle he kept for just such emergencies to close the ugly wound.

Fairlamb saw that Conley was kicking, yelling, and protesting, as the embroidery work was being done without painkiller. But moments later the job was finished, and Conley pulled up his torn and bloody jump pants and scampered off in search of his company.

Staff Sergeant Jim Stevens, who had given one of his men permission to jump carrying a guitar, landed in a heap near a big tree. He rolled over and found himself staring directly at two black boots. Terrified, Stevens was engulfed by a flashing thought: "I must be dead, because if a German is that close to me he must have killed me!" A split-second later Stevens returned to reality. The big black boots were indeed on a Wehrmacht soldier—a very dead one.

Lieutenant Andy Titko, communications officer of the 551st Parachute Infantry Battalion, was in a foul mood. He had been in a foul mood for several days. Before leaving Italy, Titko had lost his wallet containing two months' pay, his identification card, and dog tags. Then, in the last mail call before lifting off for southern France, he received a "Dear John" letter.* When his parachute opened, his foot caught in the suspension lines, but he got loose just before reaching the ground. There he crashed into a large tree, which ripped a nasty gash under one eye.

Titko's chute caught in the upper branches, and he dangled in his harness several feet off the ground. Blood was streaming down his face and temporarily blinded him. He could hear voices and rustling noises on all sides but had to remain there helplessly until a trooper came along and cut him down.

As Lt. Col. Wood Joerg, the battalion commander, wiggled out of his harness, a figure dashed up to him. It was Capt. Tims Quinn, the battalion operations officer, who had jumped with the 509th Parachute Infantry Battalion during the hours of darkness to be on the DZ when the 551st jumped.

"A beautiful job, Colonel!" Quinn enthused. "I think the entire battalion dropped right on the button!"

Joerg smiled and moved off to assemble his paratroopers. He would have to hurry: The 550th Glider Infantry Battalion was to land in minutes in the precise area that Joerg's paratroopers had dropped onto.

AT 4:10 P.M. that day, a C-47 towing a Waco glider sped down the runway at Ombrone Airfield outside Rome. At the controls was Maj. Gen. Chappell, leader of the 50th Wing of the Troop Carrier Command. It was the first of 337 tug-tow combinations to lift off for southern France carrying men of Lt. Col. Edward Sachs's untested but eager 550th Glider Infantry

---

*This "Dear John" letter had a happy ending. After the war, Lieutenant Titko married the young lady.

Battalion. Operation Dove would, in one fell swoop, deposit 2,250 men and scores of artillery pieces behind Adolf Hitler's South Wall.

Lieutenant Johnny Goodwin, the twenty-year-old executive officer of the 95th Squadron who was making his second run over southern France that day, was thrilled by the sight that greeted his eyes. In Normandy's invasion and earlier on this same day, Goodwin had flown in the darkness. But now in the light of day, America's aerial might was unfolding before his eyes.

The entire sky, from horizon to horizon, was blanketed with Uncle Sam's aircraft. There was an unending umbrella of C-47s and gliders trailing each tug at three-hundred-foot distances. Darting about like mother hens protecting their broods—and that was precisely what they were doing—were swarms of Thunderbolt, Mustang, and Lightning fighter-bombers. And at the higher levels, heavy and medium bombers described flowing condensation trails as they winged toward inland targets.

Riding with two American glider pilots, Flight Officers Leon Luczak and Howard Shupp, in their canvas-covered motorless craft were a jeep and three Japanese American soldiers of an antitank platoon of the 442nd Infantry Regiment. Until four weeks previously, the antitank men had never seen a glider nor been inside one. Then they had been informed that their platoon members were to become instant glidermen.

Luczak and Shupp had an uneventful flight, although they had to look on in anguish as one glider disintegrated in midair and another one plunged into the sea. Due to the mountains a short distance inland, C-47s and gliders had to fly at twenty-five hundred feet, considerably higher than was desirable. But the early-afternoon briefing had predicted cloudless skies and unlimited visibility, so the GPs (glider pilots) foresaw no difficulties in spotting their landing zones. Luczak and Shupp were dismayed on nearing France to see that the entire region was shrouded in thick haze and smoke.

Off to the right, Luczak and Shupp saw a column of C-47s and gliders going into a huge haze cloud and presumed that it was heading for some other landing zone. The craft carrying the flight officers plunged into a bank of smog, and moments later all gliders in their flight were cut loose from tugs.

Soaring out of the overcast, Luczak and Shupp were greeted

by a terrifying sight: An entire group of C-47s and Wacos was heading hell-bent toward them from the front—and at the same altitude. This was the same flight that the two GPs had detected off to the right a short time previously. But that flight had not been winging toward another LZ, as Luczak and Shupp had presumed. Rather, it had been off course and was seeking the same landing zone as were the gliders in Luczak's and Shupp's flight.

That errant column had realized it had flown past the LZ in the haze, had made a 180-degree turn, and now was flying back toward its target. Suddenly the pilots of the oncoming C-47s realized that a crucial mistake had been made and that a series of head-on collisions was looming; some frantically tried to pull up over the free-flying gliders of Luczak's and Shupp's flight, and others endeavored to dip down under. A wild melee erupted in the sky.

Face-to-face with disaster, the irrepressible Leon Luczak called out to his partner, "You, too, brother Shupp, can be a glider pilot and wear wings of silver on your breast!" The three stoic Japanese Americans remained silent, their faces expressionless.

Quickly the gliders in the errant flight cut loose from their C-47s, and scores of Wacos began weaving and darting about in an effort to avoid collisions. Heavy nylon ropes dangling from gliders in the errant flight dragged through the Wacos in the other group, shearing away wings and fuselages. Soldiers and pilots spilled from the damaged gliders and plunged earthward to their deaths. Luczak glanced out a side window to see a jeep plummet past, the vehicle tumbling and turning grotesquely in its earthward descent.

Chaos reigned. It was each pilot for himself. In the wild sky scramble, a few Wacos crashed head-on. All the time, Luczak and Shupp were losing altitude and searching feverishly for a likely landing place. But each time they spotted one, at least two other gliders beat them to it.

Now the flight officers' craft was near the ground, and another Waco zipped past them, missing their glider by only five feet. Suddenly their Waco stalled and plunged into the earth in a semidive, striking with such enormous force that the jeep tore loose from its lashings and Luczak was hurled through the windshield. Dazed and bleeding, Shupp and the three antitank soldiers crawled from the twisted pile of wreckage. Luczak suffered a broken neck, and Shupp was badly cut and had internal injuries. One of the Japanese Americans received a fractured skull, but his two comrades staggered off to locate the others in their antitank platoon.

Also engaged in the sky melee was Flight Officer Jack "Deacon" Merrick, a twenty-three-year-old GP from Gainesville, Texas. After maneuvering his Waco through the swirling masses of gliders, Merrick swooped in low and crash-landed into a vineyard. Next to him his pal, Flight Officer Jack "Feet" Lester, brought his glider into the same vineyard. Each craft had been carrying Japanese American antitank soldiers, and trailerloads of ammunition. Neither GPs nor passengers suffered even minor injuries.

Gathering up their personal belongings, Deacon Merrick and Feet Lester headed overland in search of a command post where they could spend the night. On the way they passed a wrecked glider and saw a dead German stretched out beside it. Curious, the two GPs pranced up to the wreckage and stared at the lifeless Feldgrau, then looked inside the twisted Waco and saw a dead American gliderman.

"I guess our guy and the Kraut had a shoot-out and killed each other," Merrick conjectured to Lester.

Hardly had the GP gotten the words out of his mouth than the American "corpse" called out from the wreckage, "Get me out of here."

Merrick and Lester were startled. They helped the wounded man out of the wreckage. He told them that he indeed had shot the German and had himself been wounded. Crawling back into the twisted Waco to await medical attention, the gliderman had lost consciousness and had revived on hearing Merrick and Lester talking.

The landing zones were spiked with hundreds of sturdy wooden poles known as *Rommelspargel* (Rommel's asparagus), named after the famed German field marshal who had "invented" the fiendish antiglider obstacles prior to the Normandy invasion. To make it more difficult for gliders to land intact, attached to the poles were shells and mines primed to detonate on impact, and thick wires were stretched between each obstacle.

Many of Wood Joerg's parachutists were still on the landing zones when Sachs's gliders started to swoop in. Paratroop Maj. Ray "Pappy" Herrmann (so nicknamed because to the youthful parachutists he was "old"—all of thirty-four) had had some anxious moments getting down from what he called "the highest tree in France," then started dashing across a wide field to reach his battalion assembly area. All the time he was darting and weaving about, trying desperately to escape being struck by the gliders that were crash-landing on the same field. Many Wacos were ripped into splinters as they smashed into ditches, trees, and poles at ninety miles per hour.

From the wreckage of some gliders there was only silence; all aboard had been killed. From others came eerie shrieks and wails of mutilated men pinned where they lay.

As he worked his way across the field of death and destruction, hardbitten Ray Herrmann muttered to a companion: "I'll stick to parachutes!"

In one Waco, Lieutenant Colonel Sachs, leader of the 550th Glider Infantry, was hurled against the tubular wall separating the pilots from the soldiers, fracturing several of his ribs. The pain was excruciating as Sachs pulled himself from the wreckage. He ignored pleas to be evacuated for medical treatment, recovered his map case from the pile of canvas and aluminum, and headed for his CP to organize his battalion.

Technical Sergeant Ralph Wenthold of Joerg's 551st Parachute Infantry, who had landed in a fig tree and was carrying such heavy gear that the tree broke in two, watched in awe as one glider came down in the orchard, had its wings sheared off by two trees, smashed head-on into another larger tree, and disintegrated. Bodies seemed to fly in each direction. Wenthold did not go to the wreckage—he believed all the glidermen and pilots were dead.

Captain Jud Chalkley, the 551st Parachute Infantry doctor, had barely finished stitching up the posterior of the injured paratrooper when gliders started coming in. The flimsy crates were hitting large boulders, trees, and Rommelspargel. Chalkley hurried to where men were frantically pulling the pilots and copilots out of the cockpits, and the surgeon counted thirty-six compound leg fractures in that one area. He and other medical men began giving the GPs morphine and setting their breaks. Most of the leg injuries were hideous, with sharp pieces of bone protruding through the flesh. When the gliders had crash-landed and smashed into unyielding objects, the plastic fronts of the cockpits peeled back into the GP's legs.

* * *

IT WAS NEARLY dark when a jeep driver pulled into the CP of Lt. Col. Dick Seitz's battalion of the 517th Parachute Infantry Regimental Combat Team. The driver had been sent by Col. Rupert Graves to bring Maj. Tom Cross, Seitz's No. 2 man, who had broken an ankle in the jump, to Graves's CP at the Château Sainte Rosseline. Graves had arrived at the château by foot at noon that day and had been warmly received by the owner, Baron Rosque de Laval, and his family. The leader of the parachute regiment had been so exhausted after being on the go constantly for three days without sleep that when he lay down on the carpet to rest for a few minutes he promptly lapsed into deep slumber for two hours.

Arriving at the château after a ride in which he had carried his injured leg over the dashboard, Major Cross saw scores of dim forms stretched out on the grounds. These were glider pilots and men of Sachs's 551st Glider Infantry Battalion, who were being treated by a corps of medical men headed by the 517th Regiment surgeon, Maj. Paul Villa.

Cross hobbled into Colonel Graves's office, and the regimental commander greeted him with: "Well, Cross, if I had known you had broken only *one* ankle, I'd have had you walk here instead of sending my driver for you." Cross presumed the colonel was speaking in jest—or was he?

The Gray Eagle told the major that the regimental combat team seemed to have obtained its objectives for D-Day. Graves's paratroopers had taken La Motte and the high ground to its south and west and had a strong force astride the road leading from Draguignan to La Motte. Les Arcs was still in German hands, but 517th troopers had control of the roads south of that village.

"You're going to remain at my CP for a while," Graves told Cross. "You can take over some of Walton's and Pierce's duties." The regimental XO (executive officer), Lt. Col. Ike Walton; and the adjutant, Capt. Robert Pierce, had both been seriously injured on landing that morning.

A short time later, Colonel Graves and his operations officer, Maj. Forest Paxton, departed to make a jeep reconnaissance. This left Major Cross, a pinch-hitter, the only senior officer remaining at headquarters. Captain Richard A. Bigler, the 517th's communications officer, burst into Cross's room and stated, "Just got a report that a Kraut force of unknown strength is in the area and probably heading this way!"

Security at the CP that night consisted mainly of glider pilots who had worked their way there and were awaiting evacuation back to Italy. All during the hours of darkness the GPs had been firing at everything within sight or hearing, so Cross and Bigler decided that if the Germans were as afraid of being hit by the wildly shooting glider pilots as were the paratroopers at the site, then the 517th Regimental CP was relatively secure.

That night at his command post in a farmhouse outside Le Mitan, a short distance to the north of German-held Le Muy, Gen. Bob Frederick was intently analyzing results achieved on D-Day by his 1st Airborne Task Force. Preliminary field reports indicated that his force had suffered 450 casualties in killed, captured, and missing during the fighting, plus another 300 wounded. In addition, the actual parachute drops and glider landings had taken a toll of 290 men, most of those sustained by the 550th Glider Infantry Battalion and the GPs. The Wacos were virtually wiped out: Of the 404 gliders in the assault, only 45 of them were thought to be salvageable.

Despite the relatively severe casualties, Frederick was generally satisfied with the situation. Not only had his ten-thousand-man force landed in southern France, but also most of the units were organized and had seized their objectives. His airborne men had captured more than a thousand Germans, and hundreds of dead Feldgrau were sprawled about the fields, towns, and byways far behind the Côte d'Azur. No one had had the time to stop to count them.

General Frederick was keenly disappointed with one facet of the D-Day operation: The key crossroads town of Le Muy had not been promptly captured by the British 2nd Independent Parachute Brigade, as called for by the plan. Frederick was furious that the British brigade had not even tried to take Le Muy, although the Red Devils had dropped intact and were organized and in position just outside the town.

Late that afternoon General Frederick had engaged in a heated dispute with Brigadier Pritchard at a bridge outside Le Muy. Frederick demanded to know why the Red Devils had not gone in and taken Le Muy and was told by Pritchard that there were too many Germans in the town, that an attack would be costly. Returning to his CP at dusk, Frederick contacted Lt. Col. Edward Sachs, leader of the just-landed 550th Glider Infantry Battalion: "Ed, go into Le Muy in the morning and run the Krauts out of there!" At the same time, Frederick started the wheels rolling to return the 2nd Independent Parachute Brigade to Italy.*

IT WAS NEARING 9:00 P.M. when those on watch aboard the hundreds of vessels lying off Alpha, Delta, and Camel beaches spotted a flight of black-bodied Ju-88 bombers winging over the inland mountains and headed directly for the coastline. Onshore antiaircraft batteries opened a withering fire on the intruders, as did hundreds of machine guns and 40mm ack-ack guns on the vessels. *LST-282*, fully loaded with men and supplies, was struck by an electronically controlled glide bomb. The shattered vessel sank in shoal water; forty men were killed or wounded.

As night pulled its ominous cloak over the Riviera, an eerie silence had descended over the killing grounds. A heavy mist had returned to the beaches and caressed the shadowy hulks of ships offshore. On occasion a lone rifle shot or a short burst from a machine gun rent the night, and periodic explosions shook the ground as the Germans blew up their own ammunition dumps to keep them from falling into the invaders' hands. Unseen in the blackness, tens of thousands of exhausted Allied and Wehrmacht soldiers fell into fitful slumber, knowing that with the arrival of dawn the killing and mutilating would resume.

----

*Colonel Rupert Graves told the author in 1985: "The curious attitude of the British led us to conclude that Brigadier Pritchard had secret orders from General Jumbo Wilson to conserve the brigade's strength, as it was slated to go to the Balkans soon in support of British interests there. After five years of war, Great Britain was running short of manpower." No one ever questioned the fighting spirit of British paratroopers.

"The Worst Day of My Life!"

Twelve hundred miles from the flaming Riviera, in East Prussia, Adolf Hitler, supreme warlord of the Third Reich, was strangely subdued at the nightly strategy conference. The session had been in progress for nearly three hours—it was nearing midnight on August 15—and all during that time solemn-faced staff officers were dashing into the Wolfsschanze conference room with one piece of bad news after the other, from all the far-flung battlefronts.

So serious was the threat posed by the Allied onslaught against the Riviera that Col. Gen. Alfred Jodl, Hitler's closest military adviser, had risked the wrath of the German dictator by having him awakened early in the morning and advised of the developments in southern France. Hitler, who had been up most of the night, as was his custom, had merely snorted at the depressing revelation and gone back to sleep. Not even when the Allies cracked open the Atlantic Wall in Normandy two months previously had Jodl dared to awaken the Führer to tell him of the landings.

As the nightly conference droned on, Hitler's subordinates were shocked by his listless demeanor and lethargic approach to the catastrophes that were striking the Wehrmacht on all fronts.

The German dictator had developed a nervous twitch, possibly as the result of injuries he received less than a month before (on July 20) when a group of conspiring prominent German general staff and governmental leaders tried to murder him with a bomb blast. Gone was the old fire-eating, confident, decisive Führer; in his place was a man broken in spirit and body.

Hitler asked several questions about the Riviera invasion, but most of his focus was upon the battle raging in Normandy—and his missing *Oberbefehlshaber West* (commander-in-chief West), sixty-one-year-old, silver-haired Field Marshal Guenther von Kluge, whom only two years before the Führer had praised as "the savior of the Russian Front."

Von Kluge had been a marked man for three weeks. The Gestapo had presented indisputable evidence to Hitler that his Wehrmacht commander in the West had been deeply involved in the July 20 assassination plot. It would be only a matter of days before von Kluge was arrested, Hitler knew. But earlier on this D-Day for Dragoon, the field marshal had mysteriously disappeared.

Von Kluge had left early that morning to confer with two subordinate generals near the battlefront and had been out of contact with any headquarters since that time. The Führer was convinced that von Kluge was in the act of compounding his treachery by going over to the Allies and surrendering Wehrmacht armies in the West. Since arising at noon that day, Hitler had repeatedly demanded to know: "Any word on von Kluge yet?"

Always the answer had been the same: "*Nein, mein Führer.*"*

Hitler was beset with other monumental worries on this fifteenth day of August. The Russian Army had torn a massive hole in German lines and was pouring through men, tanks, and assault guns; Eisenhower's armies in Normandy had shattered Wehrmacht defenses in an enormous offensive; and American tanks were racing virtually unchecked toward the Reich. Piled on top of these monumental and seemingly unsolvable woes was a continuing stream of reports from southern France of Allied successes there.

---

*Field Marshal von Kluge reappeared late that night. He had been driving around the front all day unsuccessfully seeking to make contact with some high Allied commander in order to surrender his forces. Ordered to report to Berlin, von Kluge halted his car near Metz on August 18 and killed himself by taking poison.

At this point, Adolf Hitler came as close to despair as General Jodl, Field Marshal Wilhelm Keitel, and other subordinates had ever seen him. And they had been at his elbow for five years of war. Almost inaudibly, the shaken Hitler muttered: *"This has been the worst day of my life!"*

Hitler sat hunched over in a chair as General Jodl read a long litany of gloomy reports on the southern France invasion that day. The Führer listened in silence. Grim-faced generals around the conference table inwardly braced for the customary raging outbursts by the supreme warlord in which he would denounce in red-faced fury the "cowardly and incompetent" generals who "permitted" the Allied landings to gain a toehold. But Hitler remained impassive.

When Jodl had finished his depressing summary of events along the Riviera, all present expected the usual shouted exhortations by the Führer to defend each foot of ground to the last man and the last bullet. But no such ringing pronouncements were forthcoming. Now the generals realized the reason for his apparent apathy toward momentous events along his Fortress Europe's South Wall: Hitler had moved into a sort of fantasy world, one divorced from reality; he had convinced himself that the Wehrmacht in southern France could throw the powerful Allied invaders back into the Mediterranean Sea.

Yet at the conclusion of the conference, Adolf Hitler rose from his chair and calmly announced that he was ready to consider whatever measures were necessary in the event the situation in France continued to deteriorate. The generals were dumbfounded. After months of demanding that every foot of ground in the West be held at all costs, that key ports and fortresses be held regardless of cost, the supreme warlord had executed a complete about-face—he was ready to pull back the entire Wehrmacht in France to the Siegfried Line along the German border.

AT HIS OFFICE along the Unter den Linden in drab, bomb-battered Berlin, Nazi propaganda genius Dr. Paul Josef Goebbels had been wrestling all day with a communications problem of great magnitude: how to explain to the *Herrenvolk* (master-race civilians) and members of the armed forces the massive invasion of Hitler's Riviera. After five years of war and deprivations, both the home front and the troops had grown weary. For the past two years they had been fed a steady diet of reversals and retreats on three fronts, and the homeland lay in ruins from hundreds of visits by American and British bombers. How much more catastrophic news could the German people and fighting men absorb without revolting?

The diminutive Goebbels, cunning and slavish in his worship of Adolf Hitler, shortly before midnight of August 15 flashed the "line" to be followed by Third Reich newspapers and radio stations, all of which were under his strict control. In the morning the media would publish highly fanciful accounts on the American paratroop force that was wiped out while trying to seize Marseilles (this was the six hundred diversionary dummies dropped north of the port) and the bloody repulsing of an Allied attempt to land along the Bay of La Ciotat (this was Commander John Bulkeley's tiny flotilla of speedboats cavorting about in the bay).

SHORTLY AFTER MIDNIGHT on D-Day plus one, the town of Le Muy lay dark, ghostlike, and mute. Le Muy was a prime objective of Operation Rugby, the airborne attack by Gen. Bob Frederick's men, but around the battered collection of buildings and houses nearly a thousand Feldgrau, backed by antitank guns, mortars, and automatic weapons, were dug in and waiting. Gen. Ferdinand Neuling, commander of the LXII Corps, had earlier foreseen the town's strategic value and had posted a large force there. Through Le Muy ran a north-south hard-surfaced road leading to the American landing beaches some twelve miles to the south.

At a villa less than a half mile outside Le Muy, Lt. Col. Ed Sachs, commander of the 550th Glider Infantry Battalion, had been hurriedly drawing up plans for attacking the town. The mission had been taken away from the British parachute brigade late the previous afternoon and assigned to the Five and a Half, as the battalion called itself. New to combat and about ready to launch their first coordinated attack, Sach's men in the CP were nervous about being so close to the German positions in the town.

"Hell, this ain't no goddamned CP," one gliderman said with a snort. "It's an OP [observation post]!"

Tension in Colonel Sachs's villa heightened during the hours of darkness, when it became dramatically evident that the situation around Le Muy was a fluid one indeed. Carefully concealed German snipers had been firing into the CP from the rear, while other marksmen were peppering the front of the structure from the direction of Le Muy.

Jump-off time for the attack on the town was set for 2:30 A.M. When it was time to depart the CP, Sgt. Joseph Olexy began to round up his message center personnel in the sprawling villa, which was lighted only by the flickers of two candles. Spotting a still form covered by a blanket and seated in a chair, Olexy shook the figures and shouted, ''Get up, you lazy bastard! We're moving out!'' The figure did not budge. Olexy lighted a match to see who the person was, and drew back. It was a dead German.

At 2:15 A.M. three 105mm howitzers fired on Le Muy for fifteen minutes, and then the glider battalion jumped off to seize the town. With two companies abreast and one in reserve, the Five and a Half moved through British positions along the Naturby River and approached the silent, blacked-out town. Hoping to obtain surprise, the assault troops did not fire a shot. Suddenly the peace was shattered. From within the rubble on the edge of town, German automatic weapons opened a withering fire against the glidermen, who were out in the open and devoid of cover. It was clear that Le Muy was heavily defended. The Americans, still being raked by streams of tracer bullets, pulled back to reorganize and prepare for a daylight assault on Le Muy.

Considerable chaos ensued in the pullback. Several Germans behind the withdrawing glidermen were shot, and a spirited firefight erupted between a company of Americans marching along a road and glidermen pulling back through an adjoining field, each believing the other group to be Germans.

Reorganized and strengthened by other glidermen joining the battalion, Colonel Sachs's men jumped off again at 11:40 A.M. Wheezing under the heavy burden of combat gear, weapons, and ammunition, and perspiring profusely in their wool ODs under a hot Mediterranean sun, the glidermen waded the knee-deep Naturby and headed south across open fields toward German-held Le Muy. Three hundred yards south of the river a German outpost was wiped out, the men of the Five and a Half pushed on into the first buildings of the town, and a house-to-house battle erupted.

A member of the French Underground slipped up to Lt. Paul Egan along a bullet-swept street and pointed toward a house.

"Boche!" he exclaimed. Egan dispatched four men to the structure, and they captured seven German captains and a colonel hiding in the basement, while releasing an American paratroop officer and a glider pilot who had been captured and were being held there.

When the Wehrmacht aid station in the center of town was overrun, thirty-three wounded Feldgrau and six medics were taken into captivity. In the center of Le Muy stood an ancient church, and its steeple drew much attention. From that lofty point the Germans could view the fields over which the glidermen had advanced and in the other direction could see clear to the Côte d'Azur. The Americans killed several German observers in the steeple, and whenever a shot rang out in Le Muy the steeple was fired on by every American within range of it.

Apparently unaware that the steeple held an ominous fascination for his comrades, a soldier named Paul A. Stinner decided to climb up into the pinnacle to have a look around. A shot rang out in the town, and split seconds later the steeple was peppered with American bullets. Stinner was shot in the arm.

By midafternoon, Le Muy was solidly in American hands. More than seven hundred Germans were captured in the town, and perhaps three hundred more were killed or wounded. In the greater scheme of things, the capture of Le Muy received no monumental acclaim. The next day it would receive a sentence in a roundup story on the invasion in Stateside newspapers. But to the men of Ed Sachs's 550th Glider Infantry Battalion, the capture of the key town was of the utmost significance—it was their very own victory.

THAT MORNING AT advanced headquarters of SHAEF (Supreme Headquarters, Allied Expeditionary Force), code-named Shellburst and located in a tent complex on the Normandy peninsula south of the port of Cherbourg, Allied Supreme Commander Dwight Eisenhower donned his wire-rimmed spectacles to read a telegram from the British Bulldog, Winston Churchill:

> I watched the [Riviera] landing yesterday from afar. All I have learnt there makes me admire the perfect precision with which the landing was arranged and the intimate collaboration of British-American forces . . . It seems to me that the results [in France as a whole] might well eclipse all the Russian victories.

At dawn of D-Day plus one, S. Sgt. Paul Roberson of Cedartown, Georgia, was emerging from the effects of morphine administered to help relieve the excruciating pain from two broken ankles received when he jumped the previous day with the 596th Parachute Combat Engineer Company. After wandering in extreme pain for two hours after the parachute jump, Roberson came upon a medic who gave him first aid and ordered his evacuation. In his fuzzy-minded condition, the blond, fair-complexioned sergeant recalled that he had been brought to a hospital ship lying offshore, but as he looked around the ward at some thirty wounded men stretched out on litters, all seemed to be wearing the gray-green uniform of the German Wehrmacht. And when they spoke to each other, it was definitely in the German language.

Roberson was confused. Am I having hallucinations? he reflected. Or had the American hospital vessel been sunk and had he been taken prisoner while unconscious?

Only later would Sergeant Roberson learn what had happened. With his almost yellow hair, fair complexion, his uniform soiled and torn, black camouflage paint streaking his face, and his coveted jump boots missing to relieve the stress on his broken ankles, Roberson had been mistaken for an enemy soldier by Navy medics and placed in the German ward.

When a Navy doctor stopped to treat the American, Roberson asked, "What in the hell am I doing here?"

Ignoring the question, the physician asked one of his own: "Where did you learn to speak such good English?"

Roberson snapped: "Cedartown, Georgia, by God!"

EARLY ON D-DAY plus one, Col. Rupert Graves, leader of the 517th Parachute Infantry, was outside his CP in the Château Sainte-Rosseline when he spotted one of his troopers driving up to the mansion in a large, black German car built rakishly low to the ground. The parachutist was grinning broadly as he leaped out of the luxury vehicle and turned it over to Colonel Graves. "A present from Major [Wild Bill] Boyle and the first battalion, sir," the proud trooper declared.

It was a welcome gift, as the 517th had only two vehicles, and Graves needed transportation to visit the regimental units and to get written reports to Gen. Bob Frederick at Le Mitan.

The automobile, the soldier explained, had been captured by a 1st Battalion platoon under Lieutenant Rearden. Rearden had set up a block on the road leading into Le Muy. Minutes later the German car came along and halted at the roadblock, and the neatly groomed officers inside gave the Hitler salute to the American paratroopers, mistaking them for German soldiers. Unimpressed by the salute, one of Rearden's men fired a rifle grenade at the car, striking one of the Germans in the head. In his excitement the soldier had forgotten to arm the grenade, however, and the missile did not explode. But the grenade split open the enemy officer's head, and he slumped over onto the floor in the rear in the vehicle.

Realizing their momentous mistake, the other Germans scrambled out of the big black automobile and dashed for the nearby woods. A fusillade of American rifle and Tommy-gun fire cut them down. From a lone survivor Lieutenant Rearden learned that the car belonged to the Gestapo officers now sprawled about in death. They were on their way from Marseilles into the interior of France, and when they reached Rearden's roadblock they could not believe that Americans could be in position fifteen miles inland in the heart of the Wehrmacht's defensive zone.

Now Colonel Graves peeked into the back seat. It was a mess, full of blood, and what looked like brains were scattered around on the floor.

"I would say that these Gestapo gentlemen's car is quite untidy," Graves remarked drily to the trooper who had driven in with the vehicle.

"Colonel, don't worry about that," the soldier replied breezily. With that he emptied a clip from his Tommy gun into the rear-seat floor, permitting the blood to drain out.

"See," the triumphant parachutist declared with a trace of pride in his voice, "it's as good as new, Colonel!"

THAT MORNING GEN. Aime Sudre, leader of the French 1st Armored Combat Command, was peering through a thin haze toward the beaches from a troop transport lying offshore. Sudre, along with his intense inner excitement over his imminent return to France, was a worried and frustrated man. He had been advised by Gen. Lucian Truscott that the French armored force could not land in the 36th Infantry Division's zone as planned, as Camel Red Beach and its sea approaches had not been cleared of mines. Instead of going ashore on their homeland at Saint-Maxime on the right of the invasion beaches, General Sudre and his tankers would be sideslipped seven miles to the left and land on the Delta beaches that had been assaulted by Eagle's 45th Infantry Division. Months of tedious and detailed planning by General Sudre and other high-ranking French officers had suddenly gone down the drain due to the vicissitudes of war.

The French armored leader's concern over the switch in landing beaches soon evaporated; his force went ashore at Delta without mishap or confusion. As they stepped onto the soil of their homeland, Sudre's men, as though on cue, conducted a ceremonial ritual. Tears welled in the eyes of the long-exiled French warriors as each scooped up handfuls of soil or kneeled to kiss the golden sands of the Côte d'Azur.

At 9:00 A.M. on D-Day plus one, a covey of Allied brass hopped out of an LCVP onto the beach near La Nartelle. In the official party were Adm. Kent Hewitt, commander of Dragoon's naval force; Gen. Alexander Patch of the Seventh Army; Adm. André Lemonnier, chief of staff of the French Navy; and low-keyed, taciturn Jim Forrestal, secretary of the U.S. Navy.

Only the evening before, Forrestal had been on Port-Cros, the island off Cap Negre where elements of the 1st Special Service Force under Lieutenant Colonel Akehurst had been engaged in an all day fight with a stubborn band of some sixty Germans who were deeply burrowed into concrete fortifications and who refused to be rooted out. Forrestal had insisted on visiting Port-Cros, where, calm, cool, and collected, he sat on the ground under the shade of a tree near where Akehurst's perspiring troops were battling the entrenched Germans. He spent nearly two hours watching the fierce fight.

Now at La Nartelle, as Allied soldiers and sailors stared at the glittering collection of gold braid and shining silver stars, Hewitt, Patch, Forrestal, and Lemonnier climbed into two jeeps, and with armed escorts in front and back set off inland in a cloud of dust. As the vehicles crawled through the debris-littered streets of Saint-Raphael, the smiling, hulking Kent Hewitt ordered the procession to halt. Hundreds of civilians, frightened, confused, dazed by the massive bombardment that had struck their once-peaceful town, were cautiously peering out from windows and doorways. Only a few hours previously, heavy street fighting had taken place in Saint-Raphael.

Admiral Hewitt, still grinning broadly, stood up in the jeep and pointed at Lemonnier. Recognizing the admiral's French naval cap, the civilians threw caution to the winds and surged out into the street, cheering and shouting with delirious abandon. Lemonnier, choking with emotion and with tears running down his ruddy cheeks, made a short speech. There was such a din of excited voices that no one heard what the French admiral had to say. It made no difference; the ecstatic civilians lustily cheered every sentence.

Above the turmoil, a woman's voice was heard singing the long-forbidden "Marseillaise." Hundreds of other tearful men and women joined in, and the stirring strains of the French national anthem echoed for great distances over battered Saint-Raphael. Hewitt and Patch, each hard-bitten and tough-minded, wiped moisture from their eyes. Jim Forrestal remained expressionless.

ELSEWHERE ALONG THE Riviera that morning, Allied mine-sweeping vessels and naval demolition teams were feverishly at work sweeping the Gulf of Fréjus. The project had high priority—until Toulon and Marseilles were captured, which would require at least two weeks, the Gulf of Fréjus beaches would be the principal supply route for the entire southern France force.

German engineers, skilled and diabolical, had done their work well. Not only were the mines thickly sown, both on the beaches and underwater, but also the minecraft encountered difficulties from anticutting devices, including chain moorings with attachments that fouled the sweep gear. Obstacles under the water surface, mainly mined concrete tetrahedra, were blown up by the naval demolition teams—a perilous assignment. The entire sweep of beach was booby-trapped and Teller-mined.

Three magnetic-sweeping vessels blew up five large underwater mines, then turned seaward to make another run toward the beach. There was an enormous explosion that echoed across the calm waters of the Gulf of Fréjus. One of the minecraft had hit a contact mine, and the force of the detonation hurled the boat's anchor from the forecastle (front) to the bridge, where it chopped down the skipper, Navy Lt. Samuel R. Pruett. The forward third of the boat had been blown away but, like a chicken scampering around the barnyard after its head had been cut off, the minecraft made two large circles out of control before her engines started to sputter and finally died.

Seeing the plight of the American vessel, the skipper of a British minecraft, Lt. Comdr. C. H. Pearse, ordered his boat to hurry up to help, but she also hit a mine, and the entire rear section was blown off. Commander Pearse was seriously wounded.

Minutes later, while the feverish minesweeping was going full tilt, naval personnel watched in amazement as two American PT boats suddenly raced into the mine-infested gulf and ignored frantic signals to halt or turn back. Instead, the swift torpedo boats burrowed on toward the shore, traveling at open throttle. There were two enormous explosions as each PT boat hit an underwater mine. One man was killed, six were wounded, and the sleek, speedy vessels sunk to the bottom. The survivors paddled ashore in rubber boats, where they told inquiring naval officers that they had been, curiously, "looking for fuel."

AT A GESTAPO building in Digne that noon of August 16, three haggard, bloody prisoners, each condemned to die as a "spy and terrorist," were silently awaiting their doom in a stifling, hot, dark cell. One of the disheveled captives was Lt. Col. Francis Cammaerts (code name, Roger) of the SOE (Special Operations Executive), the British cloak-and-dagger agency. Roger was the SOE's master spy in southeastern France, had been in charge of scores of secret agents parachuted into the Riviera region in recent months, and had directed the activities of countless cells of the French Underground.

With Roger in the suffocating lockup and awaiting the ominous footsteps of the executioner were another British officer, Xan Fielding (code name, Cathedrale), and Major André Sorensen, a French officer working covertly for the American OSS. All had been captured by eagle-eyed Gestapo agents four days before when, traveling as French businessmen and government officials, their car was halted at a roadblock in Digne.

Roger's arrest could not have come at a worse time—on the eve of Dragoon.

The three condemned men now felt a surge of fear as the massive door to their cell clanked open and a man in the uniform of a German SS officer beckoned them to follow him. "This is the end," each spy thought. But why did the normally cautious Germans send only one officer to escort three dangerous and desperate terrorists to the firing squad? And the SS man was armed with only a Luger, and it was in its black-leather holster.

Roger, Cathedrale, and the French officer marched apprehensively along a corridor with the SS man behind them. Instead of turning to the left in the direction of a courtyard where several rifle volleys had been heard, the three Allied spies were astonished to be ordered to turn right, toward the front door of the Gestapo building. At the gate were two sharp-eyed SS guards, and the German officer snarled at his captives, "Keep moving you sons-of-bitches!"

As they trekked through the doorway into the bright sunshine that made the prisoners squint, a shudder ran up Roger's spinal cord. Clearly he and his two companions were not to be accorded a quick, merciful death by a firing squad's bullets; no doubt the diabolical Gestapo had special treatment in mind for them—a lingering, excruciatingly painful death.

Outside, the spies were told to climb into a car in which a stone-faced civilian was seated in the front seat. The SS officer got behind the wheel and drove out into the countryside. Roger and his companions were flabbergasted. What was going on? Their intense bewilderment heightened when they drove up to a car parked alongside the road and spotted a tall, shapely young woman standing next to it. Roger immediately recognized her—she was the Lady in Red, a mysterious figure whose background was unknown but who had been working with Roger for many weeks.

The civilian remained in the Gestapo car, but the German officer scrambled out and accompanied the three stupefied prisoners to the other vehicle. The spies got into the car, the Lady in Red climbed into the front seat beside a grim driver, and the car sped away, leaving the Gestapo officer standing in the center of the road and eating a cloud of dust.

Only when the getaway car was several miles down the road did the Lady in Red begin to unfold the story of the miraculous escape. The Gestapo officer was not a Gestapo officer, but rather a Belgian who had been serving as an interpreter for the dreaded police agency. He was known only as Max. The secretive civilian who had been seated in the Gestapo car was known only as Captain X. He was a member of the hated Milice, the French police force that worked hand-in-glove with the Nazis.

When the Lady in Red, whom Roger thought to be of Spanish birth, had learned that her chief and his two lieutenants had been seized by the Gestapo in Digne on August 12, she knew there was only one remote hope for saving them: bribery. She immediately contacted her superiors in North Africa, told them of the plight of Roger and the other two spies, and asked for money for the purpose. That same night some $250,000 was parachuted in to her.

Utilizing her keen intellect and feminine wiles, the Lady in Red singled out Max and Captain X as the targets for her bribery. If she guessed wrong as to their loyalty—or lack of loyalty—to the Nazi cause, she herself would be doomed. After a series of tense and secretive negotiations in which the $250,000 carrot was dangled from a figurative stick in front of their greedy faces, Max and Captain X agreed to cooperate.*

Now, as the escape car roared along a rural road, Roger asked, "Where are we heading?"

"I've got a 'safe house' for you far inland," the mysterious woman replied.

"Oh, no!" Roger declared. "Turn around and head for the beaches. I want to meet the Allies!"

---

*The fate of the $250,000 was never learned. A few days later, Captain X was found dead in a field outside Digne under mysterious circumstances. After the war Max said that Captain X had been given the money for safekeeping and that he had never given Max a penny of it.

Urgent: Seize Les Arcs

At his CP in the Château Sainte-Rosseline on the afternoon of D-Day plus one, Col. Rupert Graves, commander of the 517th Parachute Infantry, was beset with a nagging concern. The key road center of Les Arcs, where Wild Bill Boyle and his band of fifty troopers of the 1st Battalion had engaged in a fierce fight the day before, was still in German hands. Graves contacted Lt. Col. Dick Seitz, commander of the 2nd Battalion, who had assembled most of his men north of Les Arcs. Graves told him, "Get on down there right away and give Bill Boyle a hand. We've got to grab Les Arcs!"

Even by the afternoon of the second day of the southern France invasion, the tactical situation inland from the landing beaches remained cloudy and confused. Due to the nature of the parachute and glider business in the early hours of an assault, portions of battalions, companies, platoons, and squads were often fighting as autonomous units. All had one goal in mind—seek out and destroy the Germans.

Within minutes of receiving the urgent order from the Gray Eagle, Colonel Seitz had his battalion marching toward Les Arcs, some three miles away. It was more than just a military mission to Dick Seitz—his good friend Wild Bill Boyle was facing numerically superior forces there and was in danger of being overwhelmed. Perspiring profusely under the fierce glare of the boiling Mediterranean sun, Seitz's battalion reached the outskirts of German-held Les Arcs, where the troopers dug in while patrols were sent forward to probe enemy positions.

Prowling around his front lines, Colonel Seitz heard the angry chatter of German machine guns and saw several of his men racing toward a vineyard seventy-five yards to the front. There they grabbed bunches of grapes, then spun around and dashed back for their own positions as bullets kicked up the dust at their heels. Grinning triumphantly, the winded parachutists leaped back into their foxholes.

Seitz realized that his high-spirited troopers had risked their lives not so much to retrieve juicy grapes as to taunt and show their contempt for the Germans. But he was furious; the prank could have ended in the needless deaths of the participants. But when none of his men was hit, he took a more philosophical view of the offbeat antics. By firing at the grape-stealers, the German machine-gun crews had given away their positions. Seitz called for mortar fire, which plastered the terrain on the far side of the vineyard, and soon the enemy's automatic weapons fell silent.

By the time Colonel Seitz's patrols returned from reconnoitering enemy positions, night had started to draw its ominous cloak over the battlegrounds. In order to avoid the inevitable confusion of an attack in the darkness, the 2nd Battalion commander decided to assault Les Arcs at daybreak. He contacted Lt. Loren S. James, commander of D Company, and told him, "You are going to spearhead our attack at 0600 [6:00 A.M.]."

Meanwhile, at about 4:00 P.M. that same day, Lt. Col. Mel Zais and a column of troopers of his 3rd Battalion wearily trudged into their assembly area adjacent to the Château Sainte-Rosseline. Their two-day, twenty-five-mile trek had been a brutal one. The route had taken them up one mountain and down the other. Along the way they had been bombed and strafed by "friendly" aircraft; had stopped periodically to battle German bands; and were burdened with heavy combat gear, weapons, and extra ammunition. Carrying several injured and wounded comrades had slowed their pace, and the hot sun beating down on them had sapped their strength.

Colonel Rupert Graves had seen Mel Zais and his exhausted men staggering into the grounds of the Château Sainte-Rosseline and told his battalion commander, "Take your men into those woods over there and let them rest overnight. The

Krauts still have Les Arcs, and I'm going to send your battalion down there in the morning to help take it.''

Zais and his tired troopers would have a short-lived "rest." Colonel Graves contacted the 1st Airborne Task Force commander, Gen. Bob Frederick, at Le Mitan to discuss the situation at Les Arcs. It was decided that Zais's battalion would attack immediately toward Les Arcs in spite of their fatigue, with the intention of linking up with Lieutenant Colonel Seitz's troopers in the assault on the key road center.

Rupert Graves immediately contacted Zais, who by now was relaxing with his boots off under the spreading branches of a towering pine tree. "Mel," Graves began matter-of-factly, "there's been a slight change in plans. You are to attack and join with Bill [Boyle] and Dick [Seitz] in seizing Les Arcs.''

Colonel Zais winced briefly. "When do we jump off?" he inquired.

"Eighteen hundred [6:00 P.M.]," Graves replied.

Zais took a hurried peek at his watch. His exhausted men's overnight rest had been compressed to thirty minutes.

As time neared for Colonel Zais and his men to push forward up a valley cut with numerous gullies and ditches, which would provide excellent concealment for enemy machine gunners and riflemen, Rupert Graves moved to an adjoining hill to observe the jump-off for Les Arcs. Graves had told his commanders that since the amphibious attack seemed to have been successful and supplies were pouring ashore, a maximum amount of mortar shells could be used in preparatory fire.

Promptly at 6:00 P.M., the valley echoed and reechoed with the roar as a company of 4.2-inch mortars cut loose with seven hundred rounds of WP (white phosphorus). These WP shells were even more frightening and damaging to those on the receiving end than were high-explosive rounds. On impact, thousands of fiery phosphorous particles gushered into the air and cascaded down onto unprotected foot soldiers, even coming right into their foxholes after them.

Landing on an enemy soldier's skin or in his clothing, the WP particle could not be extinguished by water; only earth would smother it, and by that time the Feldgrau had become a major casualty. The Germans long before had learned to fear the phosphorus fired by the 4.2-inch mortars (commonly called four-point-twos), and the Reich did not have the minerals to retaliate in kind.

The entire valley ahead of Colonel Zais's attacking troopers was blanketed with thick clouds of smoke from the bursting four-point-two rounds. From his vantage point on the hill, Colonel Graves was awed by the enormous bombardment carried out by the mortar crews who had landed in gliders the previous day. Graves turned to an officer and remarked, "I don't see how any German can be left under all that WP!"

The mortar firing ceased and the smoke clouds began to dissipate, but when H Company, led by Capt. Marvin D. Morris, moved forward, the abrasive chatter of German machine guns rolled across the valley as bursts tore into the leading troopers. Just after scrambling over a railroad embankment, Lieutenant Freeman and 1st Sergeant Caunce were killed by the automatic-weapons fire. But Zais's battalion pushed ahead against sporadic opposition and by nightfall had dug in on its objective for the day, the high ground south of Les Arcs.

IT WAS NEARING midnight when Lt. Col. James Critchfield's battalion of the 36th Infantry Division dug in for a short rest near La Napoule, on the road to Cannes. The Texans were exhausted after two days and a night of almost continuous marching and fighting.

General Dahlquist's Texas army had been pushing eastward along the Côte d'Azur in the direction of Cannes and Nice. VI Corps commander Lucian Truscott was intent on capturing these two world-renowned resort cities for reasons more psychological than military, although the docks at Nice would be useful to the invaders' cause. It would be humiliating to Adolf Hitler to have the Wehrmacht chased out of these two famous communities.

As Colonel Critchfield's Texans fell into fitful slumber, large-caliber shells began screaming into their positions. German batteries on Île Sainte-Marguerite off Cannes had zeroed in on Critchfield's men.

A hurried call was put through to General Dahlquist, who in turn radioed Adm. Mort Deyo, gunnery commander of the warships offshore. The energetic Deyo, who distinguished himself during the Normandy invasion by regularly rushing in close to the coastline to knock out German batteries, ordered most of his Camel Beach gunfire forces to rush eastward to silence the island batteries and other German strongpoints in and around Cannes.

Responding to the urgent order, the destroyer *McLanahan* dashed boldly into the dark Gulf of Napoule near Cannes to draw German fire and locate the big guns. Minutes later, lightninglike flashes illuminated the seascape and coastline as German guns on the Île Sainte-Marguerite opened fire on the *McLanahan*. The destroyer promptly fired back, and after an intense duel of some thirty minutes, the German battery fell silent.

Now other warships had spotted gun flashes and began pounding enemy positions—and were pounded in return. The destroyer *Tuscaloosa* was straddled by batteries located in thick-walled bunkers near the famous Cannes casino. The French destroyer *Emile Bertin* and the *Brooklyn* joined in the exchange of large-caliber shells. Crewmen on a third destroyer, the *Champlin*, cheered boisterously as one of her antiaircraft projectiles struck a Ju-88 that had attempted to bomb her; the Luftwaffe aircraft exploded in a brilliant flash of orange.

By dawn, silence had returned to the Côte d'Azur off the gambling and resort center of Cannes. But dogfaces of Jim Critchfield's battalion had gotten little sleep and soon would be climbing wearily out of foxholes to continue the attack toward Cannes and Nice.

SIXTY-FIVE MILES west of the big-gun shoot-out at Cannes and Île Sainte-Marguerite, a small flotilla of Allied vessels had slipped into position near La Ciotat, where Lt. Comdr. John Bulkeley on *Endicott* and fifteen PT boats and motor launches had deceived the Germans about the invaders' intentions forty-eight hours earlier. Now *Endicott* was back again, along with British destroyers *Scarab* and *Aphis* and seventeen PT boats. It was 1:15 P.M. on August 17.

This was to be an encore of the previous *ruse de guerre* to convince Wehrmacht commanders that the Allies were yet going to make a supporting amphibious assault along the Bay of La Ciotat. The three destroyers began to bombard the coast as the PT boats dashed about to give the impression on German radar that a large Allied naval force was maneuvering offshore.

At 5:45 A.M. Commander Bulkeley received an urgent call for help: two British gunboats reported that they were under attack by two Nazi corvettes, were badly damaged, and in imminent danger of sinking. One British vessel was out of ammunition, the other's fire control system was out, and it had no electric power. *Endicott* raced to the scene at full throttle. Once a PT-boat fighter, always one. That was John Bulkeley's motto. He would fight his destroyer just like a PT boat.

Bulkeley merely shrugged his shoulders when told that *Endicott* had fired so long and steadily at German gun batteries around La Ciotat that three of his four five-inch guns were red hot, too hot to be of use when *Endicott* closed with the German warships. Bulkeley had a simple solution: "Then we'll fire with the one gun we have!"

Endicott dashed through a thick pall of smoke to three thousand yards (virtually point-blank range) when the pair of enemy ships were spotted. They were the corvettes (slightly smaller than a destroyer) *Kemid Allah,* a converted Egyptian yacht with three-inch guns, and the *Capaiulo,* with four point seven-inch guns. Bulkeley promptly ordered: "Commence firing!" (meaning the one gun). Nothing happened. "Commence firing!" he repeated. Again nothing happened. The skipper hastily scribbled a note and rushed it down: "*Please open fire.*"

After three minutes the single gun barked—but not in the usual rapid tempo. The crew had given up trying to repair the rammer and began hand loading. During the engagement, Seaman Leonard C. Barge of Sutherland, Oregon, loaded eighty shells until his burned hands looked like raw hamburger, and his mates closed the breechblock with sledge hammers. The improvised procedure was fraught with peril; the shells might have exploded at any moment.*

Hand-loading meant a rate of fire of only one shell a minute, but the third and fourth missiles crashed into the 1,600-ton *Kemid Allah's* engine room, stopping her dead. *Endicott* took out after the *Capaiulo,* which tried to flee. Now eleven-inch shells from German shore batteries were splashing around the American destroyer. She dodged out of several straddles, then took a direct hit on a forward turret. The only casualty was a bluejacket knocked unconscious.

Another eleven-incher crashed into *Endicott* and came to rest on a bunk—a dud. It was still smoking when Carpenter's Mate 1/C Lewis Fisher of Meridian, Mississippi, bundled it in a

---

*John Bulkeley, who is still on active duty as a two-star admiral working out of the Pentagon, told the author in late 1985: "Loading the gun that way required enormous courage. It was practically suicide."

blanket, carried it on deck, and threw it overboard. Both of Fisher's hands were badly burned. The *Endicott* and the *Capaiulo* traded two torpedoes each, all misses, as the American ship rushed in to fifteen hundred yards—PT-boat range.

John Bulkeley ordered his 40mm. antiaircraft guns to open fire, and they swept *Capaiulo's* decks clear of Germans. Then *Endicott* bored in to eight hundred yards—popgun range—and her lone five-inch gun boomed. The German ship was rocked by the shell and burst into flame. Now Bulkeley's attention returned to the *Kemid Allah,* and a five-incher sent her to the bottom at 7:09 A.M. *Capaiulo* suffered a lingering death before it too plunged to the bottom at 8:32 A.M.

"Well, hell," John Bulkeley snorted as he watched the *Capaiulo* slip beneath the waves. "I wanted to board her as a prize of war!"

By boats and by lines from the *Endicott's* deck, 164 of Adolf Hitler's sailors and five officers, including both captains, were fished from the water. After escorting the crippled British gunboats from the battle area, John Bulkeley conferred with Douglas Fairbanks. "It was just like an old Hollywood thriller, with the cavalry charging to the rescue at the last moment," screen idol Fairbanks exclaimed.

AT DRAGUIGNAN ON the night of D-Day plus one, two German generals were trying frantically to contact their scattered units—without success. On the northwest outskirts of the picturesque town, with a peacetime population of ten thousand, was the headquarters of Gen. Ferdinand Neuling's LXII Corps. It was on a mountainside and surrounded by barbed-wire entanglements and minefields, and at intervals there were machine-gun posts. As the clock struck 9:00 P.M. in Neuling's office, he reflected that he was like a trapped animal with no hope of escape and no control over his own destiny. On all sides he could hear occasional small-arms fire, which meant the "hunters"—American paratroopers—were closing in on their quarry.

His communications snarled or nonexistent, the calm, courtly Neuling did not know that the Führer had reluctantly signed orders calling for the Wehrmacht's withdrawal from France, except for key fortress ports, which were to be held at all costs. Aware that his situation was hopeless and that he was in personal jeopardy from American parachute troops outside

Draguignan, the corps commander still firmly resolved to carry out Adolf Hitler's edict—fight to the last man and the last bullet. Come what may, Neuling was determined to give a good account of himself. He was an officer in the German Army, had taken a blood oath of loyalty to the Führer of the Third Reich, and his personal honor was at stake.

About two miles from where General Neuling was barricaded in his den on the slope of a mountain, a subordinate, Maj. Gen. Ludwig Bieringer, was holed up in his headquarters building in the heart of Draguignan. Haughty and aloof, the essence of the Prussian military tradition, including the affectation of a monocle, Bieringer held the title of district commander, reporting directly to the LXII Corps commander.

One of General Bieringer's tasks was to defend Draguignan. But he had no illusion that this could be done. At his disposal in the town were some 750 troops of uneven fighting spirit and ability, and there was no hope for reinforcements. On the afternoon of D-Day, thirty hours previously, Bieringer had made radio contact with a first-rate Wehrmacht regiment some twenty-five miles to the east and ordered that unit to rush to Draguignan to defend the town against encircling American paratroopers. Bieringer had not heard from the regiment since. With his communications knocked out, his radios jammed by Allied devices in ships offshore, General Bieringer had no way of knowing that the relief regiment he expected to arrive at any minute had not moved an inch; it had been pinned down by massive warship bombardment, attacked by swarms of Jabos, and was battling for its life against bands of roving, black-faced Allied paratroopers and American infantrymen who had come in over the beaches.

ABOUT TWO AND one-half miles south of the German stronghold of Draguignan at 9:00 P.M. on August 16, Maj. Pappy Herrmann, executive officer of the 551st Parachute Infantry Battalion, was poring over casualty reports. His concentration was interrupted when Capt. Edward Hartman, G-2 (Intelligence officer) of Wood Joerg's parachute battalion, excitedly burst into the CP.

"Where's the Old Man?" Hartman inquired in an urgent tone, referring to the battalion commander.

"He left with Tims Quinn [operations officer] about an hour ago to inspect forward positions."

"Well, I've received info that the Krauts had pulled out of Draguignan and that the civilians put up a hell of a lot of French flags and launched a wild demonstration in the streets. Now the Krauts are coming back into Draguignan, and they'll sure as hell take it out on the civilians for having unfurled all those French flags.''

In the absence of Lieutenant Colonel Joerg, Major Herrman promptly radioed this information to Gen. Bob Frederick at his CP in a large farmhouse outside Le Mitan.

Some fifteen minutes later, Colonel Joerg and Captain Quinn strode into the 551st Battalion command post. Pappy Herrmann handed Joerg an urgent signal from General Frederick:

"Hold present position with minimum force. Attack and seize Draguignan.''

A German General Is Captured

It was nearing 11:00 P.M. as Joerg's 551st Parachute Infantry Battalion was picking its way toward Draguignan. Leading the advance up a dry riverbed was C Company; the point consisted of three paratrooper scouts and two members of the French Resistance who had volunteered to serve as guides. If the Germans were suddenly to open fire out of the dark veil of night, the native guerrilla fighters would be the first cut down.

Lieutenant Colonel Joerg had rapidly drawn up a plan for seizing Draguignan. It called for C Company to pause outside the German-held town and for A and B companies to storm Draguignan. C Company would become battalion reserve to be summoned as needed.

It was deathly still as the long column of paratroopers trudged over the rugged terrain. The only sound was the rustling of gear and the heavy breathing of those lugging machine guns, mortar components, shells, bazooka rockets, radios, metal ammunition boxes, and other accouterments of war in addition to their own burden of personal equipment. Corporal Charlie Fairlamb, for one, felt as though his lungs would burst. It was hot and muggy. In the tall weeds could be heard the merry chirping of crickets, unaware that these human beings trekking past were but minutes away from a lethal confrontation.

"It's too goddamned quiet!" a perspiring trooper called out in a stage whisper. "Those Heinies are up to something!"

"Shut up back there, goddamn it!" called out a muted voice farther forward in the column.

Sergeant Martin Kangas and his light-machine-gun platoon were struggling along when suddenly the peace was shattered. A machine gun off to one side raked the column with heavy bursts of fire, and the troopers flopped to the ground. Kangas and his squad hurriedly set up their automatic weapon and poured streams of tracer bullets into the shadowy outline of a farmhouse from where the German fusillade seemed to be coming.

As if evolving from thin air, a French farmer came up to the Americans and, through a paratrooper translator, stated, "There's a group of Germans in my farmhouse and they want to surrender."

Replying through the interpreter, an irritated Lieutenant Slucter declared, "Well, they've got a peculiar way of trying to surrender by firing at us."

"The Boche say they're proud soldiers. They want to fire a few shots, then you are to fire a few shots, then they will surrender," the Frenchman, wearing the traditional beret cocked over one eye, explained.

"Anybody here speak German?" Slucter called out to his machine gunners huddled in a six-foot-deep irrigation ditch.

Responded a trooper from California named Frank Powers, "Yeah, I can." But he couldn't.

"Okay, then holler at those Krauts and tell them to surrender."

Powers scrambled out of the ditch, stood on the bank, and shouted, "Hey, you tediski sons-of-bitches, *alles kaput!*"

With that the German machine gunners cut loose and raked the Americans with tracers. Sergeant Kangas's machine gunner promptly fired back and was struck by a bullet, slumping over his weapon. The firing continued furiously for several minutes with white and red streams of tracers crisscrossing the night air. Then, as if on cue, both adversaries ceased firing. It was a Mexican standoff. Kangas and his men moved on toward Draguignan, leaving the enemy machine gunners to be dealt with by others.

Leading the attack, along with Capt. Marshall Dalton of A Company, was Capt. James "Jungle Jim" Evans, commander of B Company. Evans had lost his helmet and had a piece of a parachute tied around his head which, with his handlebar mustache, gave him a fierce appearance. He was not wearing his jump jacket, and he had an OD undershirt and suspenders. One of his platoon leaders, Lt. Richard Mascuch, who was at the head of the column, whispered to Captain Evans: "You look like a goddamned pirate!"

Looming through the darkness was the dim silhouette of a large cluster of houses—the outskirts of Draguignan. Except for the German machine gunners back at the farmhouse who could not make up their minds if they wanted to fight or surrender, Joerg's paratroopers had arrived at their objective without being detected or seriously impeded.

Three French Resistance fighters were at the head of the B Company column. Each was wearing dark trousers and white shirts. The white shirts worried Lieutenant Mascuch. "They stick out like goddamned beacons," he reflected. Heading down a hard-surfaced street, the French guides again caused nagging concerns among the paratroopers. The natives' hard leather heels striking the cobblestones seemed to echo for miles across the blacked-out and deathly quiet town.

"Why don't we announce to the Krauts that we're here?" an angry voice called out in a hoarse whisper. Unaware of the consternation their heavy heels and white shirts was causing among the Americans, the Frenchmen clattered on ahead.

Suddenly, heavy shooting broke out in the shadowy streets of Draguignan. At his CP in the center of town, Gen. Ludwig Bieringer looked up from his desk as rifle, machine-gun, and submachine-gun fire rattled over the landscape. Obviously, an Allied force of undetermined size had infiltrated the town.

The intense racket set off panic among Bieringer's headquarters personnel, who suddenly found themselves in the front lines. The general dashed to the front door and looked out. Firefights seemed to have erupted on all sides. "The American parachutists, they're here at last!" he reflected.

Ludwig Bieringer, an officer reared by the Prussian code of fighting to the end, was appalled by what greeted his eyes and ears. A large number of his headquarters soldiers nearly trampled each other while scrambling into an air-raid shelter. He recognized the voice of one of his staff officers, Lieutenant

Pfannkuche, calling out in the darkness, "The Americans are here! Cease firing! Cease firing!"

Not all Germans followed the orders of the authoritative voice. Heavy firing was still raging on all sides of the CP. General Bieringer rushed back inside to telephone his superior, General Neuling, at LXII Corps on the mountain slope outside town. The effort was futile; the American paratroopers or the French Underground had cut the wire between the two head-quarters.

Meanwhile, Pfc. Joe Cicchinelli, the young former boxer who was lead scout for A Company, was guiding his column into Draguignan at the same time Evans's B Company was entering. This was Cicchinelli's second visit to the town in less than ten hours. During daylight, and prior to Lieutenant Colonel Joerg receiving orders to seize Draguignan, Cicchinelli had been lead scout for a three-man patrol, headed by Lieutenant Peabody, which had been dispatched to the town to "find out what the Krauts are doing there." In that daylight foray, Cicchinelli had worked his way to the outskirts, spotted Germans moving about in the town, but reported back that there had been no sign of massing of troops or other unusual activity.

"Hell, I wasn't even shot at!" he had complained.

As Cicchinelli and the leading platoon in Dalton's A Company now were stealing along a street, the scout suddenly held up his arm. The column halted, and the troopers edged over into the shadows of the houses to each side. Cicchinelli slipped back to his comrades at the front of the column and whispered, "I don't know what's inside of that big building there, but there's a huge Nazi flag flying over the front door. Must be some Kraut bigwigs in there."

"Let's take the bastards!" Sgt. Donald M. Thompson urged.

With Cicchinelli in the lead, Thompson and troopers Ed Schultz and Bud Hook stormed through the massive front doorway, and with Tommy guns and rifles at the ready, smashed open the first door on the right and charged into the room. Startled, the Americans came face to face with a monocled middle-aged officer who had been seated at a large, ornately carved desk. Around him were several other German officers, who stood impassively and motionless. General Ludwig Bieringer slowly arose but said nothing.

"Look at that Kraut with the monocle and all the decorations," a trooper called out, nodding toward Bieringer. "He must be a colonel or a general or something.''

"Hell, he can't be a general," another declared. "A general would have scrammed out of Draguignan a long time ago.''

Unaware that they had captured the German general in command of the district and most of his staff, the four Americans were approached by Bieringer, who handed Sergeant Thompson a large mark note. It apparently was a bribe in an effort to keep the paratroopers from killing him on the spot.

Now a large number of parachutists had entered the building, and three of them were designated to march General Bieringer and his staff to Captain Dalton's CP, from where they were escorted back to battalion CP and then on up the chain of command until they reached Gen. Bob Frederick's headquarters outside Le Mitan.

As soon as the German general and his staff were marched away, Joe Cicchinelli climbed onto the flagpole reaching out horizontally over the front door and took down the huge black and red, swastika-emblazoned Nazi flag. He would send the souvenir home. His mother back in California would be really proud of her son's prominent role in capturing the Nazi bigwigs.*

By 2:00 A.M. the men of the 551st Parachute Infantry had fought their way deep into Draguignan, and Lieutenant Colonel Joerg set up his CP in the Hôtel Madeline. Word was promptly radioed to Capt. Jud Chalkley, one of the battalion's two surgeons, to hurry to town; casualties were mounting. Chalkley and the other combat doctor, Capt. John Y. Battenfield, were about two miles from Draguignan at the time. Chalkley and Battenfield had worked out a system whereby they would leapfrog each other during an attack, with one working in the rear and the other at the point of the assault.

Now it was Captain Chalkley's turn to leapfrog past Battenfield, so Chalkley and his medics started forward in the darkness for the long walk to Draguignan. It was difficult going. In addition to the treacherous, hilly terrain, the American aid men carried six casualties, one of them a Russian fighting for the Wehrmacht who had a serious head wound. Chalkley knew the enemy soldier was fatally wounded, yet he was lugged along with the other casualties.

---

*In 1985 the Nazi flag over the Draguignan headquarters was still prominently displayed in Joe Cicchinelli's Arizona home.

Firefights were raging on all sides as Chalkley and his little column edged into dark Draguignan. The doctor went directly to the battalion CP in the Hôtel Madeline, dismissed his French Resistance guides, and reported to Colonel Joerg. Chalkley was told that the paratroopers had seized a French hospital in town, and the casualties were taken there.

Captain Chalkley was greeted frigidly by a stern-faced Swiss nun who promptly made her views known: She had been a nurse for the Germans, believed in the Nazi cause, and was convinced that Adolf Hitler would win the war. The American doctor was aware that the nun greatly resented the "enemy" taking over her hospital.

"The Germans will drive you Americans out of southern France," she declared. "And it can't come too soon for me!"

Turning to one of his medics, Captain Chalkley remarked drily: "Well, at least we know where she stands."

Members of the 551st Parachute Infantry had long had a special feeling for Doc Chalkley, a free spirit who, the troopers declared, "speaks our language."

Part of the "language" the men of the 551st comprehended was the fact that Doc Chalkley always kept plenty of liquor handy, which he prescribed generously in his treatments. He would say, "Well, if you've a gunshot wound or something, a shot of whiskey won't hurt you—and it might help." When a trooper was shot, Chalkley would give him morphine to kill the pain, then hand the casualty a bottle of whiskey.

Later an admiring trooper would say: "By the time you recovered from your wound and rejoined your platoon, your comrades wanted to know if you had been treated for alcoholism or a gunshot."

Doc Chalkley was highly regarded by the parachutists for his medical ability, his willingness to share the hardships and dangers, and his courage under fire at the point of an attack. So was Doc Battenfield.

Now, inside the French hospital, which was crowded with both German and American casualties, Captain Chalkley radioed for the other doctor, John Battenfield, to move his aid station forward and "join me at the hospital in Draguignan." Battenfield promptly started forward. What neither surgeon knew was that there were *two* civilian hospitals in Draguignan— the smaller one, which the Americans had taken over, and a large one, still held by the Germans.

Carrying their casualties, Captain Battenfield and his medics reached Draguignan where he told his French guide, "Take me to the hospital." The Resistance fighter clearly was not aware either that there were two hospitals, and he led Battenfield and an assistant, trooper Perkins, through the ominous, dark streets and pointed to the shadowy silhouette of a large structure—the German-held hospital. Battenfield strode up to the front door and found that it was locked. Around him in the blackness he heard the occasional bursts of machine-gun fire. Exhausted from constant activity without sleep for many hours, Battenfield irritably pounded on the door and shouted, "Let me in, goddamn it!"

Moments later the door slowly opened and Battenfield and his medic Perkins found themselves face to face with a German officer. The adversaries stared at each other for several seconds. Recognizing that a serious mistake had been made, the quick-witted parachute doctor demanded that the Germans in the hospital surrender to him immediately. "We have your hospital surrounded. There's no way you can escape alive," he bluffed.

Actually, the only Americans directly on the scene were Battenfield and Perkins, both unarmed. Hearing loud voices at the door, a German lieutenant colonel appeared and was told of the surrender demand.

"We will surrender only to your senior commander," the *Oberstleutnant* declared haughtily. Behind the German in the darkness of the hallway, Battenfield could see the dim forms of numerous armed Germans.

Continuing his bluff, Captain Battenfield shouted back angrily: "Like hell you will! Either you surrender to me immediately or my paratroopers will storm this building and wipe you out!"

Battenfield remained stern-faced. He could feel his heart thumping furiously. Several seconds passed; then the German lieutenant colonel, speaking in flawless English, declared resignedly, "All right, to save lives I hereby surrender the hospital to your force."

The "force" was Battenfield and a somewhat alarmed trooper Perkins. While an outwardly calm and confident Battenfield remained inside the medical structure, Perkins was sent on a mission to locate some armed comrades. Much to the relief of the American captain, some fifteen minutes later a squad of troopers appeared and proceeded to round up the Germans inside the facility. Along with many wounded Feldgrau confined to patient beds, the Americans took into custody a large number of armed enemy soldiers who had taken refuge in the hospital.

Elsewhere in Draguignan, Platoon Sergeant Robert Van Horssen and his men were cautiously edging ahead down dark streets, searching each building as they went. At one large structure, Van Horssen and another trooper went inside, kicked open the first door they came to, and charged into the room, rifles and fixed bayonets at the ready. A figure sleeping in a bed in his underwear abruptly popped upright on hearing the Americans crash into his bedroom. He was a German lieutenant colonel who somehow had slept through the din of battle raging around him.

Sergeant Van Horssen motioned for the German to come with him. The German grabbed his tunic and hurriedly slipped it on. Van Horssen noticed that the blouse was covered with decorations—"fruit salad" to the GIs. The two parachutists chuckled on seeing that the enemy officer was wearing bright red undershorts.

"Let's go, Adolf!" Van Horssen barked, pointing to the door. The German protested, wanting to put on his pants.

"Hell, where you're going you won't need any pants," the sergeant exclaimed.

The two 551st men marched their high-ranking prisoner down a hill and into the Draguignan jail. With as much dignity as the Wehrmacht officer could muster, he joined thirty-two German soldiers behind bars, painfully aware that the other prisoners were no doubt snickering inwardly over the bizarre sight of a once-dignified German officer clad in an expensive, ribbon-festooned tunic and flaming red undershorts.

As a hot, muggy dawn of D-Day plus two broke out over southern France, the battle situation inside Draguignan was still fluid. Joerg's troopers had control of about half of the town, the Germans the other half. As the Americans fought their way forward during the hours of darkness, many Feldgrau had been bypassed and now were holed up in buildings to the rear of paratrooper positions.

In a forward area of "Jungle Jim" Evans's B Company, a call rang out: "Some Krauts approaching with a white flag!" Evans went out to meet the impeccably attired young German lieutenant and his aide and was told that the Draguignan garrison wanted to establish a truce and then surrender the remaining German force in and around the town.

Captain Evans and the Wehrmacht officer climbed into a jeep and drove to the command post of General Neuling of the LXII Corps on the mountain slope just northwest of Draguignan. Evans, who waited outside while the blond lieutenant entered the heavily barbed-wired CP, presumed that the emissary had been sent by some high-ranking Wehrmacht commander to arrange the capitulation.

Some fifteen minutes later, the German lieutenant, red-faced and flustered, returned to Evans's jeep. "My superior does not wish to discuss a surrender," the enemy officer stated solemnly. "You are to return to your lines immediately."

The German drastically understated the situation. General Neuling had been enraged over the action of the lieutenant, who had initiated the surrender parlay on his own. A puzzled Jim Evans climbed into his jeep and drove off, still unaware that he had been within rifle-shot distance of the Wehrmacht commander for the entire Riviera region. In and around Draguignan, the fighting broke out anew, this time more intensely than during the night.

One of Evans's platoon leaders, Lt. Bud Schroeder, was leading his men in an assault on an enemy strongpoint in a thick-walled building. Schroeder and a few of his men scrambled over a stone wall into a vineyard and were promptly pinned to the ground by machine-gun fire. With bullets just overhead, the lieutenant began slithering forward. His mind had flashed back to the Infantry School training at Fort Benning, Georgia, where instructors had pounded into the heads of students: When you are pinned down, don't try to get up or go back, but keep moving forward.

A machine gun zeroed in on Schroeder. One burst zipped past his head, struck a wall, and rocks cascaded down on him. He rolled to one side and continued inching forward. Bullets were kicking up the dust in front of his face and were actually driving dirt into his nose and eyes. Moments later Schroeder's luck ran out; he felt an enormous blow in the chest as though he had been struck by a sledgehammer. A bullet had found its mark.

Near Schroeder's attacking platoon, Capt. Jud Chalkley heard a call above the din of battle, "Doc, Lieutenant Schroeder's been hit!" The surgeon crawled forward and stuck his head over a stone wall. A large red cross on a white background painted on his helmet was clearly visible, but a burst of machine-gun fire went past him and chipped chunks out of the wall. Chalkley crawled to a small shed where Schroeder, bleeding profusely, in shock but still conscious, had been dragged. Given first aid, the badly wounded Schroeder was evacuated under heavy fire.

On Draguignan's debris-littered main street, Cpl. James Aikman, a machine gunner, and his squad were idling on the curb waiting for orders to push forward. Marching down the street toward them, three abreast and in precise parade-ground step, was a column of captured German soldiers guarded by two paratroopers. One of the Americans, Sgt. Otto Schultz, spoke fluent German and had his one hundred prisoners goose-stepping. One German refused to goose-step, and when Schultz spotted him he ran up and kicked him in the buttocks repeatedly. "Now goose-step for your Führer, you goddamned son-of-a-bitch!" the angry sergeant shouted in German.

Meanwhile, 551st Battalion surgeon Jud Chalkley had moved his wounded patients from the smaller, older hospital to the more modern one the other unit doctor, John Battenfield, had "captured" during the night. Chalkley was near the front door when it was opened, and he casually glanced up to see an armed German major and lieutenant stroll inside. Seeing the Americans moving about, the startled newcomers suddenly halted. One turned as if to bolt back outside, but thought better of it as several paratroopers rushed up with Tommy guns and shouted in less-than-perfect German, *"Hande hoch, Schweinehund!"* (Hands up, you sons-of-bitches!)

The two Wehrmacht officers had somehow reached the hospital without being seen by the American parachutists swarming over the town and had entered the hospital believing it was still in German hands.

His medical duties finished for the time being, Captain Chalkley decided to prowl around the area. He started walking up a lane, and there sitting about a hundred yards in front of him, was a German panzer, its long, menacing, 88mm gun pointed directly toward the parachute doctor. Chalkley froze, unable to move. He thought: "Dear Lord, this is it!"

In his paralysis, Captain Chalkley heard the raucous revving of the panzer's powerful engine, and the iron monster spun around and rumbled off. Possibly the German tankers thought Chalkley was a decoy to force them to give away their position.

With the arrival of dawn, Sgt. Don Thompson, Pfc. Joe

Cicchinelli, and a few comrades were prowling around the rear of General Bieringer's headquarters. They spotted an excavation that resembled a cave, cautiously entered it, and discovered five burlap sacks neatly stashed in a corner. They ripped open the containers and let out yelps; the sacks contained large amounts of German currency and a lesser amount of French francs. Probably a Wehrmacht payroll, the elated troopers concluded.

"How much do you think is there?" Thompson asked.

"Hell, I don't know what a French franc or a German mark is worth," Cicchinelli replied. "But there's a hell of a lot of money here!"

Another concluded sadly, "Yeah, but the money is good only for the Krauts and the French. It's no use to us."

A large quantity of Cognac and beer was also discovered in the excavation. Cases of it were sent to the Hôtel Madeline headquarters for eventual distribution to the paratroopers to soothe parched throats.

The burlap bags were loaded onto the rear of an old, wheezing, flatbed truck. Cicchinelli scrambled onto the rear of the truck, and another trooper began slowly driving through the cluttered streets as the old vehicle bucked and backfired. By now the shooting had died down in this part of Draguignan, and civilians, wild with joy over the arrival of their *libérateurs*, lined the sidewalks, a cheering, frenzied mass of humanity. As the truck edged along, Cicchinelli tossed out handfuls of marks and francs until all of the Wehrmacht payroll had been dispersed. The shower of currency confetti set off a wild melee as screaming, clawing civilians scrambled for the money.

"Do you think they think we're Santa Claus or goddamned fools?" a trooper in the truck shouted above the din.

"Probably a little of both," a grinning Cicchinelli called back.

By late afternoon, the echo of gunfire in Draguignan diminished, then faded out entirely. Men of the 551st Parachute Infantry had fanned out around the perimeter of the town and set up strongpoints at each road and street, blocking off any German efforts to enter and making it difficult for bypassed Feldgrau to flee. It was 5:15 P.M. when Lt. Col. Wood Joerg, from his CP in the Hôtel Madeline, radioed Gen. Bob Frederick at Le Mitan: "Draguignan secured."

"Gentlemen, We're Here to Stay!"

Five miles south of Draguignan, Lt. Col. Dick Seitz's battalion of the 517th Parachute Infantry early that morning of D-Day plus two jumped off to assault the key town of Les Arcs. In the lead, two platoons abreast, was Lt. Loren James and his D Company. Advancing alertly through vineyards and open, green fields, the parachutists reached the first houses of Les Arcs without being fired on.

The troopers heaved collective sighs of relief; it appeared that the enemy had abandoned Les Arcs. But minutes later all hell broke loose as German automatic weapons took James's men under fire and shells began screaming into their ranks.

Lieutenant James ordered his men to form a defensive line in a string of battered houses some two hundred yards from the railroad station in the southern portion of Les Arcs. That sturdy old building had been the center for massing German troops two days before, when Maj. Bill Boyle and his band of fifty had been besieged by much larger numbers of the enemy. Now Americans in forward positions saw large numbers of Germans again forming up around the station to assault James's troops. The attack was broken up before it could be launched when the paratrooper mortar squads pounded the area around the station and machine gunners opened up on the assembling Germans with heavy fusillades of fire.

Less than an hour later, Lieutenant James was told that the enemy was again forming up for an attack at the station. James relayed the information to Colonel Seitz, and a flight of P-51 fighter-bombers that had been circling the area while looking for likely targets was called in. The P-51s swooped down on the Les Arcs railroad station, bombing and strafing. Keeping low in the event of miscalculation by the pilots, who were dropping their eggs only two hundred yards to the front, the paratroopers cheered as the frenzied Feldgrau scattered to escape the Jabos.

Hardly had the dirty smoke cleared from the dive bombers' attacks than the Germans began congregating around the station for a third time. A call went out to the 4.2-inch mortars, and in minutes white phosphorous shells began exploding around the railroad structure, veiling it in a thick cloud of rolling white smoke. Enemy soldiers caught in the open were seen running with their clothes on fire. With the Germans milling in confusion, the four-point-twos switched to high explosives and began plastering the German assembly area.

Once more the Wehrmacht attack was disorganized before it had a chance to jump off. Now the Germans settled down to exchanging machine-gun, rifle, and mortar fire with the American paratroopers in Les Arcs.

As the fight raged inside the town, Lt. Col. Mel Zais's paratroopers pushed into Les Arcs from the south. Caught between converging attacks by Seitz's men from the east and Zais's battalion from the south, the defenders started pulling back and soon abandoned the town.

Les Arcs, with high hills on both sides of the hard-surfaced road leading to the Allied landing beaches, was a bottleneck for German forces trying to reach the amphibious invaders. Colonel Rupert Graves's parachutists had plugged a cork into the bottleneck.

With the capture of Draguignan and Les Arcs, the final piece in the gigantic jigsaw puzzle code-named Operation Rugby, the parachute-glider assault, had fallen into place. All 1st Airborne Task Force objectives had been seized within forty-eight hours of the first paratrooper bailing out. General Frederick's ten thousand men had carried out their mission of wreaking havoc inland from the landing beaches, snarling German communications, and blocking enemy efforts to rush reinforcements to the coastline to attack seaborne troops as they waded ashore.

IN THE MEANTIME, Lt. Col. John Akehurst's regiment of the 1st Special Service Force was still battling a band of Germans holed up inside three old stone forts built during the Napoleonic era on the offshore island of Port-Cros. For two nights and two days the tenacious Germans, armed with numerous machine guns and plenty of ammunition, had stubbornly beaten off repeated efforts by Akehurst's commandos to root them out from behind the twelve-foot-thick walls.

The cruiser *Augusta* had shelled Fort L'Éminence with her eight-inch guns on and off for forty-eight hours, and Royal Air Force Typhoons had bombed and rocketed the massive stone structures—all to no avail. But shortly after noon on D-Day plus two, Akehurst's men fought their way into one of the forts and with bayonets, grenades, and Tommy guns seized the massive stone structure. But the Germans still clung desperately to the other two forts.

A short time later, Colonel Akehurst entered the captured fort just before Rear Adm. Lyal Davidson, commander of the Mediterranean fleet, and several staff officers arrived to join him there. "What's the trouble?" Davidson asked. The question seemed to imply that Akehurst's men should have captured the German-held forts by now.

Concealing his surprise that such high-ranking brass would come to the tiny island, Akehurst explained that warship shells and airplane bombs and rockets had been bouncing off the old citadel and that his troops had to cross open ground even to reach the thick walls.

"Do you have anything 'big' out there?" Akehurst asked.

The American admiral paused and pondered the question. "I have the *Ramilles* and her fifteen-inch guns," the naval leader replied. "I'll bring her in to six-mile range."

Six miles from the target for a battleship such as the twenty-eight-year-old antiquity the *Ramilles* was virtually point-blank range. It would also place the *Ramilles* in a degree of jeopardy, for it would bring the ancient ship into easy range of German land-based guns.

As Admiral Davidson and Colonel Akehurst awaited the arrival of the first salvo from the massive guns of the *Ramilles*, they could hear the regular chatter of German machine guns erupting from the other two forts. Soon a curious rustling noise dented the hot air—the *Ramilles*'s first salvo was approaching. Moments later enormously loud explosions erupted; they seemed to shake the terrain.

The first salvo was "long," the second cluster was "short," but the third salvo exploded with teeth-jarring violence right on the German-held fortifications, covering them with a thick cloud of smoke and dirt. Watching the bombardment, Akehurst and Davidson saw white flags waving frantically through the smog. A nearby company of Akehurst's men, under Maj. Gerald McFadden, cautiously edged up to the closer fort. A drawbridge was lowered, and McFadden's troops entered the fort and quickly disarmed the dazed defenders.

The Battle of Port-Cros was over.

Admiral Davidson accompanied Colonel Akehurst on an inspection of the just-captured forts. They were astonished at the shambles caused by the warship guns and the rockets and shells. Reaching a large room used for storage, the two officers were again surprised: Stored there was a wide assortment of articles in no way connected with the defense of the citadel.

Davidson spotted a fine English riding saddle, which he had one of his aides carry for him. Akehurst took a fancy to a large supply of Portuguese sardines.

At the end of the drawbridge, Admiral Davidson and Colonel Akehurst shook hands on departing. They were in high good humor.

"Admiral, are you going to put that saddle on one of those fifteen-inch guns and ride it back to the United States?" the commando leader asked.

Davidson broke out in a hearty laugh, then was gone.

AS THE SUN was setting, the town square of Draguignan was teeming with wildly celebrating French men, women, and children. Shoehorned in among the cheering masses was Cpl. Charles S. Fairlamb and his mortar squad. Fairlamb's mortars had been firing furiously from the square during the hours of darkness and all day, and now he and his men were relaxing and watching the unrestrained celebration all around them.

Soon the grating noise of steel treads clattering on the cobblestone streets and the roar of powerful motors drowned out the din in Draguignan's town square. Moments later a column of American Sherman tanks was seen clanking toward the square, setting off an even wilder demonstration among the populace. These were tanks attached to the 45th Infantry Division, which had landed on Delta Beach two days previously and which were rapidly pushing inland against disintegrating German resistance.

Caught up in the ecstatic mood of the moment, Corporal Fairlamb and his mortarmen joined in welcoming the tankers. In their fractured French, the paratroopers called out, *"Américains! Libérateurs! Bonjour! Bonjour!"* They whistled and waved furiously at the grimy-faced, grinning tank commanders, who were riding with heads and shoulders protruding from the turrets. It was all tongue-in-cheek, the parachutists' way of reminding their amphibious comrades that Joerg's men had gotten there first.

In the meantime, the haughty German general, Ludwig Bieringer, was seated on a hard wooden chair in the headquarters of Gen. Alexander Patch near Saint-Tropez. Stiff-necked and militarily correct, the captured Wehrmacht general was received with icy contempt by Sandy Patch, then hustled off to be interrogated. Bieringer had been brought to Seventh Army headquarters in a jeep, escorted by the 1st Airborne Task Force leader, Bob Frederick, and two Tommy-gun-wielding troopers.

Bieringer, his monocle placed at the precisely correct angle, had several complaints. Frederick had not allowed him to bring an orderly with him into captivity, nor had the airborne general permitted him to be accompanied by two satchels containing extra dress uniforms. But inwardly, Bieringer had to have been thankful to General Frederick for one crucial factor: In the jeep trip from Le Mitan to the coast, the party had run a virtual gauntlet of angry, revenge-minded Frenchmen who, Bieringer was certain, would have literally torn him apart had it not been for the protective presence of Frederick and his pair of parachutists.

On that afternoon of D-Day plus two, amphibious forces were linking up with American paratroopers and glidermen at scores of locales deep behind the Côte d'Azur, then rapidly pushing onward. At an insignificant village named La Londe, men of Iron Mike O'Daniel's 3rd Infantry Division ran into a buzzsaw and were pounded by artillery and mortars and sprayed by automatic-weapons fire. The bloody fight would last all day and into the early-morning hours of August 18.

At about 2:00 P.M. on August 17, while the battle was raging in Draguignan, forward elements of O'Daniel's 2nd Battalion, 7th Infantry Regiment, were rounding a bend in the road leading to three bridges spanning the Maravennes River on the far side of La Londe. It was vital to seize the bridges in order to continue the 3rd Division's speedy advance inland.

Lieutenant George H. Franklin, leader of the point company, halted his men when he spotted a Frenchman dashing toward them and frantically waving his arms. The native told Franklin that there was a strong German roadblock just around the bend in the road and that La Londe was filled with enemy troops. Franklin ordered his stubble-bearded, mud-stained infantrymen to scramble off their three tanks and four tank-destroyers and form up into files on either side of the road. The company then moved cross-country to assault the German roadblock from the flank.

Lieutenant Franklin and his men had gone but a short distance through the fields when they were fired on by German machine gunners and riflemen in concealed positions. At the same time, an enemy antitank gun barked, and its flat-trajectory shell crashed into one of the Sherman tanks accompanying the foot soldiers. The 3rd Division men flattened themselves against the earth as streams of bullets hissed overhead and thudded into the ground around them. Several other antitank guns opened up on the remaining tanks and tank-destroyers, which returned the fire after scrambling off the road.

One of those who refused to take cover when his fellow infantrymen dropped down was S. Sgt. Stanley Bender, a squad leader. Bender had mounted the knocked-out Sherman and, with bullets splitting the air around him, shielded his eyes from the glaring sun and calmly tried to locate the source of the heavy German fire. Machine-gun slugs were playing a tune on the tank on which he was standing.

Locating the Feldgrau positions, Bender jumped down from the Sherman and ran to a ditch where two squads had taken cover. "Keep firing at the bastards!" Sergeant Bender bellowed. "I'll take my squad and charge 'em!"

Bender leaped up and ran forward, motioning for his squad to follow him. Reaching another large ditch, the sergeant and his men leaped in after running a gauntlet of machine-gun fire that had cut down four of the squad. Explosions rocked the ground as the enemy tried to pitch hand grenades into the excavation. Leaving his squad in the ditch, Bender crawled forward, and his comrades saw him emerge into sight far behind the German strongpoint.

The sergeant began walking back toward the enemy position, standing upright, much to the horror of his intently watching men. Now a German machine gunner spotted the American, still strolling erectly, approaching from the rear. The enemy weapon was spun around and sent bursts of fire toward Bender. The sergeant calmly lifted his Tommy gun and raked the German crew, killing all of the enemy soldiers.

As though on a Sunday stroll through a peaceful park, Sergeant Bender edged some thirty yards to another spitting German machine gun and killed the gunner and his assistant, then walked forty yards to a trench, where he wiped out several riflemen. In the meantime, the survivors in his squad had scrambled out of their ditch and raced forward to join in cleaning up the remaining Feldgrau at the strongpoint.

The 2nd Battalion then stormed German-held La Londe, and after a savage house-to-house fight in the black of night, the last German was killed, captured, or had withdrawn.

AT ABOUT 10:00 P.M. on August 17, a screen of destroyers, under command of U.S. Navy Capt. Harry Sanders, was on patrol off Cannes when radar picked up five unidentified vessels that appeared to be trying to sneak through the picket line of Allied warships. When the intruders failed to heed an order to identify themselves, Sanders' destroyers opened fire. For nearly a half hour, the dark seascape echoed with the roar of Allied guns, and when the smoke had cleared, Captain Sanders totaled up the night's work: The *Harding,* aided by the *Frankford,* had sunk three German gunboats and captured a fourth, and the *Carmick* and *Satterlee* had blown up a fifth vessel.

IN FAR-OFF, BOMB-BATTERED, and gloomy Berlin that night, the clever little Josef Goebbels was preparing his nation for the disastrous news coming out of the West. Warned a grim-voiced announcer over Radio Berlin: "We must be prepared for a German withdrawal from France. We must expect the loss of places with world-famous names."

Among those unspoken but implied world-famous names were Paris, Cannes, Nice, Toulon, and Marseilles.

German civilians and the military scanned the Nazi Party-sponsored newspaper, *Volkischer Beobachter*, and were shocked to read: "It is out of the question to send reinforcements to France."

Secretly, even the most zealous Nazis among the Wehrmacht's generals felt it was high time—in fact, long past time—for wholesale German withdrawals. Of the sixty divisions Hitler had in France, Holland, and Belgium three months before, fifteen had been destroyed, fifteen badly mauled, and the rest were in peril, most notably Col. Gen. Johannes Blaskowitz's Army Group G in southern France.

"Withdrawal from France" was a grim phrase for official German utterance. The prospects of actually withdrawing the remainder of German forces were grimmer still. Northern and southern France were now quagmires into which Hitler's legions were steadily disappearing. Everywhere, North and South, French patriots were rising to fight the Boche in his rear, to serve as guides for attacking Allied infantry and tanks, and to provide crucial information to help Allied air fleets pound the German troops and paralyze their movements.

AT HIS HEADQUARTERS in a spacious villa outside Saint Tropez on the night of August 17, VI Corps commander Lucian Truscott was reviewing the progress of Operation Dragoon. Things looked good. Frederick's paratroopers and glidermen had seized all objectives, and the amphibious forces had driven twenty miles inland to the Blue Line, a semicircle radiating out from the Alpha, Delta, and Camel landing beaches. The Blue Line had been drawn on Dragoon maps to indicate that the beachhead could be considered secure once it had been reached in each direction.

The heat inside the VI Corps CP was stifling, and Truscott long before had shed his trademark leather battle jacket. "Gentlemen," Truscott said to his staff officers, "we're here to stay!"

Now the general's eyes were no longer focused on a strip of ground along the Riviera. Rather they were glued on his battle maps of the Rhône Valley, the route northward to be taken by the Seventh Army to link up with General Eisenhower's Normandy forces driving eastward toward Germany. That same evening, Truscott had received a signal that American forces had sent patrols into the outskirts of Paris.

AT 6:00 A.M. on D-Day plus three (August 18), Lt. Col. Charles J. Hodge, commander of the 117th Cavalry Reconnaissance Squadron of Dahlquist's 36th Infantry Division, led his half-tracks, light tanks, and armored cars out of an assembly area near Le Muy. The column roared through Draguignan, captured the day before by Joerg's 551st Parachute Infantry Battalion, and sped toward Salerns, Aups, and Riez. Just past the northwestern outskirts of Draguignan, the cavalrymen were fired on and the column drew to a halt.

The shots came from a cave on the slope of a mountain, Hodge noticed from his command half-track. One of his tanks spun around, aimed its gun at the cave, and fired several rounds of high explosive into the opening. The entrance to the cave was shrouded with a thick cloud of black smoke and dust. Out of the curtain of smog emerged a German lieutenant waving a white flag.

"Cease firing! Cease firing!" was shouted along the column of armored vehicles. An intense silence fell over the landscape as another German came out of the cave, then another, and finally an officer Hodge recognized as a general. It was Generalleutnant Ferdinand Neuling, commander of the LXII Corps, who had been charged by Adolf Hitler with defending the Riviera.

Shoulders squared, ramrod straight, militarily correct, General Neuling, a product of the Prussian code, handed his pistol to Lt. Joseph Symes, one of Hodge's cavalry officers. The act was the symbol of the German's surrender and that of his staff and the small number of soldiers who had guarded the corps headquarters.

Lieutenant Symes turned to the recon battalion leader, handed him Neuling's pistol, and remarked, "This is for you, Colonel Hodge!"*

His face and once-immaculate uniform covered with cordite powder, dust, and grime, Ferdinand Neuling climbed into a jeep and was driven off to join the remnants of his corps in captivity. Lieutenant Colonel Hodge and his cavalrymen had little time to rejoice. Each knew that countless bitter, bloody battles lay ahead before Nazi Germany was brought to its knees.

---

*Brigadier General Charles J. Hodge (Ret.), in 1985, still had General Neuling's pistol hanging on the wall in his Florida home.

Epilogue

On the afternoon of D-Day plus three (August 18), the German Army in southern France was thrashing about wildly, trying to implement Adolf Hitler's order to withdraw from the country and at the same time to tenaciously defend key Mediterranean ports. Before it was too late, Gen. Johannes Blaskowitz, commander of Army Group G, was instructed to rush some 450 miles to the north all the men, supplies, and equipment he could muster to join up with the harried Normandy troops retreating hell-bent for the German border.

Eastward from the Riviera, two German divisions were conducting a fighting withdrawal to the rugged Maritime Alps on the Italian border where, among the towering peaks, a few defenders with a machine gun could stall an entire attacking battalion. To the west of the Riviera, feverish Wehrmacht preparations were under way for a long siege at the major ports of Toulon and Marseilles, the primary objectives of Dragoon.

Toulon would be an especially tough nut to crack as all approaches were saturated with forts, bunkers, antitank obstacles, minefields, barbed-wire entanglements, and trench networks. Marseilles was ringed by huge casemated guns, the largest of which was Big Willie, a 340-mm monster that fired shells weighing more than seven hundred pounds each.

General Jean de Lattre de Tassigny, commander of the French corps assigned to seize both Toulon and Marseilles, struck at Toulon and its 25,000 dug-in Germans at dawn on August 21. Following a bombardment by Allied warships and a heavy pounding by bombers, de Tassigny's 1st and 3rd Algerian Infantry divisions fought through the outer defenses with great dash and *élan,* then battled stubborn Feldgrau house to house. It was brutal fighting between ancient enemies; the vengeful Frenchmen, joined by members of the Resistance, asked no quarter and gave none.

Even with zealous Wehrmacht officers holding pistols to their backs on many occasions, the Germans refused to obey the Führer's stern order—fight to the death. A final-minute exhortation by Admiral of the Fleet Karl Doenitz, commander of the Reich's Navy, reminding the beleaguered garrison that "the eyes of Germany are on you," fell largely on deaf ears. Thousands of Germans were taken prisoner as the Free French clawed their way through Toulon's formidable defenses.

A week later, de Lattre's men ringed Toulon's last remaining German strongpoint, a centuries-old stone citadel. Inside, the commander of the port's garrison, Admiral Ruhfus, held out all day on August 27 as the fortification was plastered by two-thousand-pound blockbuster bombs and pounded by warships and field artillery. At midnight, Ruhfus decided that he, too, would not die for the Führer in a hopeless cause. Along with eighteen hundred of his sailors, the admiral marched into captivity.

Toulon was in Allied hands. But the battle had been costly. Twenty-seven hundred French soldiers had been killed or wounded. The Germans had lost more than five thousand killed, and nearly twenty thousand of the defenders were in French custody.

Meanwhile, for days Allied warships had been pounding

the docks and Wehrmacht facilities at Marseilles, west of Toulon. Dive bombers and heavies had been unloading thousands of tons of explosives on the port. With Toulon lost and the Germans in southern France frantically pulling back northward and eastward into the Maritime Alps, the Wehrmacht commander in Marseilles decided he was no longer imbued with the Nazi spirit. Shortly after Toulon capitulated, he raised a white flag just as French patrols were probing the outskirts of the metropolis.

Within two weeks of the Dragoon landings, the Allies had seized their two main objectives, and in less than half the time planners had projected. Although heavy minesweeping and salvage operations were required before Toulon and Marseilles could be utilized by the invaders, the German commanders of the fortress ports were either unable or unwilling to follow Adolf Hitler's dictate: "Leave the docks a desolate waste."

Unloading in Marseilles began on September 3 and in Toulon the next day. By the end of the war in Europe (May 8, 1945), 905,512 Allied troops and 4,123,794 tons of cargo would be put ashore at Marseilles, Toulon, and nearby Port de Bouc. In addition, 306,127 men, 69,312 vehicles, and 17,848 tons of gasoline had gone over the Dragoon beaches by the time they were closed down six weeks after the landings.

At the eastern end of the Riviera invasion beaches, the Germans evacuated the famed resort city of Cannes on August 24, and Grasse was abandoned the next day as the Wehrmacht pulled back eastward to the Maritime Alps. Then, like ripe plums, Nice and other towns along the Côte d'Azur fell, and the entire Mediterranean coast of France was in Allied hands by September 9.

In the meantime, youthful Gen. Bob Frederick had had time to total up the cost to his 1st Airborne Task Force in paving the way. The price tag had been high. One third of Frederick's paratroopers and glidermen had been killed, wounded, injured, or were missing. Despite the expense, Lt. Gen. William P. Yarborough (Ret.), who, as a lieutenant colonel, had led the 509th Parachute Infantry Battalion that spearheaded the invasion, subsequently labeled Operation Rugby "the most successful Allied airborne assault of World War II."

During these hectic early days of Dragoon, Ultra, the super-secret British device that intercepted and decoded German electronic messages, played one of its most significant roles of the war. When Gen. Sandy Patch sent Truscott's VI Corps roaring northward up the Rhône Valley to join with Eisenhower's Normandy forces, his columns were stretched out from the Côte d'Azur for more than 300 miles. Such a linkup could trap large numbers of Germans in southwestern France. Ultra revealed that the Wehrmacht was not massing troops along the Italian border to the east to smash into Truscott's extended—and vulnerable—flank. Armed with this crucial intelligence, Patch could drive northward at full throttle without having to drop off large bodies of troops to protect his supply lines.

With the seizure of Toulon and Marseilles, General de Lattre's French Corps turned north and raced up the west bank of the Rhône River. Near Dijon, 140 miles southeast of liberated Paris, on the morning of September 12 an historic junction occurred. Several scout cars carrying a patrol of de Lattre's Dragoon force linked up with a patrol from General Jacques Leclerc's French 2nd Armored Division, which had landed in Normandy. Dragoon and Overlord merged into one.

After the war, General of the Army Dwight Eisenhower declared that "there was no development of that period which added more decisively to our advantage or aided us more in accomplishing the final and complete defeat of German forces than did this attack coming up the Rhône Valley [from the Riviera]."

Dragoon, an operation that had seethed with controversy from its concept on almost to the actual assault, indeed was a startling military success. In one month's time, far ahead of schedule, the American and French ground forces had virtually destroyed Gen. Friedrich Wiese's Nineteenth

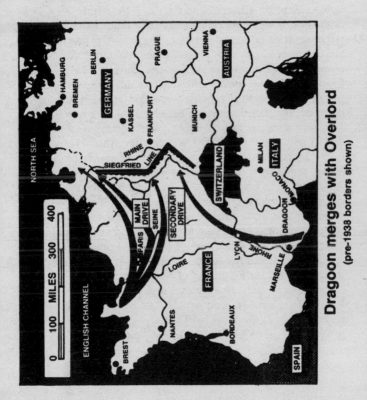

Dragoon merges with Overlord
(pre-1938 borders shown)

Army, taken more than 100,000 prisoners, liberated the southern two-thirds of France, and joined with the Normandy invasion forces 475 miles north of the Riviera landing beaches.

Yet, Winston Churchill and U.S. Gen. Mark W. Clark until their dying days vehemently held that Operation Dragoon was a monumental blunder. The British prime minister staunchly believed that Dragoon set the stage for Soviet domination of nearly all of Eastern Europe. Had General Clark's advancing Fifth Army in Italy not been stripped of most of its strength to provide forces for Dragoon, Churchill declared, the Allied armies in Italy could have driven into the Balkans, then on into Hungary, Czechoslovakia, Austria, and finally into the Third Reich. Had this been done, communism would not be entrenched in much of Europe today, the British Bulldog maintained.

"Stalin . . . was one of the strongest boosters of the invasion of southern France," General Clark asserted long after the war. "He knew exactly what he wanted; and the thing he wanted most was to keep us out of the Balkans, which Stalin had staked out for the Red Army."

Not long before his death in April 1984, Mark Clark told the author that "after the fall of Rome [on June 4, 1944, two days before the Normandy invasion] Field Marshal Kesselring's army [in Italy] could have been destroyed—had we been able to shoot the works in an all-out offensive. Then it would be on to Vienna, Budapest, and Prague."

Principal Participant
Interviews and Contacts

Col. John F. R. Akehurst (Ret.); John A. Alicki; Col. Joseph
C. Antrim (Ret.); Lloyd Bjelland; Rear Adm. John D.
Bulkeley; Roger P. Carguerville; Dr. Judson I. Chalkley; Joe
M. Cicchinelli; Ralph K. Clink; Col. Thomas R. Cross
(Ret.); Lt. Col. Jack M. Darden (Ret.); Thomas J. Dellaca;
Dan A. De Leo; Max Demuth; Charles H. Doyle; Charles S.
Fairlamb; Donald Garrigues; Col. Rupert D. Graves (Ret.);
Frank Guild, Jr.; Col. Edward Hartman (Ret.).

R. E. Hendrickson; Ray "Pappy" Herrman; John Kessler;
Col. Vincent M. Lockhart (Ret.); Dr. William W. Lumsden;
Roman W. Maire; Duffield W. Matson, Jr.; Leon Mims;
Dan Morgan; Truesdell "Pat" Moser; James M. Moses;
William Pahl; Al Peters; Charles A. Place; Dr. Charles E.
Pugh; Tims A. Quinn; Glenn E. Rathbun; Charles B. Rawls,
Jr.

James Reith; Hugh C. Roberts; Leo Rodrigues; Lt. Gen.
Richard J. Seitz (Ret.); Kenneth R. Shaker; Ernest "Bud"
Siegel; George W. Stenger; William S. Story; William W.

Sullivan; Gene Tennison; Brig. Gen. Edward H. Thomas (Ret.); Donald M. Thompson; Leo Turco; Ted Wallace; Thomas B. Waller; Solomon Weber; Lt. Gen. William P. Yarborough (Ret.).

Bibliography

Books

Adelman, Robert H., and Walton, George. *Champaign Campaign*. Boston: Little, Brown, 1969.

Ambrose, Stephen E. *The Supreme Commander*. Garden City, N.Y.: Doubleday, 1970.

Bauer, Eddy. *Encyclopedia of World War II*. New York: Marshall Cavendish, 1970.

Bekker, Cajus. *The Luftwaffe War Diaries*. Garden City, N.Y.: Doubleday, 1969.

Brown, Anthony Cave. *Bodyguard of Lies*. New York: Harper & Row, 1975.

Buckeridge, Justin P. *History of the 550th Airborne Battalion*. Nancy, France: privately published, 1945.

Butcher, Harry C. *My Three Years with Eisenhower*. New York: Simon & Schuster, 1946.

Churchill, Winston S. *Triumph and Tragedy*. Boston: Houghton Mifflin, 1953.

Clark, Mark W. *Calculated Risk*. New York: Harper & Row, 1951.

Cookridge, E. H. *Set Europe Ablaze*. New York: Crowell, 1967.

Eisenhower, Dwight D. *Crusade in Europe*. Garden City, N.Y.: Doubleday, 1948.

Guild, Frank, Jr. *Action of the Tiger*. Nashville: Battery Press, 1978.

Keitel, Wilhelm. *The Memoirs of Field-Marshal Keitel*. New York: Stein & Day, 1965, subsequently republished by Stein & Day in 1979 as *In the Service of the Reich*.

Kesselring, Albert. *A Soldier's Record*. New York: William Morrow, 1954.

Killen, John. *A History of the Luftwaffe*. Garden City. N.Y.: Doubleday, 1968.

Lewin, Ronald. *Ultra Goes to War*. New York: McGraw-Hill, 1978.

Lockhart, Vincent M. *T-Patch to Victory*. Canyon, Tex.: Staked Plains Press, 1981.

Masterson, J. C. *The Double X System*. New Haven, Conn.: Yale University Press, 1972.

Morgan, Dan. *Left Corner of My Heart*. Wauconda, Wash.: Alder Enterprises, 1984.

Morison, Samuel Eliot. *The Invasion of France and Germany*. Boston: Little, Brown, 1964.

Robichon, Jacques. *Le Debarquement de Provence*. Paris: Robert Laffont, 1962.

Schoenbrun, David. *Soldiers of the Night*. New York: E. P. Dutton, 1980.

Shirer, William L. *The Rise and Fall of the Third Reich*. New York: Simon & Schuster, 1960.

Smith, R. Harris. *OSS*. Berkeley, Calif.: University of California Press, 1972.

Summersby, Kay. *Eisenhower Was My Boss*. New York: Prentice-Hall, 1948.

Taggart, Donald G. *History of the 3rd Infantry Division*. Washington, D.C.: Infantry Journal Press, 1947.

Toland, John. *Adolf Hitler*. New York, Ballantine Books, 1972.

Truscott, Lucian K. *Command Decisions*. New York: E. P. Dutton, 1960.

Westphal, Siegfried. *The German Army in the West*. London: Cassell, 1951.

Williams, T. W. *Panic Takes Time*. London: Max Parrish, 1956.

Winterbotham, F. W. *The Ultra Secret*. New York: Harper & Row, 1974.

Booklets

Andrews, John C. *Airborne Album*. Williamstown, N.J.: Phillips Publications, 1982.

By Air to Battle. London: Air Ministry, 1945.

Davis, Bryan L. *German Parachute Forces*. New York: Arco, 1974.
Davis, Howard. *British Parachute Forces*. New York: Arco, 1974.
Warren, Dr. John C. *Airborne Missions in the Mediterranean*.
    Washington, D.C.: Department of the Air Force, 1955.

Miscellaneous

"Compilation of Lessons Learned from Dragoon," 517th Para-
    chute Infantry Headquarters to General Frederick.
The Invasion of Southern France. Washington, D.C.: U.S. Army.
The Invasion of Southern France. Admiral H. Kent Hewitt, Report
    of Naval Commander, Western Task Force.
"Order of Events, August 14–18, 1944," 517th Parachute Infantry
    Headquarters.
Seventh Army Daily Log.
Transcripts of postwar interviews with German commanders:
    Generaloberst Johannes Blaskowitz
    Generalleutnant Walther Botsch
    Generaloberst Georg von Sodenstern
    Generalmajor Edgar Theisen

Index

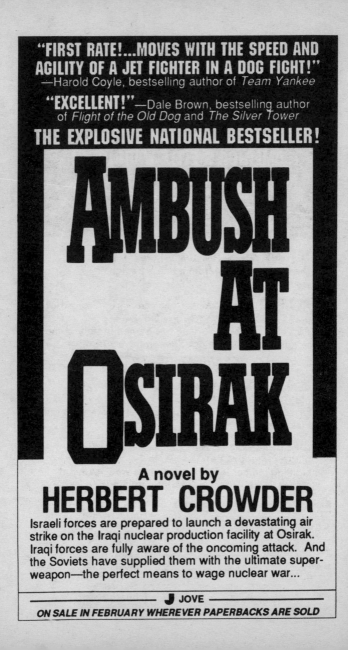

THE EXPLOSIVE NATIONAL BESTSELLER!

AMBUSH AT OSIRAK

A novel by
HERBERT CROWDER

Israeli forces are prepared to launch a devastating air
strike on the Iraqi nuclear production facility at Osirak.
Iraqi forces are fully aware of the oncoming attack. And
the Soviets have supplied them with the ultimate super-
weapon—the perfect means to wage nuclear war...